DOG FOOD

Deon Harris

This work is of fiction. Names, characters, places images, and incidents, which are the product of the authors imagination used fictitiously. Any resemblance to actual persons or events is entirely coincidental. 'No part of this work may be reproduced or transmitted in any form or by any means without the written permission from the author.

To Order Books Contact:
Progress Platform Publications
PO BOX 1025
Cedar Rapids, Iowa 52406

Cover Design: Crystell Publications
Book Productions: Crystell Publications
We Help You Self Publish Your
(405)414-3991

Printed in the U.S.A.

Copyright © 2016 Deon Harris
All rights reserved.
ISBN: - 10: 1530190754
ISBN-13: 978-1530190751

Dedication

April 12, 2013

That is the date that I picked up a pen to tell my story. It's my "time one crack at life," so when I finished speaking with a dear friend of mine, a Ms. Toneta Hollis, I was filled with a strength, will and motivation to share a part of me.

Her mother, one Ms. Ella Hollis was also on the phone and shared with me words of additional influence; "put your thoughts down on paper." That has never left my head.

I also express my gratitude to the CEO of "Un-caged Minds," Mr. Donald Reynolds, one who always gave me the words of encouragement when I needed them most. He inspired me and imparted on me a knowledge of self-determination and a blue print as I observed him. He also left me with these words; "Deon, you gotta water your seed, you not going to be here forever to tell your story, but your story would be here forever after you're gone."

This book was not made to glorify the glitz *or* horrors that come with an addiction to heroin, A.K.A. Dog Food. I pray that this story can touch at least one person that struggles in the battle with one of the deadliest drugs. It has led so many to their graves and has affected my life and that of my family for too many generations.

It is with a hope and the grace of God that we stand together, share our stories and from them unite; unite in a common interest to beat the demon, to beat the evil and to show the world we can win!

Acknowledgements

First and foremost, I thank God and my personal savior, the Lord Jesus Christ for giving me the health and breath to write this story. I am thankful for the protection and lessons through all these years that have brought me to this point in my life, a time to share my story.

To daddy's little girl, my Boo-Boo; Jasmine Paschal, my heart, true love, my everything. You are my reason for living and being the best man, the best person that I can be. I love you more than words can express.

To the man and woman that God has blessed me with; my parents, Mr. and Mrs. Charles and Sandra Boss. You have given me so much through all of the years; priceless. Please know that your efforts did not go unrecognized. All of your teachings have stayed with me and may this work reflect just a fraction of that in your honor.

From the same Dog House, my siblings; Myron, Myrail, my twin sis "The Gina" Latiesha Harris, my niece Lydiya Harris and nephew Robert Norris. Also, Onnie Jackson, thank you so much for your love and support.

Thank you to Jessie and Alexis Ankum, Pauline Lurkens and the whole Lurken's family; Albert, Alex, Anglea and

Nicole Hackett.

I'm grateful for meeting Jerry Dinnius and for his introduction to a man that I am indebted to for the enormous work he contributed to making the story, for making this story of Dog Food a reality, the editor and true god of the story, Mr. H.J. Birk. Thank you for everything and most of all, for your presence and patience.

God so does work through people and he has connected the dots to put this book together. Christopher Cungtion, my home boy, brother, friend and most of all, a brother in Christ; thank you for all your brotherly advice, honesty and encouraging words:

"you know what we do, were just passing through"

Here comes the good-part-shout-out to my real "peoples" that I have met and learned so much from on my journey; my cousins Felicia AKA "Fe-Fe", Bashawn, Pooh, Elisha, Jenifer, Felina, Lil' Pimp, Elizabeth, Tangie, Dana, Alvin, Wilie Will-Will, Tito, Rachel, Lovia, Gregory AKA "Snake", Johnny AKA "J-Bro", Jamaro, Janesha, Pooby, Angel, Rita,Rhonda, Fernado, Rochelle, Crystal, Christine, Darayl, Rene, Ricky, Niedra, Trice, Ronnie Boo, Latrell "Poola" Harris, Mookie, Joshua, Alica Harris, Raven "Rae Rae" Sparkman,

Felica Sparkman, Alica Shaw, Latrice Shaw, Tracy Swan, my uncles- Allen, Chris and Willie.   Mattie A.K.A. "Mama, Susuan "Sue-Sue" Tammy, Greg "killer" Miller, Lil' Ronnie, Dara Redmond, Cynthia Curry and the Hollis family, June

Dupree and Toya, Rosetta, Angel and the Fluker and Jackson family.

A special shout out to; Patrice Evans and family, Tiffany Rodgers and family, Jerry Miles AKA "Batman", LeAndre, Maurwa, Kalidu, Lerian, the Davis family; Vernon, Vaquatia, Taronna, Violett and to; James, Marlon, Corey, Jawan, Benjamin, Latrisha, Lil' Danny, Rudy, Debra, Clarice AKA "Angie", Robert, Nicole, Ms. Belk, Kenyatta and the Smith family, Puff, Terrance, Robin and the Holloway Family, Franklin and the Coleman family, Ebony, Twanda, Kenji and the Gladney family, Sholanda and the Pillow family, Jimmy, Samantha, Kimberly, Jerry, Angel and the Sanders family, Joseph, Vic, Francios and the Norris family, Nita, Lorenzo, AKA "Maine", Curt, Bra-Bra, Shenett, Bernedette, J.R., Carmeshia, Blood, Mindy, Jennifer, Jessica, Tiffany, Aliva and the Hegarty family, Bo, Quincy, Ace, Na-Na, Gino "the Gift", Burpie, Killa, Larry AKA "Trav", Don Juan Harrison and Kenneth "Boo" Hart.

To my main men; Thomas "Slick" King, Cavel! Smallwood, Sam "Bino" Hinton, Dre, Adonis "AC" Carswell and family, Richard "Richie" Hodges & family, Willie "Squillie" Harris, Corey "Mac Buddy" Wright, Markus "CKI", Robinson "Bay-Bay" Patterson, "Moose Head" William "Pokie" Moore, Prince "P" Rush, J-Rock, "Al" Cole mankie, Paul "P" Porter, Barry "face" Moss, "Lil' Chris" Davis, Lil' Mike, Myron, "RR" Rodgers, Damon Richardson, Terrance "T-Dub" Wright, Tabitha Maro, Pete Langford, Rick

Pemble and John Sherwood, Jerome "Jay" Austin, Aletha Hughes and family, Sarah Marie Reed, Tara Griffith, Dixon, Tyrone "Ty" Griffith, TP, Mechie "Qualow" Ivy and Montrail "4" Butcher.

To my Partners, the ones who saw the magic take place right before their very eyes; Chip, T.D., T.C., Charles "Pookie" Jackson, Twin A.K.A Lawrence, Dermont "Juice" Broussard and to my main man "Fullie", Cortez Johnson and family, Dion "The Sleeping Giant", Gregory Sykes and to Wayner "Musso" Black, Eric
"Quake" Richmond, Niecho Thorton, Marcus Wellington, Karren "Frank Nitty" Bradley, Ant, "Sleepy" Knox and "Worm G".

To all the grammar schools that helped to shape my adolescent mind: Henry Suder, Nathaniel Dett, George Gershwin, Perkin Bass, Guglielmo Marconi, Matthew Henson, Herbert Spencer and to John Marshall High School whose halls will always be in my mind.
Thank you to the Taylor Street, "Gateway Recovery Program" on the west side of Chicago, for influencing my mind; I wasn't ready at the time, but now I am! Thank you Ms. Barbra Bethford, Jackie Pearson, Parish, Ken and the entire staff.

I would like to also thank the IDOC Boot Camp of DuQuoin for all of the physical and combat training that I still maintain today.

Thank you to the Kennedy family that planted a seed in my spiritual growth and to Pastor Michael Kennedy for all the mentorship.

To the places of custody, of which many would deem ugly, I found to be a blessing in the lessons learned; Cook County Jail and Linn County in Cedar Rapids. Also, to the Honorable Judge Linda Reade, for I could not have written this book without her; I may have never found the courage and strength to put my story down on paper.

To the FCI Pekin staff; you have all seen me transform from an unruly boy to an accountable and responsible man over the last eleven years, especially to R. Thomas for his understanding and support and to B. "K Dog" Kearns.

To all of those that I have brushed against inside the walls and wire for just a moment in my journey, this is for you as well, we have come from the same streets and the same struggles.

Last and certainly not least, those that have been affected by the tragedies and those that have been lost during them (may they rest in peace); Sadie B. Harris, Cleotha Hodges, Lula K. Hodges, Annette Harris, William "Will" Holloway, Duane "Duball" Franklin and Johnell "Munchie" Harris. To Terry Brooks, Areatha Ann Roberts, Mona Lisa O'Bannon-Fuller, Patrice "Poochie" Steel, Cecil "Zeke", Charlie Boss, Melvin Boss, Marnette Boss, Lilly Bell Casey, 2 Pac,

Notorious B.I.G., Eazy-E and Mr. James Bolden a thank you goes out and to Mr. Richard Matzke, my first editor who passed during this and to Crystell Publications.

To the most important of this project, those that read it; my fans and supporters, may God continue to bless you all. I pray that I have delivered to you, the best of me, my heart and soul.

....and to JB who said, "this book will be a success,"... West Side!

Prologue

The west side of Chicago, or the "CHI" as was taught when you were very young, was a rapidly growing and dynamic area in the late eighties. Dre was just another kid growing up on the block trying to make it through the sixth grade. Most of his education to this point was from the school of hard knocks and things didn't seem to be much different at his new school.

"Alright lil' Nigga, then I'll see yo punk ass after school!" threatened the foot taller boy as he walked away from Dre. The crowd had begun to settle in, apparently creating an apprehension on the part of the larger boy despite his advantage of size. This lead only to a deferment of the inevitable; an after school event.

The kid disrespected Dre as much as one can in the sixth grade. Slighting ones family or economic status was about as personal as one could get and when it occurred, you addressed it. If you allowed it to happen, you just invited more of the same from others.

Dre wouldn't stand for it, regardless of the difference in size. *It was the size of the heart in the fighter,* Dre told himself, *not the size of the fighter.* Dre stood his ground, facing the much bigger kid that had just made fun of his shoes. *Payless shoes or not, I'm not backing down,* Dre repeated to himself with absolute confidence and conviction.

It was the 2:30 bell that indicated to Dre it was time to return to the earlier business at hand, the business of disrespect. His brother and sister awaited him as he exited the school building and approached the already forming crowd. *I'm not backing down,* kept playing over and over in Dre's mind.

One of the kids pointed at Dre as he approached," Don't run now!" he warned with a snide and condescending tone.

"I ain't runnin' from nobody!" trumpeted Dre with equal curtness and purpose as he squared off with the taller boy that stood in the circle of kids that had now completely formed.

The larger kid stole off on Dre like something bad, causing the typical adolescent reactions of; "oohs" and "aahs." When Dre caught a glimpse of his other siblings, dim images from his blurred vision as he took repeated shots to his face, something in him was triggered. He was filled with a rage he had never felt before. It filed him in an instant, as if a type of survival mechanism and it made him feel ten feet tall.

Dre took off his coat despite the cold winter air and began to dance like *Sugar Ray* and proceeded to work the other kid with similar flare and style as the *Champ*. The "oohs" and "aahs" were now replaced with a silence and awe as Dre demonstrated that the larger kid was little more than talk. The big kid found nothing but retribution from the fists of the boy that danced in those *Payless* shoes.

The silence soon dissipated and the air was replaced with cheers from the kids as Dre landed shot after shot; right, left, upper cut, upper cut and all sorts of combos from around the world! As the bigger boy hit the ground the crowd and Dre felt the ground beneath them move a little, they could almost feel the pain Dre laid on him.

The western sun began to nestle lower in the sky, serving as a backdrop to the scene and separating the crowd by only their shadows as Dre stood proudly over the boy.

"I whooped your ass with these *Payless* shoes!" declared Dre as he looked down over the fallen figure. His heart was racing and his hands hurt.

The crowd's laughter of mockery was thrown at the boy as Dre's wit kept them engaged in the events. This soon subsided as a teacher grabbed both boys. In such haste however, she almost fell on the slippery ground. This gave cause for an even greater uproar, inviting more laughter, especially from one, Sedrick "Slick" Young, a trend setter on fashion, ergo,

"Slick."

Due to the exuberant expression by Slick, the teacher also invited him to join the other two boys.

"I didn't have nothin' to do with no fighting! Why you want me to come back in the school?" argumentatively inquired Slick.

"Well Mr. Young, since you think everything is so terribly funny, you can stay after school and share all of your stories and enlighten me," profoundly replied the teacher with a seriousness that seemed to only come from elementary teachers when someone was in trouble.

What seemed like forever later, the boys were released, each going their separate ways; Dre and Slick in one direction and the beaten' boy in the other.

Dre and Slick made small talk and in the midst of their youthful antics and introductions they had come to find out that they lived very near one another. During their walk, Dre couldn't help but notice how all the pushers riding by blew their horns at Slick, demonstrating to Dre how heavily involved Slick's family was in the *traffic* of the neighborhood.

"I see you got up with that Nigga, *glamour Joe*? Claimed Slick, with a sarcastic emphasis on the *glamour Joe*, referring to the boy Dre had beaten, but with respect on the rest.

"Yeah, that Nigga was tryin' to case my shoes," admitted Dre. "Man, fuck this shit, I need to get me some cheese to cop me a pair of those Nikes you wearin', those the ones he had on when he won the dunk contest last weekend!" declared Dre.

"I know how you can make some scratch for the *Nikes*, a jogging suit and a *Starter* jacket Joe," temptingly offered Slick. "Fact, we can go down on Madison and Keeler at *Price Barber* Shop and even meet Michael Jordan!" emphatically bragged Slick.

"Straight-up man?" Now I see why they call you *Slick*!" announced Dre with a sense of envy and admiration folded in an adolescent anxiousness.

As the two boys enjoyed Dre's comment, Slick's uncle pulled up on them in an '88 short body *Park Avenue* with five point rims, a custom rag top and a chrome bottom that read: *I'm Hurtin' 'em.*

Easy E's, "No More Question" was bumpin' as the scene was attractive and appealing to an impressionable boy from the streets; Dre was hooked on the spot.

When Dre jumped into the car with Slick, he was entering a new world, a new continuum of existence that would shape and direct the rest of his life; only one thing, the boy that wanted to be a man, didn't even know it.

That same night, Slick started showing Dre the ropes as they worked security on the block. Dre was taught how *not* to let the police roll up on you and how *not* to attract unwarranted attention. Dre's young age often precluded "warranted" attention by the authorities; that was until they saw his face around too many scenes too many times. This resulted in one, of many, pursuits that Dre would evade due to his quick mind, quick speed and youthful endurance.

Soon, Dre found himself donning the *Starter* jacket, wearing the *Jordans* and even had a chance to meet the man himself. He was entranced by the lifestyle that offered him a chance to feel like a man. These were the streets of CHI, and to Dre they were paved with gold; they were built on *Dog Food*.

Chapter 1
Little Child Running Wild

Each exhaled breath took on a life of its own as the cold air captured it and then catapulted it against the front windshield.

"Damn, I gotta find me one, I can't find me no motherfucker out here," he said under his breath, watching the traces of his last words float up into a swirl against the window.

He rubbed his eyes that burned from a night of too much of one thing and not enough of another. His desperate attempts to clear the windshield with his hand only resulted in smearing the frost more and more. The smoke from his cigarette was billowing in the opposite direction of his breath. It was a cacophony of events; the puffing of his cigarette while rubbing his face and trying to wipe the window; a futile effort.

His *Newport* is near its butt, his eyes are blood-shot and he is rocking back and forth as his head is turning side to side. He is looking, seeking, searching for his mark. With each movement his breath quickens like a steady drum roll, but there is no drum other than the drumming in his head accompanied by the ensuing nausea; he needed a fix and he needed it bad.

"This fuckin' gorilla is starting to shake in his cage," he announces to the competing noises coming from his '84 Regal and those in his head as he rolls down the driver side window.

The smell from the *McDonald's* off Madison Avenue wafts in the air as the winds blow hard on the west side, filling his nostrils and his belly with aroma just long enough for him to focus; *there it is, his guy, the mark!* His pulse quickens, his breath stops, he is focused, he is zeroing in on his prey; *he belongs to me*, he thinks to himself, *that boy belongs to me!*

Turning off on Karlov into the McDonald's parking lot he begins to develop a clearer picture of his mark as he draws closer; slight build, in his forties and too soft looking to put up much of a fight, an easy prey makes for an easy day.

Flicking what is left of his square out the window he is hit with the cool, crisp, tight air. His lungs gulp, his eyes squint and his jaw flexes. The taste in his mouth is atrocious, his eyes burn, his whole body hurts and he can't lose the feeling that he is going to shit himself.

His mind is racing; *does he jump into the guys' car or does he follow him to a less public place?* He placates as he looks at his dashboard. *What's the play?* He asks himself. Seeing the gas gauge below "E" he realizes his only option is to jump out of his car and into the strangers' car.

He puts his car in park, pulls up the hood of his *hoodie,* grabs the .38 sitting in the passenger seat and shoves it into his pocket as he steps from his car. He no longer feels the cold, the numbness hits his hands immediately, and his nose is running like a faucet, his eyes watering and his shoes crunching the hard barren ground beneath him.

With each stride his mark is made clearer and clearer, he is determined, he is ready, he needs this. He puts his hand in his pocket to make sure that the .38 is still snuggled where it was just a second ago, giving him confidence and security despite the line of sweat running down the middle of his back and off his forehead under the *hoodie.* He is beginning to feel the cool sensation of the beads of sweat as the wind whips across the parking lot, but not even the eastern wind can match his adrenaline as he unconsciously holds his breath and reaches for the *marks'* passenger side door handle.

His fingers touch the metal. Feeling the cool sensation his breath stops, and anticipating what is about to happen, his heart halts. He leans forward to enter.

"Hey, Dre, is that you? Dre?" is shouted from behind him, causing him to jerk his hand away just before pulling the car door open, spinning in the direction from where the voice came.

As he spins towards the noise he peers through the window to see the white man, his *mark*, sitting in the driver's seat reading what looks like some type of report.

"Slick!" shockingly responds Dre, "My, nigga, what's poppin'?"

Dre almost shouts as if overcome with a sense of relief and joy as he calmly pulls his hand away from the door handle and places it back on top of the .38 in his jacket pocket.

"I see you're still up to your old tricks," as Slick approaches with a swagger that only the street can teach, finishing his sentence without taking a breath, "I need you to run the Tip for me today."
"Don't even trip, you know I got you. I'm kinda fucked up, give me something to get my sick off," pleadingly but with what dignity Dre could muster.

Slick had a natural athletic build and carried himself with confidence, a feature beneficial to the world he was in, where action took precedence and he was a man of such accord.

Slick reached into his pocket and gave Dre three blows and told him to follow him. Dre was still respected in the crowd, plus, everyone knew that if Dre was around the spot, the dope had to be good. As Slick went into McDonald's, Dre got back into his car; both men anxiously awaiting their respective consumptions.

Dre slowly and cautiously placed the blows on his lap, looking down on them as if they were a lifeline, like oxygen. So desperate to release the pain, he opened the first one and ate it as if it were *Fun Dip Kool-Aid* all in one. As the medicine hit the back of his throat while crossing over his tongue, he could taste the cutting agent. He could feel the warmth fill his stomach.

With each heartbeat his aches subsiding, disappearing as gently as a breath vanishes into the cool winter air. As the pain diminished he was filled with an ecstasy, like that of sunshine pushing through the rain on his wedding day.

As he blew his nose, he shit himself. *Fuck, how could this lil' powder be so powerful,* he wondered as he poured the other two onto a CD case. In one snort, the powder was gone, just like a magic trick, saying to himself, *"now you see it, now you don't".* He was laughing to himself and feeling so good all over, like a different man. He reached in the back and pulled out his fitted cap, sitting back down he realized he had an issue; *what am I going to do with the shit stuck to my ass?*

He didn't have time to go shower, so he rationalized; *I can just go into McDonald's and take off these shitty drawers.*

As he was getting out of his car, so was his mark. Dre,

feeling much better now, had more pressing issues, like the fecal matter up in his business, so he was not too interested in him.

Then he saw it. In absolute disbelief, *the fucker showing the glimmer of a badge, a bullet proof vest and hosta. The early bird do get the worm, I just missed a case or worse yet, a death bullet,* Dre thought to himself as he exhaled a deep sigh relief.

Dre looked up to the sky and said, "Thank you Jesus," with a humble nod of his head.

Slick was still waiting for Dre as he exited the McDonald's. Dre's car wouldn't even start it was so far below the "E." *Just imagine if he took the mark and then tried to get away,* he thought to himself, *and he was an agent to boot! Shitting himself was a nice consolation at least; it was something he could clean up and he wouldn't have to serve time for.* Dre smiled as the thoughts rolled through his mind. He jumped into the truck with Slick and adjusted his cap.

"You step in some shit or what, check the bottom of your shoes!" exclaimed Slick, "you got it smellin' like a fuckin' horse barn or something."

The creases on his brown skinned forehead were showing his frustration as he turned up the music. This was no new look for Dre as Slick had a tendency to carry a frown and appear upset even though he wasn't.

They drove off thumping to *Spice 1* "Money Gone," puffing from the 15-inch woofer slick was pushing. The gray Suburban had tinted shade and chrome rims with all the accessories of necessity; TV, DVD, video games. It was a sweet ride; it was the whole deal.

"Let me get your thumper?" asked Slick as he pushed a button on the stereo and a secret compartment appeared magically under the steering wheel. "It's too early and you know how I love my Music. How's that dope hitting you?"

"Ooh, it's bomb, I got a good drain Joe," *like a little child running wild* he thought to himself. Dre's eyes rolled back into his head to the rhythm of the music, echoing in his head a sweet lullaby, making him feel all warm and safe inside. On the outside, like a statue, a fixed smile appeared on Dre and the lines on his face were so still he looked like he had been frozen in time.

Chapter 2
Welcome to Crook County

The only thing making Dre feel alive in route to Cook Jail was the constant nausea resulting from the last two days of being locked up and without a fix. The ride from area 5 police station on Harrison and Kedize brought back memories, far too many of them. The nine other guys in the paddy wagon reminded him that there was more reality to his situation than the nausea, one that he didn't like.

Shit, I'm back, going through this bullshit again. I'm glad the turnkey made sure my prints came back on time to get this ball rolling, was the only comforting thought Dre could focus on. He glanced around the wagon and saw the look in some of their eyes, the scared, unknown look that accompanied a first time 'Rodeo'.

"Hey Joe, what you locked up for?" one of the guys asked

Dre.

"Mindin' my own fucking business Charlie," Dre replied with a curt, breaking the uneasy silence with laughter all around.

Dre was handcuffed to a guy near a window. Dre's focused gaze out the crack between the metal bars was broken by the subtle plea.

"A young blood, reach down to the floor with me," whispered his cuff partner.
"For what?" Dre demanded.
"I got somethin' in the sole of my shoes; I'm tryin' to get to."

Before the last word was out, Dre knew that it was one of two things; "Rocks" or that "China White" called "Blows," A.K.A. *Dog Food.*

Inclined to accommodate his partner with a wish, they bent down together, revealing the small tin foil packages; *Dog Food!*
Dre lit up like a Christmas tree, eying such a present.

What seemed like only moments later, Dre was wakened from his brief nod as the paddy wagon was pulling up to the basement of the Cook County Jail and the boisterous sound emanated from the big gated bars as they clashed together closing behind their entrance. No sooner had Dre focused in on where they were, the doors flew open to the sight Dre couldn't stand.

"All right, every motherfucker get up, let's go! Walk in a single file line in two's," yelled the officer out the corner of his mouth, looking back and forth like a small dog looking for a bone.

Traveling in twos was difficult, in fact it was the only way they could move as they were handcuffed together, *master of the obvious* came to mind as they shuffled in small steps due to the shackles around their ankles as well as their wrists. *Just the smell of this shit is a hell hole;* Dre grimaced to himself, making his stomach start to turn again.

The holding cells were full of guys from every direction of the wind; South side, West side, East Side and North side and even some representation from different skirts of the suburbs around CHI. Many of the guys are heading up stairs to see the judge, hoping they will be able to escape the madness of going through processing and seeing the dick doctor in the basement!

Dre could see the situation he was in and admitted to himself; *I already know I gotta do some County time, I got a probation hold.* His contemplation was brief as it was broken up by all of the nervous small talk around him and Dre just nodded politely as that was all he could do considering the stuff he just snorted in the wagon was still fresh on the brain.

Dre knew that after court upstairs was finished, the guys that *got no probable cause* stayed there to get released. The other guys who were looking at getting bonds, whether it be $100 or even $10,000, headed downstairs to get searched, ID'd, fingerprinted and seen by the dick doctor.

Dre was walking in a long, cold, dirty tunnel flanked by walls of needed repair, worn by the years of visitors and the absence of care. Dre imagined all of the gang chiefs that had actually handled their business in these very tunnels. He was filled with a sense of pride and walked with his head high; he was walking in the footsteps of legends.

"A Dre, when we get in the bullpen, you think I can bomb one of your squares off you?"
"Man Joe, I don't got shit to smoke on. When they got me I was smoking on a filter damn near." Both men laughing as the last word came out of Dre's mouth; anything to break the monotony of the moment, anything to escape the scene.

The Sheriff broke the group of approximately seventy guys into three separate bullpens to facilitate the process in an orderly fashion. The first thing required was the relinquishing of all of their personal items. Dre knew full well that guys would be tryin' to keep money on them to smoke up every square or cigarette they could or they would be tryin' to get drugs upstairs without getting beat half to death by the Sheriff.

The stench in the bullpen was atrocious; it was a stale, pungent odor, the kind that would make a Billy goat puke. The smell was consistent with the images; guys curled up in the corners, all balled up *dope sick* on the floor, withdrawing from not having their fix; from missing their *Dog food.*

The room is bustling with the spreading of the latest gossip of who got caught with whose dope on whosever spot they were working. The going rate was $1 to $5 for a cigarette.

They are calling guys in to ask them questions regarding their state of minds; *are they thinking of killing someone or themselves?* This is followed by seeing the dick doctor. They take a metal *Q-tip* and insert it into the head of your shit and move it around like they are trying to screw the cap off a bottle. Then they throw you up against the wall for an x-ray, followed by a picture for your ID before they process you to classification: maximum, medium or minimum security.

The background is filled with voices and the faint echoing of V 103 F.M. as Dre is walking through the bullpen scanning for a familiar face. Sure enough, he spots a cousin of one of his homeboys who is motioning Dre over.

"What up Joe?" the man hollers over the crowd while simultaneously holding up his hand and spreading out his fingers in sign.

Just as Dre is about to reciprocate the gesture, he was called out by the lieutenant with a gesture from his hand; condescending and with authority.

As Dre approached the officer, *Wham!!* Right upside the head and across his ear, Dre is smacked so hard that his ears are ringing like he just left a concert, pulsing and throbbing.

"You throwin' gang signs up in my jail?" said the man in the crisp pressed shirt. "Now go sit your ass down!" demanded the man in white.

Dre walked away knowing there was nothing he could do, not right then, not right now. He walked away saying to himself; *I'll kill that punk motherfucker.*

All the while, the man who threw the sign at him to begin with, is laughing hysterically, something Dre did not appreciate either. Watching the man bent over in laughter, Dre was reminded that the high was just slapped outta him.

It was approaching the fourth quarter and by now the guys had made their phone calls to notify their loved ones and to tell them where they were and what their bail was set at. If there was a bond and their people paid the bail they would be released. If not, they were heading upstairs onto the decks.

It was a long arduous seven-hour process in all and it was finally time to go onto the decks, right before the "coup de grace" that is; the strip search.

"We want every mother fucker to get on the straight line

and strip down to nuts and balls!" shouted the Sheriff.

Dre can only laugh because of the redundancy of a nut being the same as a ball. His laughter is soon shattered by the constancy of the demands and increased agitation in the Sheriff's voice.

"Don't shake a mother fuckin' thing either, and if you get a smart idea by tryin' to take some dope upstairs, you got another thing comin'!"

Breaking his threats with an even stare across the room, breathing heavy as his mouth has worked harder than the rest of him over the years as his gut now sagged over his belt.

"I wish you could ask the last couple of mother fuckers about that, but they still at Medical at Cermack!" he trumpeted.

"So if you got anything, whether it is weed, blows, rocks, tees blues, tac, leaf, pills, anything, even Tylenol, put it in the middle on the floor. You won't be charged with it and we won't kick your ass!"

"Now, when you are done strippin', turn your asses around and press your nose against the wall unless you want the dog shit beat from you by me or one of my partners here!" cautioned so arrogantly the voice behind the badge, as the rest of the less than physically fit deputies put on their black leather gloves to join the search.

There is always a dumb one, Dre thought, and this time it was the one next to him. He was trying to smuggle some dope in the tongue of his shoe. So the beating proceeded as promised.

As four of them took turns on the man, the Sheriff reminded the group that, "there is always one, I knew there would be one stupid mother fucker! I just knew it!" as he gave the prisoner a personal boot for good measure.

"I swear!" is streaming from the man's mouth along with liquid and blood, "those ain't my shoes, they my uncles! Help me, somebody help me, please!" the voice pleaded to an empty response.
"Well, stupid fucker, you shouldn't have worn them, it's your bad day today," punctuating the last comment with a fist to the temple.

Dre knew with all that was going on next to him, all the vibrations happening, keeping his nose to the wall was best, unless he wanted some of that drama. He had already had enough from the white shirt "Lou" earlier when he got slapped into next week. Dre kept his nose to the wall.

Moving through the procession into laundry was a warm welcome compared to the previous demonstration of stupidity and brutality.

"What size Doc suit you want Joe?" one of the guys asked, an orderly who knew Dre from a previous stint, making Dre feel welcome and like a regular. He wasn't just shovin' Dre a shirt and pants like the average "Rudy Poot."

After they picked up their clothing, Dre lead a pack up to Division 6 with about twenty guys going on different tiers on the deck.

After a full, eventful day of talking shit and eating it along with all of the drama, and coming down off his high, Dre was tired, just plain tired. *Man am I ready to get me a lil' rest so I can make a phone call in the morning to call my baby,* were the only comforting words that crossed his lips as he turned onto the deck.

Welcome to a few months of hell, Dre thought to himself, *welcome to Cook County Jail!*

Chapter 3
Shooting Gallery

The ring broke the silence, startling Sally as she sat contemplating last night's sermon message. The ring echoing throughout the room was interrupted mid-tone as Sally instinctively grabbed the receiver.

"Hello" she said rushing her words into the phone.

The words had not entirely escaped her mouth when they were met with equal eagerness on the other end.

"Hey Aunt Sally is Dre there?"

Aunt Sally would recognize that voice anywhere, *Munchie,* she said to herself in a whisper.

"Naw," sighing Aunt Sally, "he is back in that damn County!"

"For what?" retorted Munchie as more of a reaction than a complete thought resulting in a question.

Munchie and Dre had a long history together. Their mothers were sisters and as a result they went through a lot of the same things together, too much actually for boys their age. Their exposure to drugs and the effects that drugs have were almost second nature to them. They had a history that primarily involved drugs and alcohol. There was no changing it or going back, they were products of their environment.

"Ain't no telling with him, most likely to do with some dope," conceded Sally, her voice trailing off, as Munchie pressed his ear harder against the receiver so as to catch every word.

"He haven't called me yet Munchie, 'cuz he already knows what I'm going to tell him."

Aunt Sally had seen most everything a woman needed to see in a lifetime, plus some, and while sympathetic, she knew that lessons in life are what make us stronger and wiser.

"He got himself into this mess, he can get himself out," finished Sally with what seemed like a rehearsed finiteness.

Pausing just long enough to hear the subtle breathing of Munchie and the once faint background of *Master P's,* "No Limit Soldiers," now thumping in the background.

"Auntie, when you talk to him, tell him to give me call."

"I will Munchie. By the way, how is your Dad?"

"We cool Auntie, be glad when y'all come down here," emphasizing "here" in a way that only Munchie could.

"Well nephew, I'll be sure to give him the message when I hear from him and tell your Dad I said, what-up and all my love."

"Love you too Auntie," Munchie tried to sneak into the phone before he was met with the dial tone.

"Munchie!" resonated from the living room just as the dial tone vanished from his ear.

"Aye, son, come and help with the squares," continued the demanding voice.

Munchie knew the art of tearing aluminum foil into squares and he was obedient to a fault to the instructive voice coming from the other room; it belonged to his dad, Terry.

Terry reminded you of a cross between rapper Beanie Sigel Scarface; dark skinned, long hair, medium build and carried himself with a certain confidence. Terry was a no bullshit direct mother fucker that bent to no man. While Munchie and he shared similar looks, their demeanors and natures could not be further apart, they were on opposite ends of the personality spectrum.

Even though Terry was not around much while Munchie was growing up, Munchie admired him and wanted to be around him and was always seeking his approval.

When Munchie walked into the kitchen, Terry was sitting on 20 grams of *Dog Food* and he was sifting the heroin from a plate he was shaking into a blender.

"How much you need?" wondered Munchie, not certain if he asked it aloud or only to himself.
"Cutting about 2 grams' street," answered Terry, confirming to Munchie that he had said it out loud.

The dope Terry had was so potent that prior to him adding the *Dormin* sleeping pills you could see dust clouds from the powder, swirling out of the baggies. Terry learned long ago that if he would add seven capsules of *Dormin* to every gram of *Dog Food* it would keep customers from over-dosing due to its potency. Terry himself would occasionally snort some through his nose and blow smoke out of his mouth, it was one way for him to test and show its concentration.

"Is you going to weigh all dat?" interrupted Munchie.
"Naw son, them mother fuckers ain't crazy enough, 'cuz if they try to short me for anything, I'm goin' to rob the shit out of them," Terry laughing in unison with Munchie.

With Munchie tearing and breaking the foil into squares, Terry could focus on blending the pink sleeping capsules like he was mixin' a fruit drink. The sound of the blender resonated off the walls and other equipment, a tone that Munchie was far too familiar with.

Jumping in his seat, Munchies' head snapped towards his Dad. Over the blender came a pounding on the door, like someone wanted to break it down, not to announce their arrival. Terry stopped the blender and very calmly instructed Munchie to turn the music down. They could read each other's face; the police.

In one motion, Terry was up, walking across the living room, already giving Munchie instructions to stay put as he grabbed his 357 from under the couch.

"If you hear any serious commotion, throw all of this shit in the sink and poor water on it!" Instructed Terry.

Glancing out the peephole with worrisome concentration, Terry sighed with an exhale that seemed to have no beginning or end. You could sense his anger over the relief as he ripped the door open.

"What the fuck?" Who the fuck told you to bring yo' stupid ass over here?" Who told you to come knockin' like the mother fuckin' police? Who Pete? Who?" hammered Terry into the face of the skinny, short-haired, big eyed man standing in the hallway.

The man's eyes grew even larger than two dollar quarters

from staring down the nose of the cold 357 Terry held steady in his hand. The barrel was silent, echoing nothing back, only looking at him with no concern; the closeness of death, just a triggers' pull away.

"T!" desperately stammered Pete, "I meant to hit you up on the cell, but I'm sick as a dog, I just need a lick, I need to be medicated baby."

Pete had been good for Terry; he showed him how sweet the cash was from Cedar Rapids connections. Usually Terry would not allow anyone in his crib, especially when he was mixing a bomb up on dope, but in this case, Terry would make the exception. Plus, Terry could tell from Pete's eyes and nose that he was close to getting sick. The last thing Terry wanted was Pete's insides all over his living room floor.

Terry was confident that Pete wouldn't play any games and he knew Pete was a straight-shooter; he injected his dope straight into his veins, unlike Terry who snorted it. Terry knew, from this, that Pete's dependency level was high and the wad of Benjamin's in his pocket even made the proposition all the more attractive to Terry.

"Bring yo ass in and go downstairs in the basement; I'll be down; whatcha you want?"

"Bring me a half a gram," announced Pete, throwing it into the air like the lyrics to a well-known song.

To Terry, a song he had heard far too often, nonetheless, it was music to his ears. After all, he was in the money business; the business of *Dog Food.*

"Got your works on you?" trailed Terry's voice over Pete's shoulder as he headed down the stairs.

Terry hated needles and thought people that shot dope were fools. While those who shot thought they were cleaner and didn't waste as much as those who snorted it. Either way, it was $150 dollars to Terry and Pete could take it any way he wanted to.

With his 357 already back under the couch, Terry entered the kitchen and instructed Munchie to put a half gram on the scale.

Grabbing it from Munchie, their eyes met. Terry gave him a nod of approval and headed off out of the kitchen and down the stairs, with Munchie sheepishly following.

"Here you go," offered Terry as if Pete had just been served at one of the finest restaurants in town.
"That will be $150 dollars' nigga!" Terry announced, articulately mimicking a white cashier's voice, causing both men to smile and even laugh a little.

As soon as the money left Pete's hands, his belt was

around his arm, desperately tightening it, waiting for the veins to surface. He tore the white cotton from the end of his cigarette and placed it gingerly on the table. With a nice amount of heroin in the spoon, he added a few drops of water and wafted it over his flame with the precision of a surgeon. When Pete could see the bubbles and hear the crackling, he absorbed it with the cotton and filled his needle for the anxiously awaiting arm that was now throbbing from the restriction of the belt and the need to feel the rush. The 60cc's glistening in the firelight, waiting to find its way into Pete, waiting to find its way home.

After so many years of use, the veins can collapse, they become harder and harder to find. The arm is typically the first track taken so it is one of the first areas to become difficult to use; Pete was no exception. Struggling to find a vein, without a blink, Pete took off a shoe and quickly released the golden honey into his foot.

Pete's face immediately transformed from one of despair and panic to one of tranquility and peace, Munchie stood silent in the corner of the room watching this transformation and wondered to himself what it must feel like.

Pete's eyes rolled back into his head as he started that rocket ride into the sky in search of a falling star. He was flyin' off the shot, off the power; the power of *Dog food*.

Chapter 4
Mr. Bone

Three weeks had passed and Dre was starting to see the transformation of his complexion. His skin was *clean and smooth and lookin' good,* he thought to himself as he stared into the polished acrylic mirror. As his eyes scanned the outline of his own face he could tell he had put on some weight with all of the eating and sleeping and no drugs. He recognized a part of the old him but could see the new him emerging. He stood there feeling good physically and contemplated his situation; his life, his beliefs and those that influenced him the most. Above all there was God. There was his mom Sally Hall; she was a motivation and influence as she was a recovering addict herself. Then there was Mr. Bone, probably one of the greatest influences on his life, a man he respected.

Almost as if manifesting his appearance through thought, Mr. Bone walked into his cell like a spirit on the wind, breaking

Dre out of his trance.

"Hey Dre, I gotta go to the doc later, but Ms. Mindy should be dropping a package off later."

Mindy was one of the female Sheriff Deputies that worked the tier while also on Mr. Bone's payroll. Dre appreciated her visits lately, compliments of Mr. Bone of course. Mr. Bone was a man of discipline and control. His mannerisms and articulation was purposeful and with tact, he was a gentleman. The years of incarceration were good to his physical appearance as a man in his late 50s, early 60s he was in great shape and his face was not nearly as weathered as one of *so* many years would typically be. Prison did give him that benefit. He had a life sentence in the Feds on drug charges, but was in the County for allegations of murder.

It was nothing for him to look into a person's eyes and see right through them, right to their core. He could sense what they feared, what they were feeling, he could see into their heart if not their soul. He was meticulous with the details of his dealings and it was because of these attributes that he drew people to him, his aura had a power to draw people close to him if he wanted it and Dre was no exception.

"Dre, you clean up pretty nice, now you gotta always remember you can be the customer or you can be the controller of the game," spoke Mr. Bone almost in a whisper, but one that you could hear clearly as if he was standing right next to you.

"I felt what it's like to be a customer," mumbled Dre as he reflected back on when he first made it on the deck. He was so dope sick he had to move his cot next to the toilette so he wouldn't puke or shit on himself. The withdrawals were almost unbearable; the cold sweats, sleepless nights, the shaking like your bones were going to bust through the skin and the feeling that you couldn't *move* any part of your body as you lay helpless on your back. Mr. Bone was there, helping him to his feet and to the shower, putting him in a chair allowing the hot water to sooth the pain a little. Dre had no energy, he couldn't eat. He was summarizing in his mind how the dope had gotten to him; how the *Dog Food* would eat him up while he was taking it and how it would spit him out when he stopped taking it. He was feeling on top of his game now and he remembered all those years of taking so much shit from people when he was messin' with the *Dog Food*.

"It's okay," softened Mr. Bone, reading and feeling the expression on Dre's face, "keep all of that pain up front and you'll never have to return to it, but don't for one-minute think that the pain is non-refundable or you special in any kinda way!"
"I'm drinkin' what your pourin'!" trumpeted Dre," I know he's out there in the parking lot lifting cars waiting on me, getting cock diesel strong!"
"Yeah, you better believe it, that demon will be around for the rest of your life, until your dying day. When you six feet in your grave, then he's finding another soul," assured Mr. Bone

looking through Dre as if he could see the soul stealer.

Mr. Bone quietly exited to go to the doctor as the rest of the tier was heading to "rec." Ms. Mindy was coming with the package and even though everyone knew the package was for Mr. Bone, no one said or did anything about it. Hell, he had most, if not all, of the Sheriff's Department on his payroll. Mr. Bone was one of the largest distributors of heroin and cocaine in Chicago, if not in the entire Midwest and even though he was looking at life in prison, he was like AT&T; he could still "reach out and touch someone."

Ms. Mindy was approximately 5'-7", with crystal hazel eyes, dark skin, measuring 36-24-38 and with long flowing hair; reminding you of *Kiesha* off "Belly" the movie. She was in her mid-twenties with no children and like so many ghetto girls began working for Mr. Bone early on. The payoff was large for her and considering she had a uniform and some keys to turn she was just that much more valuable to Mr. Bone.

She swayed into the cell, poppin' her bubble gum, with wide hips and a mean switch, smelling like sweet perfume.

"Hey Dre, I got a package for you, fair exchange, ain't no robbery, so let me get some of that dick!" she proclaimed with a smile and a hunger in her eyes that turned Dre on.

She grabbed the balloon out of her pussy and washed her juices off of it over the sink. The visualization of that pink wet pussy was more than Dre could stand; his dick was harder than that metal sink she rested against.

"You not going to get no dick by standing over there," rushed Dre, feeling his throbbing manhood, knowing full well that he needed to penetrate her; he needed to fill her completely.

Ms. Mindy put the sign over the door like someone was taking a shit or the cell was being shook down in case anyone returned from "rec" prematurely.

The walk across the cell was only three feet from Dre but it could have been the Mojave, as Dre's thirst for her was nothing short of having just walked across a desert for weeks with no water.

When their bodies touched it was as if they collided. His heart raced and his dick throbbed for her as he rubbed her with one hand as the other unzipped her pants. He could sense her pussy feeling the need for him as her red thong barely covered her pleasure mound; inviting Dre in. Her full voluptuous breasts spilled out of her top, bearing her firm hard nipples, reassuring Dre that she needed him, needed to feel his touch, needed to feel his manhood. Dre was all over her like an octopus. He could smell her sexuality mixed with her perfume as Dre pushed her panties to the floor. She pressed hard against Dre, all of her heat gushing all over him, he couldn't stand it. He caressed her passionately, ravenously and without limits.

"Dre," begging Mindy, "I can't take it anymore, slide that fat dick in my pussy from the back," moaning as she turned away from him, throwing her ass cheeks in the air as her head fell towards the ground. Dre could feel the cold steel of the sink as he bent her over it, he was so hard and hot, and she was so wet and soft, a perfect match.

Dre was reaching around the front and gently caressing her love bump as she thrust against him, her ass slapping against his midsection. His dick was so hard and deep, driving harder and harder with each moan of his name.

"Oh Dre, oh Dre," she whined, while grasping for air," make this pussy cum Dre, don't you love this platinum pussy... oh ah ah ah ah oooooh shit! Dre fuck me harder, don't stop, I'm about to cum. Oh yes, right their Daddy, right there!"

Dre was pumping like never before, sweating with juices all over, with both hands on her sides throwing himself deep inside her, "I'm going to cuuuum," he gasped out into the thick air. With one powerful thrust that met with one of hers.

"Oh, yes!" they both released in voice and of each other, filling each with their own juices and desires, both collapsing in ecstasy and triumph.

They made small talk as she dressed and Dre zipped up his pants, still smelling her on him and their sex in the air. She walked out leaving him behind, but with a smile, letting him know that she was once again so very satisfied.

Mr. Bone often left the package with Dre for some time. Dre was convinced that it was a test to see if Dre was serious about beating the addiction, about controlling it and not having it control him. He was testing Dre to see if he could trust him. Mr. Bone's motto was "if you can't trust one with the small things, how could you trust them with the Empire?"

Mr. Bone wanted to groom Dre, he wanted Dre to be a part of what he had built, so he observed. He wanted to show Dre a world beyond his imagination, more drugs than he had ever seen and a lifestyle that people only talk about. Mr. Bone had eyes and ears everywhere and he didn't mention his intentions to Dre, but he did keep an accounting of their conversations over the time they were together. It was a six months that would forever change Dre's life.

Chapter 5
The Heart of a Woman

Walking through the last gate of the Cook County Jail was liberating. Dre could feel his freedom with each step closer to the door. When he stepped out into the fresh air off Division 6 and headed towards California Street, his lungs burned with the air of liberty.

The sun on his face was warm and comforting, it made him feel safe in a world that was so often a threat; he was at a peace. The colors were more vibrant than he could ever remember, like God had just painted a fresh coat across the Universe. He dropped to his knees and thanked the Creator.

Rising to his feet he declared to himself, *let me get myself together, I'm carrying on like I just did six years or something!*
Crossing California, heading towards the bus, Dre was still absorbed in the beautiful day. His trance was broken

by the sound of a loud horn and yelling. It was Slick!

"A Dre, get yo ass over here my Nigga," sounded the voice as he came to a stop for Dre and backing up in traffic. *Good thing it was 10:00 in the morning,* thought Dre, *and not rush hour.* Who knows what Slick would have done in that traffic.

When their eyes met Dre could see the happiness mirrored in Slick, illuminating how they both felt; happy to see a familiar face. Dre jumped into the passenger side and Slick pulled off before creating too much of a scene.

"Welcome home Joe, you already know I was keepin' tabs on ya and I knew you only had a probation hold, I paid the bond on the other case," as Slick slanted his head to the side and then forward as if accepting an award. He knew Dre was thankful.
"That was good lookin' out my Nigga and I appreciate you droppin' that money on my books and sending me flicks and magazines, straight up! Straight up!"
"That was the least I could do for you, after all it was partly my fault you were locked to begin with," bowing his head in respect for Dre and what he had just been through.

The beat of the music in the background pulled Dre into the scene, into the reality. Slick smoking on his blunt, happy to see Dre and Dre happy to see Slick, each one looking forward as if looking into the future together as Jay-Z played,

"Where I'm From."

"Whatever happened to my Regal?" inquired Dre, remembering the last time he saw Slick and how he saved him from a world of troubles from not robbing that guy who ended up being a Federal agent.

"Did it get towed or what?"
"Man Joe, you know I got cha, I went and picked it up the same day you got locked up."

"You think we can go pick it up Slick, I gotta run over to Mama's crib and go see Tonya."
"Yeah, yeah, I dig that Joe," conceded Slick. "Hey Dre, you wanna run the spot for me tonight?"
"Is your fuckin' crazy man, I just got out of the fuckin' County!" Dre hardly able to breath from the blatant audacity of such a question.
"You right man, my bad. If you wanna wake up or something I got the bomb on the blows. I know you want one Joe, it's been over six months," as Slick tried to diffuse Dre and send up a peace offering.

Plus, the more Dre was into the blow, the more Slick could handle him.

"You can't change a Zebra's stripes you know!"
"Yeah, you sure can't, but I ain't no Zebra and I have control over what it is I can change and that's me," defended Dre as he

pulled down the visor to look at himself in the mirror.

As he studied his reflection he recalled all of those late night talks he had with Mr. Bone. Dre realized that a Nigga would offer him dope before he would offer him something to eat or a couple of dollars; *always tryin' to keep a Nigga in the gutta,* bounced through Dre's mind and he didn't like it.

"Damn you look good my Nigga," admitted Slick, "and I see you got your mind right. Now let me take you to the mall to get you all right!"
"I'm cool man, you can give me a couple dollars and drop me off where the Regal at and I'll get up with you later on."

Slick stopped at Roosevelt and Kostner. It was *Raybonds Body Shop,* where Slick had them replace the transmission, tune it up and put on some new tread so it would be ready for Dre when he got out.

"It's up in there, they're expecting you," Slick instructed. "I had it towed because there was no fuckin' gas in it!"

Oh, yeah, that's right, Dre thought to himself. Only to have his private thought stolen by Slicks' laughter. Dre followed suit. It was funny. They both knew it and laughing felt so good to Dre. It had been too long.

They had known each other since the sixth grade. Slick was the one who introduced him to the dope game. Dre had seen it from his Moms and other family members, but Slick gave him a closer look.

"Man, good looking my Nigga, straight up, straight up!"

Good lookin' for what? You deserve it Joe," Slick throwing heavy emphasis on "Joe," reminding Dre that they were old school partners, together since back in the day.

As Dre was exiting the truck, Slick reached up and grabbed an envelope from underneath the visor and handed it to Dre. Dre walked away with some bread in his hand thinking; *damn, that is a good dude and that's my Nigga! Jay-Z's* "Dead President" was thumping as Slick drove away.

Dre jumped into the Regal and opened the envelope, $2,500 worth of crispy $100 dollar bills and a new pack of Newport's sitting on the dash.

Dre looked at the pack of smokes for a second, shook his head and grabbed them, tossing them out the window thinking to himself; *I don't need no more of these, I am going to be the controller of the game, depending on nothing or no one.*

He started up the Regal and headed down Roosevelt beating to *2 Pac,* "Me Against the World." While he was anew, the scene was old. The same people walking around doing the same thing, like zombies in search of their next fix and all of the different hypes working the tips with their dull complexions and hollering, "Rock Blows Park!"

"Man, thank you Jesus for giving me the strength," as Dre looked up into the sky. His heart was heavy and full. He was thankful and he was heading home.

Dre unlocked the door with his keys and walked through the living room hearing his "Moms," Aunt Sally, in the kitchen with a soft back drop of gospel music by *Be-Be* and *Ce-Ce Winans,* "So Addictive."

"Hey Mama!" greeted Dre as she was opening the refrigerator door. The sound of the voice filling her heart with warmth and as she turned Dre could see it in her eyes; the pride, her youngest boy, her baby, priceless.
"Just look at my baby! Come here DeAndre and give me hugs and kisses!"
They embraced each other as the tears fell from both of their eyes. Dre always felt comfortable there and so did Mama. When they were in each other's arms things were good, things were right.

"Look what you got me doin'," expressed Dre sheepishly, as they pulled away from one another wiping their eyes. They looked at each other for what seemed like an eternity, frozen in time. They were more than kin, anyone who observed their interactions would tell you they shared part of their souls. She was his Mama and he was her boy, with no bond stronger.

"Sit down baby and let me make you somethin' to eat. You look so healthy and your eyes are so clear. Oh, it makes me so happy to see you like this," bragged Mama as she transitioned into reciting Matthew 6:22,"the eye is the lamp of the body," she continued," so if your eyes is healthy, your whole body will be full of light." She looked up and said in a soft whisper, "thank you Jesus."

Mama Hall was a recovering addict and she gave herself full-time to the Lord and to her recovery. She did not sugar coat a thing, she said it straight; she had been there, she knew better. Despite Dre's using she still supported him. She could remember the times they would get high together and a part of her felt responsible for his using. Five years clean for her and six months clean for Dre, both of them feeling well and proud of themselves and one another; it was a blessed day.

"I'm all right Mama, I'm about to take me a shower and go see Tonya," was the easiest way he could turn down Mama's cooking.

Mama liked Tonya and the relationship that Dre had with her. Mama could read the game on any woman, she had been in the streets and she knew what was what. Mama was the queen of all game even before she was saved and all clean. It gave her comfort that Dre found someone that wasn't running game and was a positive influence on him.

"Baby is you going to stay out of trouble? Give your life to God so you can stay off that dope, only Jesus can fix it when it's that big," gently preached Mama from her heart and not from judgment.

"Everything else is played out and I want to see you live and not just be existing. I would love to have a grand baby one of these days too!" Mama was smiling from ear to ear passing Dre a look of compassion and sincerity.

"Mama I'm going to get myself, excuse me, let me rephrase that, I got myself together, so don't worry your pretty self. By the way, do you have a fountain of youth around here?" Dre was trying to flatter her and compliment his Mama in an attempt to redirect the conversation off of Dre.

"I know what you're tryin' to do," busted in Mama.

"What? Me? Nothing mama!" Dre was laughing out loud now and he had a sparkle in his eyes, it had been awhile, and it felt good.

"Dre, make a meeting with me this week and go to church with me on Sunday. Promise me, please Dre," pleaded Mama.

"Okay, Mama, you got that!" Promised Dre.

Mama threw her arms around Dre and showered him with hugs and "I love yous." The pride in her was overwhelming; she seemed to float out of the kitchen.

Watching his Mama walk away he recognized the similar facial features they shared. Mama was still a head turner as the years of punishing her body did not take its toll like it normally does.

Her skin was smooth and clear, she was beautiful. Dre used to hate it when they would go somewhere and guys would ogle her as if he was walking with his sister or his girlfriend. *Mama, I love you,* Dre said to himself as he walked to his bedroom.

As Dre entered in his room his mind switched gears; he was one to meditate or *talk to God* as he would put it. *I already made my plan so I can give a fuck less what society says about how they perpetuated the images and mindset that it's cooler to say I'm a drug dealer than working legit 9 to 5,* flashed across his minds' eye. *Shit, I'm about to go from being a dope user to one of the heaviest dope pushers,* he said to himself, convincingly aware that it was possible if he stayed off the drugs. He could do it. He was ready to be the controller not the controlled.

Picking up the phone to call Tonya Dre had a good feeling inside. Things were in a good place, things were right.

"Hey my hunny-bunny," filled Dre's ear, as Tonya picked up the other end, "I miss you sooo much!"
"I miss you too. I'm sorry I'm just talking to you, but I have been ripping and running most of the day."

Tonya could hear how clear Dre sounded from not using, it was sexy.

"Baby, you miss me huh?" Dre asked picking up on the vibe and had to go there, this was his girl.

"You don't even need to ask me that Dre." Tonya had her moments when he was away; the sadness would engulf her and she would have to fight it and let it go, knowing that she would see him again.

"Baby, that's over, you're here now," she kittened into the phone.

"What's on your agenda for tonight?"

"Pleasing my man of course!"

"That's what I love to hear!" All excited and anxious, "check this out; we're going to get a room downtown in the hotel overlooking the Chicago skyline. Look your best baby, and I will do the same. Need to get me a haircut. We goin' out on the town tonight!"

"That sounds like a plan. I already know that when you get a haircut and dress to impress, you the finest man in town!" Tonya declared with an unwavering confidence as she played with the pen in her hand she had picked up off her desk.

She was at work, but the vision of Dre and he going inside her was making her wet and she started to tingle and throb between her legs. She missed him in every way.

"Okay baby, pick me up. Better yet, just drive by the house and we will take my car."

"Aight girl, it's a date at eight! I love you."

"I love you more!" Tonya rushed into the phone.

As she hung up the phone she looked at the clock and noticed it was time for her to wrap it up. Tonya was a sophisticated college graduate who was very family oriented. She was a banker who dabbled in real estate; her portfolio was a few houses and growing. She was down for Dre to the fullest, but wouldn't take no bullshit from him. Despite how tough she was with Dre, when he was at his lowest she was there for him too. Even when those around her questioned what she was doing with such a guy, why she was "wasting her time with him," she stood strong to support her man. She saw something else in him, she saw the man he could be. Mama said that Tonya saw aspects of her own father in him, thinking of the adage; "a woman looks in a man what she sees in her Dad."

She was not an advocate of Dre making a living out of hustling. She was a 5'-5" drop dead gorgeous bombshell. She had deep brown eyes and a brilliant smile that would light up any room. She had smooth soft brown skin and a short Halle Berry Style do. She was always wearing the latest in fashion and she looked her best natural, with no make-up. She kind of reminded you of Gabrielle Union in a way, not forgetting the tight body from proper diet, exercise and no drugs. She was Dre's perfect woman!

Tonya and Dre were high school sweethearts even though they went to different schools. Dre met her when he was getting kicked out actually. To this day, Dre could remember those moments with Tonya and she reflected fondly on those days as well. They were deep into each other.

Tonya wanted to get ready early and surprise Dre. She needed to shower and change because her panties were still wet from earlier when she pictured Dre inside her. She never told anyone but she was a real freak in her unique way when it came to being with Dre. She just loved that "dope-dick"; she couldn't get enough of it. It was so hard and so big, bigger than a police "billet club" and she wanted every inch. Sometimes however, Dre would go so long that she would need to stop because she would get sore from how long he lasted and how hard he would thrust. She didn't understand the magic powers of the dope dick until then. At times she swore he was so deep in her that she could see his thrusting push up against her abdominal wall.

In the shower she couldn't help but play with her soapy pussy. The warm water was caressing her body along with her own fingers, rubbing her thighs, inching closer and closer to her pleasure garden, her pussy was so wet her fingers were covered in cream, in her cream, she was almost there.

"Oh Dre, Oh Dre, Yes, Yes, Yes!" Climaxing to the vision of her on his face and feeling the magic of his ways. Oh she loved how he made her feel.

Tonya was admiring herself in the full-length mirror as she was applying lotion to her toned body, all pores open and she was electrified from her orgasm and couldn't wait for the real thing. The beat of R-Kelly's "Etcetera" bounced in the back ground as she danced around her bedroom, feeling it, ready for it, ready for the night with her man!

This is what about to be going on, she hissed to herself. *My hair is already done, a bitch just went to the shop yesterday and about to sweat it all out but for a good cause.* She admired her finger nails and her feet, they were done to perfection. She knew Dre would be sucking on her small feet later and play "this little piggy" in his compassionate voice, the one that made her melt. She smiled.

Across town Dre was getting dressed. He was looking strong, dark and handsome. He had his hair cut and was sporting a smoke gray Giorgio Armani suit with his block toe black gators and all accessorized out. He knew Tonya would be wearing what he liked so he was wearing what she liked.

Tonya was feeling it in her beautiful evening gown by *Marchesa Notte*, with the shoulders out and back dropped down just above her ass. It was the same shade of gray as Dre's suit; they matched to a "T." She was clutching a matching color *Lauren Merkin* leather purse and supporting a pair of 6" *stilettos*. She rounded out the perfect package with a pair of diamond earrings, necklace and bracelet from Tiffany's. She was sparkling and right.

Dre pulled up in the Regal at eight sharp and when the two of them were actually together, how they complimented one another lifted them up even higher, they were it. Dre's father "Storm" would tell him," it don't matter what you do, but how you do it" and they were doing it up right! They were fresh and fit perfectly with the ambiance and style of her new BMW X5.

Dre couldn't believe his eyes, she looked like a superstar. Tonya felt like one and Dre's eyes just reinforced it. She was in love, with the moment, with him, with everything. He embraced her and lifted her off the ground, remembering that she had a gown on, he set her down gently. She was his princess; he placed a kiss upon her lips gently and opened the door for his lady. The running board lights of the X5 silhouetted her outline, it was a chariot made for his princess.

Luther Vandross was playing, elegantly swaying the rhythm through them and their moment, "promise me, promise me you'll leave me never, promise me we'll be forever" as they headed downtown on Lake Shore Drive to the *Drake* hotel.

Dre had one hand on the wheel and the other in Tonya's hand singing the words to her as serenading his princess in a pale moonlight. He didn't want the moment to end and neither did she.

The suite of the hotel captured the Chicago skyline and *Johnny Gill* "Girl it's Your Body" was playing on the system. Dre mixed them some drinks and they talked. Dre made an exception to his rule and enjoyed a couple shots of Yak (Cognac) and Tonya enjoyed a glass of wine. They both peered out the full length windows taking in the Chicago skyline, each dressed to kill and the alcohol heightening their sensitivity to their own sexuality.

"I miss you baby," Dre offered in a caressing voice, leaning towards her with the Chicago Skyline silhouetting her body.

Tonya looked directly into Dre, she pulled him in with her eyes, commanding him, taking control of him with just one look.

Dre was helpless to such desires and her beauty, he took her in his arms and their clothes fell to the floor as if they were tied on lightly with a simple string. They were naked, surrounded by the city, embracing one another, tightly, never wanting to let go.

Dre was trying to consume every part of her body, her breast filled his mouth, and they were so subtle and ready for him. He could feel Tonya's heat, her passion, her desire.

"Fuck me Dre, please fuck me!" she begged.

Dre slowly turns her around tapping her ass as he enters her from behind. Tonya is gripping the sheets as her breasts bounce to Dre's rhythm. All caution is thrown to the wind, as passion takes control. In this moment, it changes, Dre starts making love to her. She senses the change and it sends her to another place, he is pleasing her not just physically but emotionally, she is losing control like never before.

She screams his name in absolute passion as she explodes all over him. In turn Dre grabs her intently around the hips and dances in and out of her, slow and then fast, grinding towards a crescendo of climatic altitude.

"Oh, baby, oh Tonya, I am 'bout to cum, I am so," as he thrusts every ounce of his being into her, leaving his seed. His head falls forward just as hers rises; they kiss a gentle kiss that only spent lovers can.

As they shower and dress themselves, each one cognizant of the other, the special moment they just shared, the feelings they had for one another, it felt good.

"Damn, you look good. You are so beautiful!" Dre commented with a twinkle in his eye even after all of the sex. It made Tonya beam.

"Thank you, you look damn good yourself. You make me feel like the actual queen that I am," she conceded to Dre with a warm smile and a gentle rub of his back as they headed out the door.

"Anything for my love, anything," he whispered as Dre grabbed her hand and held it tight. They were lost in one another's company; setting out to enjoy the night, hand in hand, together. They only had eyes for each other, so much so, that they didn't notice the set of eyes that was on them.

Chapter 6
Troubled Man

Three weeks had passed since his release and the boredom was setting in. Dre had been to church and was making the meetings while searching for a job. The $2500 was down to approximately $90 and that wasn't *going* to keep him much longer.

Mama lived in a nice section 8 housing development, nicely furnished and full of *love,* but Dre needed more, he needed to really live, not just exist.

"Its 9:00 baby!" Urges Mama as she opens his bedroom door, "are you going to get up and look for a job today?"
"Yeah Mama, I'm about to get up and get myself together," as he shuffles under the warm *covers* that stop just below his chin letting in the intoxicating aroma of mama's cooking as it streams through the now opened door. *Hmmm, that smells delicious* Dre thinks to himself as a smile broadens across his face.

As Dre crawls out of bed he can't help but think, *damn, I gotta get my own spot.* He took comfort in the fact that Mama would never kick him out. The hounding of her about him getting a job was wearing on him and all of the church meetings were a little more than what he had bargained for. He believed, he just devoted himself in a different way.

As the sun bounced off the walls it formed a warm blanket around him. Through the glare, on his nightstand, was a picture of her, of Tonya. He sat and contemplated his position and wondered why he hadn't taken her up on her offer. Dre concluded that he wasn't that type of man; if they were going to live together it would be in his crib and on his terms. He pulled on a pair of pants and a tee and walked towards the smell, almost floating towards the odorous delight.

"Good morning Mama," as he kissed her on the cheek, "hmmm, that smells so good!"

"Good Morning DeAndre, thank you. Now eat it up before it gets cold," she said with almost a caution. It wasn't a caution towards the food, rather what she was going to talk about.

"Baby," Mama started almost sheepishly, "I hope you don't think I am pressuring you, but I know what an idle mind would do, especially with all of the free time you have; it's the making of the devil's workshop if you're not careful. I pray every day to keep my sanity and my sobriety and I take it one step at a time, one day at a time. It's not easy Baby, it's been five years and I still have thoughts of getting high. Because I know how hard it is for me, is why I ask you to attend the meetings, for you. You and I think alike and I don't want you going back to the drugs, to that life. It is not just doing the drugs, but selling them too. It's a proven fact, if the drugs don't kill ya' the, lifestyle will," Mama expressed almost as a concession to a fate that may not be avoided for Dre.

"I hear you Mama," as he focused in on devouring his breakfast.

"Don't just hear me DeAndre, but show me you are listening, take action. Do something, not for me, but for yourself," she pleaded as she turned away from Dre so as to not let him see the tears forming in her eyes.

"I'm not always going to be here and you're my baby; of all the children, you are my baby. You are one of the smartest, but you are human, not always making the right decisions. By His grace and mercy we are still here," as she lifts her head towards the sky peering out the kitchen window the tears fall down her cheeks, "we need to change ourselves if we want things around us to change."

"Mama," Dre says in a confident comforting voice, seeing the pain in her eyes in her posture causing Dre to feel the pain too. "Mama, we're going to be all right. I don't know what I'll do without you and especially this good cooking! I think the best thing to do is get a catering truck and start selling this food made by my Mama!"

As a huge smile comes across Dre's face, Mama's heart is filled with joy. Her boy had come a long way and she was so proud of him. They laughed with one another, sitting there in the comfort of the kitchen that held so many memories; this was another one, one they would both cherish.

Their moment was disrupted by the thumping of what sounded like a dozen 12" woofers. It was no doubt, Uncle Terry's van pulling up the driveway accompanied by *Master P's* "No Limit Soldiers" vibrating the kitchen windows.

Dre hustled to the door to let them in and was greeted from the car by Terry as he slid on his fitted cap.

"Hey nephew!" Terry shouted out, waking up any neighbor that were not already throttled from their slumber by the dozen woofer's rambling down the road.

Dre was happy to see his Uncle Terry, but he was elated to see his favorite cousin Munchie!

"Give me a hug Nephew!" Terry demanded with a rough compassion, "I heard you was locked up!"
"What's up Cuzo, you shou'll lookin' good," Munchie said into Dre's ear as he followed Terry in embracing Dre with a hug.

Mama was happy to see Dre so pleased and to be a part of the reunion, but she also knew Terry was trouble and a fool, and an old fool at that. She stood silent in the periphery with her hands crossed, patient and subtle.

"Hey, they had a nigga locked down, but they can't hold a good nigga down! Straight Up, straight up!" echoed Dre across the presence of Terry and Munchie. "They had me for six months, six long months for working on Slick's spot and a probation violation hold."

"I called Aunt Sally and she told me what had happened, you being locked up and all. Where's my Auntie anyway?" as *Munchie pushed passed* Dre into the house.

"She's in the kitchen," bounced off Munchie's back as he was already three steps ahead of Dre.

Munchie had lost his mother two years ago to cancer and Aunt Sally was like a mother to him now. Sally reminded Munchie of his mother and made him feel comfortable and accepted unlike his Mama did as it wasn't always easy for Munchie.

"So, Nephew, you ready to get some real money?" Terry threw into Dre's face.

Dre could hear the candy in his throat, how snorting that *Dog Food* would strain the larynx, making his voice scratchy and *froggy*.

"Unc, you don't even need to ask me that," responded Dre with a confident indifference, "Who the fuck we gotta rob or kill, cause you talkin' real money; straight up, straight up!"

"Nobody Nigga, the money already in the bag!" retorted Terry with an indifference of confidence.

"What money? Where at?" bit Dre.

"I'll let your cousin tell ya."

As Dre and Terry entered the Kitchen, Munchie was entertaining Aunt Sally with his stories.

"Hey Saphie, how you been?" interrupted Terry.
"Hey Terry, what I tell you about calling me that name? If you can't call me Sally, then don't call me at all!" playfully barked Aunt Sally.

There was a serious undertone despite her jolly demeanor. Sally knew that one had to change everything to really escape their ghosts and she wasn't too pleased with the memories attached to that name.

"Okay Sally," conceded Terry politely while snatching up a piece of bacon off the plate," I'm sorry, your right," with a trail of light sarcasm not allowing Sally the complete satisfaction of an apology or moreover the admission of Terry having done something wrong.

Aunt Sally had to bite her tongue, she knew Terry was a fool and starting something would only end poorly and there was no benefit in such endeavor; not today anyway. If looks could kill however, Terry would be lying on the floor.

"Munchie?" cutting the thick air, "what is this your Dad talkin' bout some paper?"
"That's why we up here Dre, I was just telling Auntie if you wanted to come down to Iowa. I don't think you remember that I was in a car accident shortly after my Mama died. Well, I was, and I just got the check this morning."

"Really? For how much?" Dre was eager to learn of the amount and little interested in the accident that warranted such a sum.

"You might want to sit down for this one cuz'," offered Munchie, but unwilling to postpone, "thirty thousand," rolling off his lips like he had won the *Mega Bucks* lottery.

"You bullshittin'?" enthusiastically shouted Dre, looking at Mama and in an undertone, "sorry Mama," because he had just cursed in front of her.

"Yeah Nigga!" chimed in Terry, "we ain't playin', the money is in the bag in the van!" as he nonchalantly pulled a square and started to light it.

"Take that outside!" Trumpeted Aunt Sally, "You already know I don't allow no smoking in here!"

"Damn Sally, I remember when you would smoke, it was cool then," complained Terry.

"You said the magic word Terry, *use* to!"

As Terry and Dre carried their conversation onto the back porch Terry tilted his head while lighting up and looked at Dre as he exhaled across the porch, "it is good to see that your Moms got her head on straight."

"Yes it is," confirmed Dre, "and naw, I'm cool, I don't smoke no more," as Terry gestured to Dre to light one up as well.

"I see your Moms has really rubbed off on you."

"Naw, I had made my mind up in the County, I was about to get out and make me some money. I'm tired of being a dog chasing my tail around in a circle and eating my own shit, dat *Dog Food!*"

"I hear ya Dre nephew, but I ain't ready yet with chasing my tail around in a circle and eating my own shit. As a matter of fact, I feel like eating some right now!" as Terry slowly and methodically pulled out a tin foil 20 package of blow from his pocket.

Right there, just like that, *lickity split,* Terry snorted and licked the foil, crumbled it into a ball flicking it off the back of the porch while pulling a drag off his square all in one motion.

"Yeah, that's the good shit," as Terry snorted in what residue was left in his nostrils, while rubbing his nose with the palm of his hand.
"Hey, what works for me, may not work for you. When you sick and tired of being sick and tired, you'll make the right decision; straight up, straight up!" confessed Dre, being made more as an offertory for Terry's benefit than a personal claim of epiphany.
"Nephew, I'm too fuckin' old to be changin' and I've been fuckin' with this shit since 14 years old, and I pushing 50! I wouldn't know what the fuck to do clean and sober. That is one reason why I respect your Moms so much. I remember when we use to all get high together and pull all kind of capers. You were just a spring chicken then." As Terry looked off into the past, you could see in his face he was telling the truth, or so he thought it was the truth.

It was a part of him, it was who he was and there was nothing or no one that was going to change that.

"Speaking of Mama," echoed Dre, "just like what I was telling you, I don't feel all of her plans either. I mean I don't have the desire to get high, but I wanna get this money and she want me to make meetings and go to church, get a 9 to 5 job. I'm just not feeling all of that; pain is the game and we all gotta pay and play for ourselves."

"Nephew, just be thankful you still got a Mama here that's concerned about your well-being. I wish like hell mines' was still here. It ain't a day that goes by I don't think about my Mama and wish I could give her all the joy and heart my soul can give," confessed Terry with a compassion that was foreign for him. It made Dre uncomfortable but at the same time it was real and authentic, a side he seldom saw of Terry.

The moment took both of them away, Terry embraced Dre and Dre returned the affection. There they stood on Mama's porch embraced in understanding and awareness, they made a connection and they both felt it.

As Terry and Dre walked into the house with their arms around one another's' shoulders, Terry asked Sally if Dre could go with them down to Iowa.

Sally was startled as she looked up to see the two men embraced as they were,

"I am not sure what happened on my porch, but I like to see such strength and camaraderie. Dre is grown, he can make his own decisions, if he wants to go to Iowa with you, he goes to Iowa, and I cannot hold his hand forever."

The tone of her voice was somewhat condescending and Dre could read between the lines, "C'mon Mama, don't lecture me in front of them."

"Whatcha you mean in front of *them?*" interjected Munchie, *"We is family!"*

The manner in which Munchie delivered his interjection made the whole group break up into laughter. Munchie reached into his pocket and pulled out a wad of cash and handed it to Aunt Sally and told Dre that they would be in the car waiting for him.

"You don't need no clothes either 'cuz, I'm buying you all new gear, like the Lox's said; *I tell all my niggas ridin'; you don't need a dime!"*

Uncle Terry and Munchie hugged Aunt Sally goodbye and headed out the door.

"Dre, you be careful," cautioned Aunt Sally, "you keep your eyes open and stay prayerful and watchful."
"You know I'm going to do that. I love you Mama."

They hugged each other. The hug was different than when he had first walked into the kitchen so many months ago. It was more. It was not a hug goodbye, it was a hug that said; I love you, you are a part of me and I want you safe just as you are in my arms right now.

Dre walked out the side door with nothing but the clothes on his back.

Aunt Sally, Mama, looked out the window as Dre quickly stepped into the waiting vehicle. The door opened and out rushed, "Ride" by *Master P.* It was a sunny day as Mama had to squint to see the last clear image of Dre as he ducked into the van.

She closed her eyes and said a prayer. She prayed that God gave Angels for around the van, keeping their travels safe and that Dre did not follow Terry's path into the pit of darkness, back into the hold of the *Dog Food.*

Chapter 7
The Ride

Terry flew down Lake Street toward Ciero like he had just robbed a bank. Master P, "Ride" was playing and Dre and Munchie were kicking back in the captain's chair feeling large. The music is thumping so loud that the cinder from his ash was glowing to the beat, ready to fall at any moment.

Terry flicks his cigarette out the window and turns down the music from the streering wheel control as he looks down on all the passerby's. The van sits higher than most vehicles and Terry likes that point of view, from the top looking down.

"You show him that money in the bag son?" yelled Terry over the music as he was turning it down.

"Yeah, I see it, its Benjamin's for days; straight up, straight up! If it was mines I'll be headed for Brazil where all those sexy exotic ladies are, like I'm on the run from the feds!"

"Yeah Cuzo," adding to Dre's fantasy, "We're about to sepnd it go down here to go shopping and buy us some water skies an all types of stuff, just like we in Brazil."

Fighting through the laughter Terry punctuates, "hey, don't forget we about to flip some of that shit to lil' Nigga in Iowa, not Brazil!"

As the laughter trailed off, Munchie thought about what Terry had said, but he didn't say anything. Munchie knew that one way or another the money would go away and when it did Terry would still be there.

"Nephew, you think you can call a mother fucker and get me a half of book of cocaine, a heavy eighteen ounces? I already got the connect on the dope, I wanna go back down to this sweet ass fuckin' state double breasted!"
"Unc, don't even trip, I'll call Slick up, let me see your phone Joe," replied Dre with confidence.
"Give 'em your phone son!" hollered Terry to Munchie in the back of the van, while bobbing his head to the beat and rapping; "this ride, this is for the killers and dealers still 'bout it, 'bout it Nigga, now the world gone feel us." Terry was gritten' with that mask on gangster, *Dog Food style*!

Dre is pressing his phone against his ear listening to it ring on the other end.
"Who this?" snaps the other end of the line.
"This me Partner!" with Dre emphasizing "partner" to his

man slick.

"Oh, what up Joe, what's poppin' baby?"

"Man, I need to holler at cha, ASAP. I need a half a chicken."

"A playboy, what you talkin' bout Joe?" Slicked hummed back into the phone. He knew Dre wouldn't be on any bullshit, but he didn't recognize the area code on his caller ID and he wasn't in the habit of taking any chances.

"Ai'ight meet me at T's and B's in fifteen minutes, that's cool Joe."

Catching Slicks vibe, "it's all good, like MC Hammer; straight up, straight up!"

"Shit, we can do better than that, how about five, we riding down Lake Street, just about to make a right on Pulaski."

"Who is we Joe?" interrupted Slick, while emphasizing the "we."

"Oh, shit man, I forget, I'm with my Unc Terry and my Cuzo Munchie."

"Man, yo crazy ass Unc? He ain't tryin' to get none of that counterfeit paper off on a Nigga is he?" wondered Slick out loud.

"Man, you trippin' Joe, you think I'll be up with some shit like that with you? Straight up, Straight up!" replied Dre.

"Tell Slick, do he want this mother fuckin' paper or not and stop asking all the mother fuckin' questions like he's Pueblo Escobar or something," rattled Terry from the driver's seat.

Terry caught Slick in his review mirror. He slammed on the brakes causing Dre and Munchie to fly forward, but Slick, somehow, reacted fast enough to avoid a rear end collision. Terry let his foot off the brake laughing to himself and to the world that he didn't give a shit about. Dre managed to find the phone on the floor of the van.

"Man, yo Unc is still crazier than a mother fucker, what he got in the back of that bitch? He got it bumpin' all over Joe!" came out the other end as Dre was putting the phone back to his ear.
"About a dozen twelve's," bragged Dre.
"In a minute Joe," and Slick was off the line.

T's and B's was a clothing store right on Madison and Pulaski. A place where all the hustlers in the hood would go to when they ain't tryin' to go to the malls or private stores if the paper ain't right. Dre and Slick had been shopping there since middle school. This was back when the Chiefs had accounts, one could just walk in, give a name, and they knew they were good for it; their credit was accepted just from a name. That would get a guy a suit or two.

Dre and Slick entered the store together with Munchie trailing and Terry staying with the van. It had been some time since Dre had been there but the workers and owner greeted Dre by name. Dre had made a reputation for himself, plus they had seen Dre and Slick grow up on those streets.

'What's up Joe, you all getting' a big package baby?" asked Slick.

"Yeah, my Cuzo just got a settlement, cash settlement!"

Just then Munchie walked up to Dre, handed him $1,000 saying; "get some outfits cuz. I'm heading to Footlocker to get me some Jordan's and I'll grab you a pair too!" as Munchie turned away

Dre could still see the smile on Muchie's face, the pride that accompanied the hand off of so much cash. Dre was happy for him and he was happy for himself, he was about to get some new threads.

"Damn, ya'll spendin' money like its water or like it grows on trees or something!"
"Man, you crazy Slick," retorted Dre as he picked out some Roca Wear and Sean John suits along with some white Tees and a couple of fitted caps, " you cool Joe!" Dre concluded as he put the last hat on his head.
"Just get me a hat," countered Slick as he watched Dre sport that last one.
"I don't got no problem with that; straight up, straight up!"

They headed back to the van where Munchie and Terry were waiting and Slick told Dre to grab the money and to jump in with him.

"That's cool Slick, they got no problem with that," answered Dre.

Dre put both bags in the van and appreciated the deal the

owner gave him. Dre had the blue Detroit Tiger's with the "D" on it and Slick was hoisting the black San Jose Shark's with the "S" on it, each of them cocked a little to the left. They looked like two twins on a commercial.

Dre had asked, "Slick, what's the ticket?" when they were heading back to the van. Slick proceeded to explain to Dre that he would need $3,000 for the half.

"Straight up Joe?" asked Dre in slight disbelief, "$3k, straight up for the whole 18 ounces?"

"You my Nigga Joe," replied Slick. For Slick it was a way to show Dre how much he appreciated their friendship, their association.

Slick always admired Dre but knew that Dre would forever be held back if he stayed under the thumb of the Dog Food. When Dre was free from it however, Slick knew that Dre would achieve greatness, more than any of them could imagine.

Uncle Terry popped his head in the van opening the door as the food wafted in. He had three brown paper bags with Italian Beef and fries and three sodas with straws. They were hungry. Dre had been so wrapped up in the clothes and dope scene that he forgot he was hungry. *Good call Unc*, Dre thought to himself.

"So, what's up," started Terry, "What's that motherfucker Slick want for that half of thang?"

"You not going to believe this Unc, $3,000!"

"Hell naw'll, I ain't tryin' to buy no eighteen ounces of bullshit, when I cook it up it only be six ounces! I'll fuck Slick up and every mother fucker that favor him, even his babies," laughing out the last verse.

"Real talk Unc, real talk. He owes me from when I caught that case for him. He see I'm on a come up; straight up, straight up!" popped off Dre.

"Alright Nephew, you in like flint, shit I can pay for this my mother fuckin' self as Terry reached into his pocket and pulled out a bank roll that would choke a bull and shed $3k worth of crispy hundreds.

"Unc, check this out; I'm 'bout to get in the truck and ride with Slick. Ya'll follow me, we going over on Central Park," Dre instructed while stepping out of the van.

Terry and Slick drove out of the lot separately, but both bumping like they both had gorillas on the loose at their back doors tryin' to escape with all eyes on them from that bass; thumpin' and humpin'.

Terry was spinning *Master P's*, "Make 'em Say Huh" while Slick was rolling *Hot Boys'*, "Help."

They headed down Pulaski toward Roosevelt making a left at *George's Music Room* where a long line stood. They proceeded down Roosevelt between Harding and Springfield until they reached Central Park, a cool ten blocks down. They both pulled into the alley with Uncle Terry following Slick and killing his motor as they rolled up.

"Damn, who got all them Niggas down the street acting a fool like that?" asked Dre estimating a good 80 to 90 people in that line down the block.

"That's one of my blow tips. I'm acting a complete ass Joe, we pulling about 20 stacks a day, no bullshit," answered Slick.

Twenty grand is a lot of dough, Dre thought to himself as they walked up the stairs in the Row house. You could see the heavy traffic; whites, Mexicans, blacks, all flavors, like a *Baskin' Robbins*. As Slick reached into his pocket to get his keys he turned to Dre and Slick giving him the low down.

"And we doing nothing but doubles too Joe!"

That's twenty dollars, no singles, and for twenty-four hours a day, as Dre did the math in his head.

When Slick opened the door Dre's eyes were stolen by the vision on the couch; she was a light skin red bone, wearing the tightest shorts he had ever seen and a belly top, it fit her all too well.

Slick, almost impervious to the scene, walked straight in, threw his keys on the glass table and prompted almost by cue, "what's up baby? That's my man Dre," as Slick nodded towards Dre standing just inside the door, "and this," continued Slick, "is my fine lady Regina."

Slicks crib was all laid out; he had state of the art technology including flat screens, surround sound and all accented by imported furniture.

"Man, you got this mother fucker laid out; straight up!" complemented Dre.

"This ain't shit, I got one overlooking that water by Lake Shore Drive up north," whispering to Dre, losing all modesty with such a one up. "Oh, and a badder looking bitch too!" as he slowly walked away from Dre concluding, "I'm just sayin'."

"Just let me pick up so I can get up outa here."

With that command by Dre they walked into one of the bedrooms and Slick went to the window sill and pulled the paneling back and took a whole brick out and handed it to Dre. The Kilo was still in the wrapper with the symbol on it, just like in the movies.

"Here you go baby," blew Slick, "it's been three weeks since you been out and you ain't asked a Nigga for shit and you still ain't fuckin' with that dope, you 'bout to come up Joe."

"Man, baby good looking straight up! You already know it's a quiet town I'm about to tie it down! Slick, let me break this in half so I can give Unc one half and I can stash the other one; straight up, straight up?"

"Hey man, you don't have to go through all of that, put it on the table and grab that *Gucci* bag off the chair; there are two halves in there already. I was going to grab it, but fuck it, I am going to just chill out and fuck Regina's sexy ass while I count this paper!"

They walked back through the living room, Slick smacked

Regina on the ass and tossed her the $3,000. Not many knew it, but Slick couldn't really count or add his money, that is one of the reason he always had a girl around him, not to mention all of the other reasons, one of which he would be exercising in a minute.

They exited the place and walked towards the truck and van that was parked just outside. They hugged and Dre jumped into the van. They looked each other in the eyes, knowing what the other was thinking. They were both thankful that they were doing things together again and they felt good about things. If they had only noticed the other set of eyes down the street watching them as well.

"Man, it took you long a fuckin' nuff, what ya'll was doin? Wait a minute, don't tell me, ya'll was converting the shit from Coca plant like he grew it," laughing so hard you thought Terry would bust a gut.

"You gotta lot of jokes Unc," replied Dre, not too amused.
"No, what I need is, me a couple of packs of those blows down there. I've been watching the traffic since we been parked. Whoever spot that is, is making a killing for real, for real!"
"That's Slick's spot too!" informed Dre. "Shit, I should've gotten my grams from that Nigga too!"
"When you get those Unc?"
"My medicine is the first thing I get. As soon as I come off the expressway and I put it in the stash spot, the spot where that half brick is going too."

"Hey son, you jumpin' in the driver seat as soon as I pullover up here. When you do, turn around I need to get me three packs," instructed Terry.

As they turned around and headed back you could hear the selling; a shorty was yelling, "Rocks blows Park, Rocks Blows Park, Rocks Blows Park!"

"Hey shorty" snapped Terry, "give me three packs!"

The shorty told him, "Park with $300 out your ass," like Terry was some lame or something. Terry's initial thought was to rob his young punk ass with no gun. He could see that he was no street Nigga, he could smell the weakness, he was a pussy bitch that just got off the porch and got his first piece of pussy from a damn crack head. Terry realized he had too much to lose right now and that this shorty wasn't worth it. When Terry approached the shorty, he tries to pat Terry down and finds only a look of cold-edged-tough-stay-outta-my-shit.

"You think I'll be trying to rob somebody with this roll here?" as Terry pulls out his fat bank roll.

The lil' Nigga knew this was no average Nigga and let Terry through without saying another word.

Terry got his three packs and on the way back as he passed the shorty,"Soft ass Nigga," rumbled out of Terry' mouth.

The shorty, while agitated and in his feelings, knew better than to try and do something.

Munchie had timed the pick-up perfectly, just as Terry stepped into the open he stepped into the side door of the van, just like a scene from the "A-Team".

Once settled in the van, Terry opened the three packs, each holding six foils each for a total of 18. Each was a $20 blow with an extra blow for the pack worker but the tip Rollin so hard that Slick paid them $500 dollars a shift regardless.

"Hey, son, get ready to get on the highway and land this plane on home, cause your captain is ready to zone out. One more thing, Dre, that traffic like what Slick was on, that's a no-no down where were going. We do everything by the phone.

Traffic is a guaranteed one-way ticket to one of those red neck prisons down there Nephew, it's Fed Capitol!"
"I hear ya Unc, I hear ya," replied Dre.
"That's cool, we need to put that thang in the stash spot anyways," as Terry opened two 20's onto the CD case and concentrated on rolling a $100 bill. "Damn this shit gotta good hit to it," Terry confesses as the music softly plays in the back.

Most of the speakers were in the back, so when Terry was back there he didn't like it thumpin'. He liked it down low. He liked it smooth, just like his blow.

Dre hops in the back for a front row audience with Terry, "Unc, here you go" as Dre hands Terry the bag out of the Gucci bag.

With Munchie driving, the windows tinted and the blinds up, they are in their own private lair on wheels.

"This look and smell good Nephew," claims Terry as he exhales from a long winded whiff of the goods, "some of this is yours too baby."

Dre conceded with a nod and the three sat silent for the rest of the trip back to Mama's. Each one envisioning their own version of today's events and what the future held and the part they would play.

They made it back to Mama's house in no time. Dre hopped out with his *Gucci* bag, walked through the gate, unlocked the door and entered an empty house. Mama was gone so Dre took advantage of the situation and stashed his portion in some shoe old shoe boxes he had at the bottom of his closet.

He left as fast as he entered and with the *Gucci* bag over his shoulder. He was feeling large and in charge; new tight fitted cap, new *Jordan's* and a new perspective. With his favorite cousin in the Captain's chair, and ·his Unc in the back, Dre took shot-gun and was feeling good. Life was good at that moment, the future was his and he couldn't wait to have it.

"Dre, you good now?" asked Munchie as they pulled out of the driveway.

"One more thing, let me go get some of my CD's," answered Dre as he looked back at Terry, his head bobbing up and down like a yo-yo. Dre ran back in and returned with his CD folder.

Dre popped in *Biggie feat Jay-Z,* "I Love the Dough," while Munchie headed towards the expressway out of town. They filled up for gas just prior to entering the 290 expressway toll road heading them back to Iowa; Dre and Munchie talking shit and enjoying one another's company.

"Cuzo, we going to get some matching big boy clean Chevy's!" remarked Munchie with some finality.

"We're going to hook them up tuff! Straight up, straight up!"

"I know that's right, us CHI mother fuckers is too tight," sounding like Nuisance from Psycho Drama.

Dre looked to the back of the van eyeing Terry as he floated about along with each bump on the road. Dre remembered that feeling, better than sex and money, the euphoria, the Eden, a Paradise.

Terry was out, he was gone. His fingers held onto the burning square in his hand, ashes grown long from the lack of interruption of a drag. He was taking another trip with only his soul to guide him on his journey fueled by the *Dog Food*.

Chapter 8
When it All Falls Down

The *Welcome to Iowa* sign was refreshing; it meant they were almost there. Munchie had been the pilot, flying solo since Dre had retired to the rear captain's chair to catch some shut-eye. Terry was still out so Munchie relied on Keith Sweat to keep him company, most recently, "Make it Last Forever." When Munchie had the choice, he opted to stay away from Rap, he wasn't much of a fan and only listened to it because Terry and Dre liked it and he wanted to fit in.

Munchie was sporting his new fitted *Polo* cap and his *Versace* shades to block the rays. He was looking fresh. Truth be told though, Munchie demonstrated more feminine qualities than masculine, an issue that was not openly addressed. He tried to hide them from Terry and his Cuzo, Dre, but they all knew. They loved him regardless and didn't treat him any differently.

Munchie couldn't help it they figured; he grew up around a bunch of girls, always cheering and jumping rope. There was his mom, grandmother, sisters, aunts, cousins. It was girls, girls, and girls. No wonder his testosterone levels were so low and his estrogen levels so high.

Munchies' daydreaming to the constant hum of the road was interrupted by the ring of the phone in the Captain's chair next to Dre. It startled Dre awake.

"Hey Cuzo, the phone is ringing," informed Dre, not completely awake to assess from where the ring was specifically coming from only that there was a ringing sound.
"I can't answer it, I'm driving," trying to talk over the Keith Sweat melody with some angst as they, the phone and Dre, interrupted his place of thought.
"Aight, Aight," conceded Dre, "I'll get it." "Hello?"
"Hey baby, I need to holler at cha, can I swing by or are you going to meet me?" asked the voice on the other end.

Dre was completely taken back, half asleep and some strange voice is asking too many questions.

"Who the fuck is this?"
"It's Pete!"
"Hey, it's Pete," Dre yelled up to Munchie.
"Tell him that my Dad gone right now, we'll call him at that number before 30 minutes are out, do he got some tissue on

him?" resonated Munchie.

"Yeah he got some tissue," responded Dre after repeating into the phone what Munchie had said.

How Munchie handled himself reminded Dre that Munchie knew the dope business. He had a baby face and wavy hair making him look like a lame, but he was the epitome of "don't judge a book by its cover." Dre respected Munchie for that.

"Yeah, I'll wait until my Dad get up outta his zone in like 10 or so min and tell him Pete called," instructed Munchie as Dre was moving from the back to the front passenger seat.

"Aight, I see ya'll got this shit down to a science; straight up, straight up!" boasted Dre. "By the way, who is Pete?"

"Pete's one of the customers my Dad let come to the house cuz he knows everybody and he bring my Dad plenty of tissue," answered Munchie.

"Tissue? That's what y'all call money?"

"Yeah, it's softer than paper but heavier than lead," confirmed Munchie, "it's the whole combination; it is fragile but can cause chaos; it is powerful and garners respect. It is addictive, it is evil, and it is good. It is everything and at the end of the day it's what cha needin' right?"

"Cuzo," chuckles Dre, "you crazy as shit!"

"We there yet son?" resonating from the rear of the van, Terry is awake.

"About 30 minutes pops!" immediately fires back Munchie.

"You think you got everything figured out," commented Dre to Munchie in a low tone.

"I do!" exclaimed Munchie,

"Oh, I do," he said with a sense of finality.

"Hey Dad, Pete called while you was asleep."

"How long ago did he call? Did he say whether or not he had some tissue on him?" queried Terry.

"He had some," answered Munchie.

"How many rolls?" anxiously asked Terry.

"I don't know Dad; I was driving so Dre had to answer the phone. I had Dre tell him that we would call him back on his number," articulated Munchie, indicating to Terry that he had things under control while Terry had vanished into the pale moon light.

"Tissue" was denominated in $100 bills and "rolls" were how many they had.

"The Captain has awoken," yawned out Terry as he stretched his arms towards the ceiling of the van and exhaled slowly, "hand me that phone Dre."

Dre threw Terry the phone in the back as Terry caught the phone in one hand while he sipped some soda out of his straw. They had been in the van for hours by now, ever since they were at T's and B's. Terry was awake and restless.

To cure the ache, he lit himself a square and hit a button on the phone.

"Hello!" shot back from the other end.
"Hey mother fucker, what up Man?" Terry shoved into the phone.
"I need to see ya!" answered Pete.
"How many rolls?" asked Terry while exhaling his last drag.
"Five rolls," declared Pete," five," he repeated.
"C'mon by the crib, you stinky mother fucker," laughed out Terry as he hung up the phone.

Terry loved the tissue.

"Take that bullshit out of the CD player!" demanded Terry. "Put in *The Colonel of the Tank* and rid this soft-ass, cryin' ass Keith Sweat bullshit!"

Munchie obeyed and put on "Bout it, Bout it" by *Master P* and then Terry was back; amped and motivated, but needed a little more of a boost to get right. He opened him up two more of slicks' twenty dollar blows, poured them together on the Newport cigarette box, brought the box up to his nose nice and steady and inhaled. In one sniff all the white magic dust was gone, poof! He could feel the warm sensation as it shot across his membranes and into his head, what a rush, what a feeling. *Dog Food.*

"Ten minutes Dad and we're there, do you want me to stop off somewhere before we get home?" asked Munchie.

Munchie exited off the interstate entering the town of Vinton, Iowa. Dre was amazed at how clean it was. There was no trash and a collage of people appearing to be walking aimlessly about, but pleasant.

"Damn, Cuzo, where we at, Mayberry?"
"Cuzo, you in the *Land of Milk and Honey* and an Aunt Bea on every block!"
"Naw'll, you in the fuckin' better stay your ass low key kingdom is where you at!" exclaimed Terry. "These punk ass white folks call each other by their whole name, oh, that's *Joe Blow* or *Sally Walker*. Dre, don't let this clean shit fool you for a minute, they tryin' to keep this bitch clean and they can't stand a Nigga from Chicago. These hatin' ass Nigga and especially the Cops, you gotta watch these hoes too, they sneaky asses. Fuck, shit, everybody is fuckin' everybody. Hey let me stop running my mouth, I ain't got no license to be on the pulpit, plus, I gotta take me a piss like yesterday. Pull over the next chance Munch."

Munchie pulled up to the gas station and Terry jumped out to take a piss and grab some squares. Dre was in awe at how clean everything was, even the gas station parking lot, no decades old oil stains, no worn out signs or tore up curbs; it was clean. Dre had to roll down the window to see if it smelled as clean as it looked.

"Damn, it smells different too! Straight up, straight up!" Dre expressed as he opened the door to get out and stretch his legs with Munchie.

"I'm tired than a mother fucker, we've been haulin' for two days now," complained Munchie.

"Shit, ya'll came and picked me up about 10, no later than 10:30, we've been on the road ever since. What time is it?" wondered Dre out loud.

Munchie glanced at his *Fossil* watch, twisting it ever so slightly changing the reflection of the clear day sun so he could see the face.

"It's 6:46 Cuzo and we about to hit the town tomorrow," announced Munchie, "so I am about to get me some rest."

Terry walked out of the station just as Dre was wondering what this town was all about. He was carrying a carton of *Newports* and a plastic bottle of *Orange Crush*.

"Here Dre, hold this a minute," as Terry handed Dre his carton of squares and jumped in the back of the van.

The two block drive to the apartments was a short two blocks. After riding for so long, the sense of time changes. Two blocks was a blink compared to the hundreds of miles they just put on. There was enough time however, for Terry to stash some of his stuff.

"Hey Dre, let me put this thang in that funny lookin' bag of yours," stated Terry more than he questioned.

"Sure Unc," replied Dre as Terry shoved a half of brick deep into the bottom of the bag.

"Whose fuckin' cell phone is this?" sternly inquired Terry as he slowly lifted his hand out the bag.

"I don't know Unc," shot back Dre with a nervousness, "it must have been in there since Slick's crib. What's the number on it, I'll dial it."

Terry rehearsed the number to himself and couldn't help but notice how much it resembled his old number back in the CHI.

Terry tossed the phone to Dre just as they pulled into the parking lot, "home sweet home, mother fuckers, home sweet home!"

They all piled out of the van, tiresome and lethargic. Munchie was still sportin' his shades and had his Polo cap retro.

"Don't worry about the bags," expressed Munchie, "I'll get mines later, just grab the money bag."

"I got the mother fuckin' dope bag," hushed Terry, "and the money bag; UUUhhh'' just like *Master P,* while enacting his *Daddy Cool Strut* with the hands to the side and everything.

"I'm grabbing mines, takin' a shower' gettin' douggie and callin' Mama to let her know we made it safe. And I'm callin' Tonya," expressed Dre almost exasperated.

While walking back to the complex carting all of their stuff, less Munchie's bags, Terry walked up on Dre.

"You still fuckin' with Tonya? She got yo ass pussy whipped or that's the dope dick you put on her ass from day one!" laughed Terry while swinging the Gucci bag. "That's a good girl Nephew, real talk, that's a good girl."
"Hey, we got a swimming pool in the back Nigga," instructed Terry.

Munchie managed the key ring to the door, he had about 30 keys and 4 alarms on it, so it took him a minute to find the right one. Once in the apartment, Munchie grabbed the remote and hit up the volume to Master P's "Ice Cream Man."

"I'm going to go lay down," conceded Munchie, "I'm beat."
"Aight, later Cuzo," Dre replied.
"Son, one more thing before you lay your ass down; look in the bathroom and please, please, please," with a James Brown tone and rhythm, "get me the two bottles of *Dormins* from the cabinet."
"Aight Dad."
"That's my boy," imitating the cartoon voice of *Spike* and his son.
"Ya'll be trippin' for real!" expressed Dre as he sat observing this interaction.
"Oh, I have fun with my son, we ain't always promised a tomorrow," echoed Terry.

Munchie promptly returned with the Dormins and then headed straight to bed.

"You 'bout to shake this shit?" asked Dre.
"Yeah, I gotta a custo 'bout to bring me 5 rolls of that Scottie for ya Body."

Terry took a half brick of Cocaine out of the Gucci bag and 25 grams of heroin, *Dog Food,* out and walked towards the kitchen with the fourteen $20 blows that was left over from what he had from Slick and told Dre to grab the two bottles of Dormins. Terry opened up two more of the twenty dollar blows and snorted them just as a loud knock came over Master P's "Ice Cream Man."

"Nephew, go open that, it's Pete's stinky ass," instructed Terry as he was compressing the 25 grams of dope in his hands.

As Dre was going to the door to open it something told him to look through the peep hole first. He couldn't even get his eye to the hole before the barrage of chaos rushed on him. The door flew off the hinges, splinters flying everywhere, leaving Dre to put his arms up to cover his face from the blast. The door took him at the shoulder as a loud, thunderous voice hollered out.

"Everybody get down on the ground, this is the DEA, don't no one move," as the herd came trampling in with business on their minds and heat in their hands; M-16 assault rifles all around and every make of hand gun as they were packin' their favorite brands. They were dressed in black like they were going to a funeral and kept yelling; "show the hands, show the hands and everyone on the ground, everyone on the ground" as if they were taking down a squadron of insurgents. The light reflected off their helmet shields and blurred the eyes of the charging force.

Terry reacted quickly, tossing the 25 grams in the trash that was right by the edge of the counter.

"Is there anybody else in the house?" was asked as they escorted Munchie in handcuffs out from the back of the apartment. No one answered their question.

They put all three in the middle of the living room and placed them in cuffs. They had to get Dre off of his stomach as they moved the door out of the way.

"What the fuck ya'll here for and where's ya'll fuckin' warrant?" excitedly and inquisitively demanded Terry.
"We are here for you, Mr. Dent," answered a calm, monotone voice out of the sea of uniforms, "or should I say, Mr. Terry Dent.? You are under arrest for three counts of selling narcotics to an informant on a protected location, 1000 feet!"

"Ya'll fuckin' bitches," was the only retort Terry had, "Ya'll fuckin' bitches!"
"Are there any drugs or firearms in the apartment that we

should know about before we search?" asked another voice?

"Do ya'll mother-fuckin'-jobs, crackers, that's what ya'll get paid for!" argued Terry as he struggled to free his hands that were cuffed behind his back, wanting to spit on them.

Another agent bent down towards Dre,

"Who are you sir? We know Mr. Dent only has one son, a Mr. Johnell Hall."

"Don't tell those punk mother fuckin bitches shit!" yelled Terry just as the butt end of an assault rifle found his stomach, bending Terry over searching for a breath.

The one that seemed to be in charge of the operation told the agent who had just hit Terry to take him out to the car. In obedience, two agents, each flanking a side of Terry, escorted him out. You could hear Terry cussing and fussing until they were out of the ears reach.

The look on Munchie's face was telling. For him to see his father dragged out like that was as if he was just hit in the stomach with the assault rifle. He was sick and he was saddened. He couldn't believe what was happening and he couldn't breathe. His chest had constricted from the panic and his pulse was racing as a tear slowly fell down his face. Inside he was screaming, he was screaming at the Agents, he was screaming for his father, he was screaming at the world, a world that was being shattered around him with every inch that his father was drawn away from him.

"Okay," says the Agent as he draws his hand up pointing a finger at Munchie, "we know you are Johnell Hall, Terry's son. We've had you guys under surveillance for some time now and all those trips back and forth to and from Chicago; you two certainly have logged the miles that's for sure. We've seen all the activity at the gas stations, grocery stores and at Lindell and the Westdale Mall in Cedar Rapids. I'm betting that you are going to pass this guy," as he redirects his finger towards Dre, "off as your cousin," the voice concludes with an arrogance and confidence.

"Somebody check his ID!" commanded the Agent.

A shielded face roughly searches Dre and tosses the agent in charge his wallet.

"Well, well, well. Shit, I am in the wrong profession; I should have been a psychic! I see here we have ourselves one DeAndre Hall from Illinois, and I bet my last dollar to a bucket of shit that he is from Chicago!"

Dre had a look of disbelief, despair and confusion all in one. *What the hell he had gotten himself into,* he shouted to himself, thinking that everyone else heard it as well. His life was fast forwarding through his mind and then reversing; he was seeing images of Mama Sally, Tonya, Munchie, Terry, all of them. Most of all, however, no matter how he played things out in his head, *he was fucked,* was the conclusion he kept coming to.

"Well Mr. Hall, today is your lucky day," started the agent addressing Dre, but was distracted by the parade of items passing them by. They had seized the *1/2* brick of cocaine, the 357 handgun, and twenty-seven thousand in the bank bag; mostly $100 bills and some 10,000 stacks still wrapped with the tape on.

"Excuse me officers," interrupted Munchie in a sheepish yet serious tone, "but that money in the bag is mine. I just received a settlement for an accident I was in and I have the paperwork and credentials to prove it."

"Mr. Hall, we are not disputing that, but as of right now this money will be seized and confiscated along with the rest of the things due to obtaining the items as the result of a drug trafficking raid. As of right now, we don't know whether or not it is drug money, we can only let a judge decide that," replied the agent.

"That's my money," relentlessly pleaded Munchie, "ya'll can't take my money; ya'll already took my Dad!"

Now Munchie had crossed the line between afraid and defeated and was bordering on the hysterical. His father and now his money, it was too much for him to handle.

"Cool out Cuzo," as Dre tried to inject some control and perspective into Munchie. "Everything will work itself out, it will be ok," finished Dre in as much a calming voice as he could find at the moment considering the circumstances.

"Now that is good advice," proudly interjected the agent, looking straight at Dre. "This is a smart and bright guy," he continued as he turned to look back at Munchie, "unlike his uncle," the agent concluded as he finished with a slow sweep of the head back towards Dre.

"So, Mr. Smart and bright guy, what the fuck are you doing down here in my town? What were you about to do?" threatened the agent.

"I'm just down here visiting my cousin and Unc," explained Dre in an innocent tone and sincere reflection.

"Yeah freakin' right! With a half kilo of cocaine! I sure in the hell wouldn't want to be around for your birthday visits. Maybe that's when you brings, what? Two or three keys of cocaine," the agent threw in Dre's face.

"Listen," said a calm, level demeanor in the background stepping out of the shadows, "we will need to make a call to Chicago to verify a few things, like you are who you say you are.

In addition to that, we are taking all of the party favors including the dope, the cash and the *Dirty Harry.*"

His articulation was authoritative and direct, it was obvious that he out-ranked the agent that was thrashing Dre and Munchie for the last 30 minutes. While they did not appreciate the situation they were in or the guys in that living room, that tone and those words were a step towards a positive result to a possibly horrific situation.

"I will need a number to call someone to verify that you are who you say you are," as the new voice came into clear view, nodding his head at Dre.

"Sure," replied Dre, "the area code is 773," and while he provided the remaining digits, Dre was struggling inside.

The only one they could call would be Mama Sally. He didn't want to put her through any more than she already had. She had warned him and now, not but 24 hours later, the DEA are calling her. Dre had no other choice; he only hoped Mama would understand. She knew Terry and she had been around, so Dre concluded that she knew what to do.

"Whom will I be speaking with and what is your relationship?" asked the agent.

"Sally Hall, my Mama," offered Dre in the background.

"Hello," was the sound that broke the ringing tones emanating from the cell phone in the agents hand.

"May I please speak with a Mrs. Sally Hall?"

"This is she," answered the clear, gentle voice on the other end of the line.

"Hello, Ma'am, I am Captain Rivera of the Narcotics Task Force and we have a DeAndre Hall here with us. I am calling to verify his identity. He provided us with this number. What, may I ask, is your relationship to him?"

"I am his mother sir," stated Sally directly and purposefully.

"Ok, Ma'am, can you tell us his date of birth, social security number and age? Also, any distinguishing marks, like a tattoo or scar?" posed the inquisitive mind of the Captain.

Mama hall gave all the right information. It was amazing, having as many kids as she had and to have remembered all of that info on Dre was remarkable. Dre loved his mom, this just added to it. She would always be there for him, he could count on her. It hurt that she had to go through this, but she was tough and Dre needed her at this time. It's what they did, they were family.

She provided detail, even down to the scar that Dre received as the result of a car accident a few years back. The accident that gave rise to the two tombstones of, *Rest in Peace Will and Duball* that he had tattooed on him.

"Thank you Ma'am," the agent said with a sense of acceptance and appreciation.
"Is DeAndre in any kinda trouble?" asked Mama Sally before Captain Rivera could hang up the phone.
"No Ma'am, he was just at the wrong place at the wrong time. Thank you for your cooperation," Captain Rivera offered as he hung up the phone.

The Captain spun around to face Dre and Munchie and as he did he snapped his fingers as if a good tune just came on the radio, one he knew and gave him found memories.

"Ok, so this is what we are going to do," he started. "We are going to take some pictures, pictures of the scars on your forehead and the tattoos and then you will be free to go."

Words of delight for Dre, words of delight; they could take pictures of his entire body if they wanted to for all he cared.

"You are lucky we are not taking you in for fingerprinting

and to be bagged and tagged along with that money," the Captain concluded with a degree of finality. You could sense that he had enough.

"But where's my damn money at?" trumpeted Munchie from out of nowhere.

"Like I said, you two are lucky that we are not baggin' and taggin' you along with the money," the Captain replied with angst in his voice. He was expecting some sincere gratitude not attitude.

Munchie stopped talking and his head fell towards his chest in defeat with a sigh of concession.

Captain Rivera did an inventory of Dre and Munchie and the two of them together were carrying a total of $590; Dre had $90 cash and Munchie $500.

"See fellas, I'm not that mean. I am going to let you keep this money. That could have been additional evidence for drug money," explained the Captain with a soliciting voice, looking for a thank you.

Even though Dre was thinking it, he was not going to pacify the Captain and thank him verbally, ever.

"We are about to give the apartment the up and down, so you are not allowed to take anything from it," explained the Captain. "In addition, one of my officers has already conducted a thorough search of the van and here are the keys. We are going to un-cuff you now," the Captain continued with slight hesitation in his voice as he nodded to one of the other agents to assist him.

They removed the hand cuffs from Dre and Munchie. As soon as the pressure was released from Dre's wrists, the sense of freedom overtook him. He vowed to never be handcuffed again.

Munchie was beside himself, he had lost his money and his Dad; two things he had waited so long for. It hurt and Munchie felt helpless, a feeling he never wanted to feel again. He stood quietly.

As Dre and Munchie were leaving they could hear whispers behind them with one voice standing out above the rest.

"Don't worry fellas, we'll get those two Niggas. Trust me, it's in their blood, they can't resist the temptation. Like kids in a candy store gentleman, like kids in a candy store, but this time it's our store we, are the owners."

Dre and Munchie did not look at one another, they kept their heads down and kept moving, neither said a word, they hardly made a breath. They were full of emotions and had $590 between the two of them and just the clothes on their backs. They last twenty-four hours had been a shift of fates, but, they were free.

"Fellas, I have a hunch these guys are not going back to

Chicago. Trust me, you'll see, they're up to something and they're sticking around."

The last thing that flashed through Dre's mind as they stepped out into the open of the apartment complex was how close they came to going in again, and it was all in the spirit of *Dog Food*.

Chapter 9
Golden Time of Day

The sun was cascading down in the West on a perfectly clear evening. The only sound in the van was the hum of the tires. There was no Master P, there was no Keith Sweat; there was no music. There was just silence between them, but within, the introspection was speaking volumes. The loss of a father for one and almost the loss of a dream for another but it was a beautiful evening and they were free; it was a golden time of day.

"Cuzo'," delicately opened Dre, "I just about know how you are feeling."

Before Dre could finish, words flew out Munchie's mouth as if he was just waiting for an invitation.

"Cuzo, what just happened? They took my Dad, they took my money! They're both gone!" Slamming the heel of his palm into the steering wheel.

"They can't take your money," comforted Dre, "you got the papers saying that it's legit and that you just picked it up."

"Yeah, I hear you, but how long do you think that will take and how long do you think my Pops is going to be locked up?" asked Munchie with a sadness that hovered in the air.

"That all depends, but we'll worry about that later, 'cuz there's nothing we can really do about it right now," encouraged Dre.

"I guess," responded Munchie, still melancholy, "we will learn more when we go visit him."

"Let's just head back to the crib, they ain't playin' down here Cuzo!"

"Cuzo, I don't feel like driving all the way back to CHI tonight and a hotel would drain all this lil' money we got quick. I got this lil' white chick that was diggin' me in CR at the camp ground. I have an idea," coolly said Munchie, smiling from ear to ear.

It was refreshing to see Munchie come out of his emotional coma and it was inspirational to Dre as well.

"Hey man I follow you. I didn't know you and your Pops hit the grounds in Cedar Rapids. I'm in the passenger seat, I'm following you, you da driver and da navigator!" replied Dre with the same type of smile, not mischievous, but playful.

Dre was a master at breaking tension and infusing

laughter when laughter was needed, it was a gift, one of many that he had.

They both started laughing. The laughter may have been excessive relative to the punch line, but relative to what they had just gone through and where they were emotionally, it was one of the funniest things they had heard. It felt good to laugh, so they did.

Twenty minutes later they pulled up to a house on the corner of 15th Ave and 5th Street in Cedar Rapids. They slowly rolled out of the van and headed to the door. Munchie rang the doorbell and a heavy set white girl answered the door.

When Munchie quit fidgeting, he proceeded in his most masculine voice,

"Hey baby girl, this is my cousin Dre and we need a spot to chill at for the night."

In a giggly response, blushing as she looked at Dre. "That's no problem, come on in, and oh, Dre, my name is Claria."

She opened the door wider for them to enter.

As she closed the door behind them she rushed past them up the stairs yelling to them that she was in hurry and had to get to work.

Their timing was astute. They needed to take a break and she was heading out. They would have the place to themselves.

"Do you need a ride sexy?" shouted back Munchie still trying to maintain his macho voice.

"Look at my lil' Cuzo with the ladies. Are all the white girls down here this nice?" asked Dre.

Claria came racing down the steps and told Munchie that she didn't need a ride, thanked him, told them to make themselves at home and headed out the door.

The house was silent, Munchie and Dre were alone with their thoughts. It was an opportunity for Dre to tell Munchie the news.

"Munchie, I still gotta 1/2 brick in the CHI, you think we can go get it and flip it down here?"

"Stop playing DeAndre, heck yeah!" exclaimed Munchie with great enthusiasm almost to the point of disbelief. "We can flip it right here on this block," continued Munchie, "me and my Dad hustles right in town and Pete lives here too!"

"Is Pete the guy who called the phone when we was on our way down here?"

"Yes Sir!" trumpeted Munchie with a new found energy.

"Aight," said Dre, "let's get us some rest and we outta here first thing in the morning."

"Cuzo I ain't even tired now, it's only 10:30, let's roll, get it and come back," demanded Munchie.

Dre and Munchie hit the road. Not but a few hours earlier they had dodged a bullet and were feeling the pain of the downside of the business. Now, with the prospects surrounding a half brick and what they could do with it made all that vanish, it made all the pain go away; the power of the *Dog Food*.

They were back at Claria's place by 6:00 the next morning. They had a half brick in hand and were ready to get paper, but they needed to get some rest. It had been a long twenty-four hours.

By 9:00 a.m. Munchie was up and on the phone with Pete starting to turn the wheels.

"Hey Pete, I need to holler at ya," shot Munchie into the phone promptly after he heard "hello" in the other end.

"I can't make it to where ya'll at, I'm not mobile like that baby, that's why I couldn't make it yesterday," disappointingly admitted Pete.

"I'm right around the corner, I can meet you at the *Hy-Vee* on 1st Ave. and 15th, explained Munchie.

"Cool, I thought you guys were still in Vinton, I'm on my way," confirmed Pete as Munchie was already hanging up the phone.

Munchie and Dre decided to flip all the ounces and give Pete one for getting rid of them. It would be less traffic and a quick flip, well worth it.

Pete was already there by the time Dre and Munchie pulled up. They drove up next to Pete and opened the side door of the van to let him in.

"Hey Pete, I got something. If you help me get it off, I'll look out for you," exclaimed Munchie.

"Okay, cool. Where's Terry?" asked Pete.

"Oh, he's just chillin'," abruptly answered Munchie.

"Listen, I got some ounces of powder I need to get rid of; you can break it down in quarters, eight balls or grams," continued Munchie, redirecting Pete's attention away from Terry and to the business at hand.

"What's the ticket?" asked Pete.

"$1,250," answered Munchie confidently.

"C'mon baby," pleaded Pete, "leave me some room."

"Aight, $1,200 and I got something for you when we

done with it all," conceded Munchie.

"My flavor?" asked Pete," I could use a wake up about now."

"When we done, I'm going to have your eyes rolling in the back of your head!" bragged Munchie.

"That's what I want Baby, that's what I want," urged Pete.

"When you're ready to shop, bring the tissue and only you to this address," instructed Munchie as he held out a piece of paper. "The place is located at 15th Ave and 6th Street."

Pete jumped outta the van and into his ride and burned off.

"Why did you tell that Nigga that you had some blows on you?" inquired Dre with some irritation in his voice," now he's going to be lookin' for some."

"I'll make it up to him. All the things and all the money he owes my dad, he should love to be doing me a favor," answered Munchie.

Dre and Munchie headed back to Claria's on a mission. They needed to shower and change, they were starting to smell themselves. They found an old school scale under the kitchen sink Claria told them about and they went to work carving it up into eighteen ounce sets. They kept things low key in Claria presence, as the less she saw the less she knew. For all Claria knew they were weighin' and baggin' weed or even drops of shit. Dre wasn't showing his hand to anyone. Even if most of the guys that came down from CHI operated with the white girls this way, Dre wasn't just another guy, he was clandestine to be more. He could feel it inside.

Pete was knocking on the door not more than thirty minutes later. Munchie was sporting some of the new clothes that he had left in the van that were not confiscated back in Vinton. He looked refreshed and ready for business.

"Here," said Pete as he thrust $2,400 into Munchie's hand," I need two of those ounces!"

Dre had a look of amazement on his face, he was bewildered; $2,400 for two ounces just like that! That damn near paid for the whole brick that Slick had given him.

Pete was back again fifteen minutes later asking for three more ounces for $3,600 cash.

"Damn, that Nigga acting a fool, straight up, straight up! That's five ounces in less than an hour. Pete is a fucking ATM machine!" announced Dre.
"I told you this was the *land of milk and honey,*" reminded Munchie.

Pete repeated this routine another five times pushing all the ounces but one.

"Munchie, I need you to go with me to drop this one off," sheepishly touted Pete.

"Pete," cautioned Munchie," I am not a delivery service for dope."

Dre didn't know Pete that well, but it was an odd request. All that was going through Dre's head was, *I knew this was all too good to be true.* Dre concluded that Pete was either an undercover informant or they about to get poked. They had over $20k large in the van and it made Dre paranoid as shit.

Munchie was surprisingly calm, cool and collected. He patiently drove Pete to the location he indicated to drop the dope. Pete handed Munchie a stack of cash as he was exiting the van.

"Here you go, $1,200, now hit me with it baby!" spewed Pete.

Munchie reached into his jacket collar of the *Nautica* hood and gave him a half ounce of powder and $200 of the $1,200. Munchie made it work as he shorted all of the other ounces to make this last one.

"This can't be my flavor," argued Pete, "this too damn big to be mines!"

"Check this out," assured Munchie in a New Jack City Nino Brown tone, "take this powder cocaine and that $200 I just gave you and I'll make it right for ya when I get back. Trust me, we cool."

"Aight lil' Terry, cause they wanting that *Dog Food* baby."

After all, Pete had a good day and made an extra $50 off each ounce, eighteen in total.

Pete hopped out of the van leaving Dre and Munchie to their own devices. They waited for Pete to be clear of the vehicle. Without saying a word they looked at each other, the smiles on their faces gradually spreading until the exploded in victory cries! They were screaming at the top of their lungs like the guy from *Goodfellas;* the scene when the kid hears on the radio his own robbery. They were movie stars baby, movie stars!

"Man Joe, you couldn't told me that you can make this type of money down here this quick," expressed Dre in a manner of disbelief.
"It's the first of the month Cuzo," replied Munchie," people payin' their rent and getting' their fix!"
"You damn near replaced what they took from you Cuzo!" observed Dre.
"We need to get back to the CHI and get some ounces of dope and coke baby," stated Munchie.
"Aight Nino, I see Pete about that business, straight up!"
"I wish I would've had something for Pete though," admitted Munchie.

Munchies thoughts were abruptly halted by a loud ring

emanating from the rear of the van. Dre and Munchie looked at each other in silence, naturally holding their breath. Neither of them said a word, but their eyes were shouting volumes.

Dre slid into the back, picked up the phone and answered the call," Hello?" he whispered into the phone.

"This is a prepaid call from an inmate in Linn County Jail, Terry Dent, would you accept?" was music to Dre's ear.

"Yes, yes!" hurried Dre into the receiver. "What's up Unc?" inquired Dre.

"Hey Nephew," with an expression of exhaustive relief, "I'm alright."

"Listen," Terry continues, "I'm in Linn County and yes the Feds picked the case up so I'm probably looking at some time, but don't tell my boy, not just yet."

"I got you Unc," avowed Dre.

"Hey, who's on the phone?" yelled Munchie from the front.

"It's your Dad!" sang Dre back.

"Let me talk to him, let me talk to my Dad!" yelled Munchie with great excitement.

"Let me talk to my boy, but make sure we talk again before we hang up," instructed Terry.

"Ok Unc, will do," as Dre was handing the phone to Munchie. The hand off was amiss as Dre flew to the side when Munchie tried to swerve off the road, almost hitting another car in the process to take the call.

Almost in a panic,"Dad? You okay?"

"Son, you already know these punk bitches can't break your Pops!" with effort towards trying to convince.

"Dad, we comin' to see ya, do you need anything and where are you?" asked Munchie.

Dre said Linn County in the back ground as Terry informed Munchie he needed some supplies.

"I need some white unclear clothes," pausing briefly," better yet, ya'll come and see me right now son, I love you," Terry offered into the phone, hitting Munchie in the heart. The last few hours hustling put things out of Munchie's mind, but this was a reality check and it was coming back and hitting Munchie hard. He loved his Pops.

"Put Dre back on the line will ya?" asked Terry.

Munchie handed Dre the phone almost in a trance, he was numb and he was confused. He and Dre just scored big but it wasn't the same without his Dad there with him. Munchie was sad and his chest hurt directly over his heart.

"Hey Unc, wassup and how did you get this number?" asked Dre.

"Look on the handle of the phone in your hand, it is almost the same as the one I had back in CHI. I memorized it when we found it in the bottom of that colorful bag of yours."

"Now look," restarted Terry with seriousness in his

voice," I need for you to do the Cook County style with me, some boxers on that damn defense. I'm feeling really queasy and you know it's only going to get worse. Do ya'll got some money on ya, cause I see they confiscated all the bread and shit!"

Dre knew what Cook County style was, been there done that; sewing or gluing dope into whatever you brought. A hem with a double stitch, for example, would do the trick. It was a code proprietary to the Halls; their game on.

"I don't know where to mingle at and yes we got money," answered Dre.
"You go see Pete," answered Terry to Dre's mingling question, "Munchie will take you to him."
"Aight Unc, we on our way and I'm on it," replied Dre, omitting the news of their recent business development with Pete.
"Aight Nigga, tell my son I love him," with compassionate emphasis on the "love him."

It made Dre smile and kind of sad at the same time. He appreciated the relationship they had and he also knew how important Munchie was to him and he was to Munchie; the bond between a father and a son.

Dre and Munchie had gone from $590 to over $20k in a few days and were feeling less of the world on their shoulders. They went to *Wal-Mart* and bought Terry some boxer briefs and T-shirts so they could take them into the visit. The tunes blasted again, things seemed right. The period when there were no tunes just didn't fit with them or with the van. This was their ride, their enterprise on wheels and it should always be hoppin', not stuck in the mud! Dre's mind was already into the future; *he was about to turn the motherfucker out!*

"Cuzo, we about to go see your Dad and then we rollin' back to CHI, but first let's go see Pete so I can hook up these whites for your Dad!" instructed Dre.

"Aight Cuzo, Aight!" echoed Munchie.

Munchie and Dre stopped to see Pete, he introduced them to a guy and settled ten blows at $50 a pop; a small $500 from their large roll.

Dre was thinking to himself, *I'm about to get Nigga rich and only hustle in the winter time down here. Straight up, straight up!*

After they picked up some crazy glue for the whites they headed to the *Red Roof Inn* to get a room. They paid in advance for two weeks as it was out of the immediate locale they would be hustling but close enough to get back and forth conveniently. Dre planned on surprising Terry with a ten pack instead of the one hitter. Dre smiled at the reaction he anticipated from Terry when Terry would discover it in his cell.

Not having product all over Claria's house or in the van with them was another benefit of securing the hotel room. Dre was careful like that, the streets had taught him a thing or two and now he was reving up to cash in on what it owed him. His carefulness typically paid him back with dividends and this was no exception and the reason he had the half brick. The hotel was going to be the temporary safe house to store their stuff until they could find something more permanent. Dre believed in the adage; *you never sleep and eat where you store your stash.*

They hooked the whites up and went to visit Terry, leaving them with the officer on duty. They wouldn't go directly to Terry, but they would find their way to his cell eventually.

Just seeing Munchie and Dre caused Terry to beam. When Terry walked up to the glass he was walking stiff and a little sickly. You could tell going straight was affecting him, but he was staying strong and he knew the process. He knew that it would take some time, but he would make it through it. It was not his first rodeo.

Munchie jumped on the phone and peered through the glass at his Pops,

"Hey Dad!"
"Hey son," replied Terry in a comforting, loving manner reserved for his son. "I'm going to make this quick. Look, I've seen my indictment and I'm being charged with a firearm and the half block of coke. They didn't mention anything about the

twenty-five grams of dope. It must still be in the damn garbage can."

"Dad," Munchie interrupted," the police put us outta there and locked the door with a pad lock!"

"You gotta break up in that bitch then," instructed Terry.

"These peoples ain't playin'! You want us up in there with you, huh?" chimed in Dre as he overheard what Terry was telling Munchie.

"I understand, but that's a damn shame, $13k going to waste like that!" exclaimed Terry.

"You already know," stated Dre slowly and carefully, "I am not leaving my Cuzo nowhere by his self, straight up straight up."

Dre was talking loud enough for Terry to hear him without using a phone. There was no one else in the visiting room anyways, so Dre didn't mind.

"Hey ya'll it's good seeing you, but I got some shit to get to. I love you and keep ya'll damn eyes open and come back to see me tomorrow," ended Terry.

He hung up the phone, stood up and walked away, never looking back. To some it may have seemed cold, but to Dre and Munchie they understood. Despite his rough demeanor, Terry was feeling the pain of losing his freedom and losing his son at the same time he was feeling the pain of coming off a forever high.

Dre and Munchie both pressed their palms up against the glass and gave it a pound out of respect for Terry. They walked away as well, never looking back.

As Terry turned on to the deck a smile crossed his face because he knew it was just a matter of time and he would be in the stars, he would be unpacking and tracking the stash in his whites. He couldn't wait for the feed; he couldn't wait for the *Dog Food.*

Chapter 10
Ensue, Ensure, Everything

They left Linn County around the noon hour, the sky was blue and the large light clouds filled the gaps. It was more brisk than Dre liked but the air was fresh and they were free. It was strange how whenever you left a facility that held people, like a jail or prison, you always felt a little more free than when you arrived, even as a visitor.

They had no need to pick up any of their stash so they decided to head back to CHI. They logged more hours in the last few days than they would log in a month in town. The miles were wearing on them and on the van. They needed a change.

"Cuzo, we gettin' a new whip when we get back!" announced Dre.
"How 'bout matching whips, the twin Chevy's I was talking about?" asked Munchie in a seriously fantastical manner.

Munchie was serious about wanting them, he had always dreamed of having matching rides with his Cuz', but to make it a reality was a whole other matter.

They decided to fill up at the gas station just prior to entering the interstate. Dre was pumping the gas, cognizant of the smell of the fumes permeating in the cool afternoon breeze, mesmerized by the events of the past few days as they played through his head.

"Woosh!" went the tires as they almost took Dre out at the knees, causing Dre to awake abruptly and angrily from his moment.

"What the fuck yo' problem Joe? You blind or something?" were the immediate words out of Dre's mouth.

They were instinctively directed at the driver behind the wheel of the car that almost ripped his legs off.

The driver was pulling up to the pump across from Dre as if he was in the Daytona 500. His mouth was as fast as his driving.

"You need to get YOUR ass outta da way or grow some bumpers on your ass!" instructed the black Dale Earnhardt Jr. wanna be.

Dre could tell by his plates that he was a pretender, whispering to himself, *this a wanna be tough ass Nigga from*

CHI, thinkin' I'm some lame ass or somethin'.

Dre had met many like him before and he knew the most efficient way to handle him; with diplomacy.

Dre slowly and calmly walked over to the car as the man was getting out and when he was out he introduced the guy to his ambassadors; Mr. Right and Mr. Left and then Mr. Right again. Dre dropped a three piece on him so fast the guy never knew what hit him. That was diplomacy the *Hall* way; direct and to the point with no ambiguity or miscommunication.

"You grow some bumpers on your own ass," Dre retorted as he towered over the man as he crumbled to the concrete almost hitting his head on the pump on the way down.

The Halls had a way with their hands, it was almost a tradition, not spoken of but passed down from generation to generation; the Uncles and the cousins always offering advice and insight into the use of the hands whether it was boxing, Karate or any other martial arts or movements. Those were lessons Dre never missed. In fact, even Munchie had the touch.

As Dre jumped into the van Munchie was already laughing with a degree of awe, Dre was fast, Munchie had forgotten how fast.

"Damn Cuzo, you knocked that Nigga out like Tyson!" cheered Munchie.

"He got what was coming to him, what his hand called for.

Tellin' me I needed to grow bumpers on my ass," Dre mumbled out with angst, "he know now they on my fuckin' fists, it was time for him to pit!"

Dre was doing all he could to not absolutely lose his composure to laughter. It was funny.

They attacked the bags of candy Munchie bought at the store, it had been some time since they had eaten a full meal, actually since they had eaten at all.

It was approaching four o'clock by the time they pulled into the windy city and landed on Central Park. Slick stood out as he was flashing his white gold chain, sparkling on and dangle to his navel while wearing a *Rocawear* short fit with the fisherman in front of his candy-red flip-flop painted '73 Malibu with 100 spokes and *Vauges,* all decked out with TV's flipped on visors, bumping out, *Foxy Brows 4-5-6.*

Munchie pulled up alongside Slick on Dre's side of the van.

"What up Joe, what's the business," greeted Slick.
"I need to holler 'bout some business, straight up, straight up," answered Dre.
"Hey Joe, we can't discuss no business like this," reminded Slick as he was swayin' to the tunes feeling all bossed-up with his shorties and workers all around him.

It was his moment and Dre let him have it.

Munchie caught a park and stayed in the van while Dre and Slick hooked up.

Dre followed Slick into one of his ghetto fabulous cribs. The same thick ass sexy girl was there on the couch and she was watching the Jamie Foxx Show. *Regina?* Dre questioned to himself.

As they walked into a back room, Slick opened the meeting.

"Talk to me baby," while rubbing his hands together like he was *roasting over an open fire.*
"Man, I got over $20k, I need to get double breasted, straight up, straight up!" explained Dre.
"Shit, you didn't make that much off that brick?" sarcastically questioned Slick with a grimace across his face.
"This was only off half!" exclaimed Dre as he continued on a foray of how fast everything happened; how they hit the bulls-eye.
"I told you your ass was about to get money Joe," bragged Slick, pulling on his blunt.
"What you'll give me for the $20k?" asked Dre. "The only thing I need is gas and a case of Dormins, 'cause they don't sell none down there," finished Dre.
"Shit," replied Slick, "I need to go down there with ya'll Joe!"
"I'm just getting my feet wet," admitted Dre confidently, "when I make it to the deep end you already know I'm coming for ya. Shit, you giving me a life preserver

straight up, straight up!"

"You know I wanna see you win!" exclaimed Slick as he exhaled a hit from his blunt. "Just like I wanna see you win a whole book at 17 stacks and I'll give you the quarter brick of dope. You getting' this shit cheaper than I get it. I'm be outta business fuckin' with you," finished Slick in a jovial yet mature tone, leaning towards a seriousness.

Dre got the money and paid Slick. They had a key of coke and a quarter brick of blow; they were ready to roll. As they were heading outta town on the expressway when Dre told Munchie to turn it around. Dre needed a fix; the loving kind.

Dre was filled with a missing. He needed to see Tonya, but first he would do her right, he needed to get her some ice cream. She would enjoy eating it and he would enjoy feeding it to her. The simple things in life, he appreciated, and this was one he didn't want to wait for.

They headed west out by North Avenue and pulled up in front of her house, the ice cream cold in Dre's hand. He sat in the passenger seat ready to spring into action like a lion on the prowl.

He reached the front door, his fingers no more sensitive to the coolness of the cream in his hand. He slowly and purposefully rang the doorbell, leaving Munchie back in the car.

"Hey Hunny-Bunny," came out of Tonya as she wrapped herself around him like a warm blanket on a cold night. She always felt so good to Dre.

"How you feelin' baby?" posed Dre as he kept one arm wrapped around her slender waist as his other arm rose up slowly from behind his back to reveal the prize.

The smile on her face coupled with her grabbing him tighter as they entered the house reminded Dre just how well they fit together. Of all the women Dre had messed with, when it came to loving, they did it best. She knew him so well, sometimes better than he knew himself it seemed. She made him feel good inside, made him feel good about who he was as a person, no pretending, but being real.

"I was wondering when I was going to see you again," claimed Tonya.
"I been down in Iowa with Munchie and Terry," flashing his killer smile while handing his princess the ice cream as if it was a bag of jewels.
"Oh, this for me baby?" she asked in a sexy, innocent voice killing him back with her appreciative and desirous stare. It shot right through him, right to the core and right through the heart.
"You know my favorite flavor Hunny-Bunny," she seductively smoothed over him verbally while she grabbed one of his cheeks. "Kiss me," she commanded.

Dre obeyed, tasting the Black Walnut swirling off her tongue and into his mouth.

Dre followed Tonya into the kitchen mesmerized by the pendulum shaking of her ass; left...right...left...right, bouncing from hip to hip. She could feel the heat of his stare so she gave it a little more shake. Her juices were building up again and her itch was moments away from being scratched, or so she hoped.

Thoughts of taking her right there, right now, ran through Dre's head; to shake that thing up and down and not just sideways. Dre couldn't do it. If his money wasn't in order, no sex, no love. He was determined to create his own destiny and nothing was going to get in his way. His historical hurdle, the Dog Food, was no longer controlling him, he was free to conquer his demons, to conquer the world and he would do so with a vengeance.

He had the dope to make the money, he had the contacts and he had the conviction so he needed to keep his head, think clearly and to think ahead. Tonya was not a distraction and he needed to keep it that way. She was his girl and he loved her.

Tonya came out of the kitchen with a bowl of ice cream, two spoons and a smile that could melt the polar ice caps. They sat down in front of the large screen but their eyes were only on each other. Tonya slowly slipped the spoon out of her mouth and into Dre's. He could taste the blend of the ice cream and Tonya all at once it was more than he expected, something greater than Black Walnut, it was "Black Heaven" He could feel her desires mounting.

"Take your shirt off baby, I want to lick this off your body," Tonya demanded Dre.

Dre knew he had to put the hammer on her; she was so hot, so horny and with this ice cream, so sweet.

"But I can't stay long baby, Munchie is out in the van waiting," Dre admitted trying to break her spell.

"Give me a quickie," Tonya begged. "Take your clothes off and I'll be back with a blanket," she suggestively commanded.

Before Dre knew it she was back, butt ass booty hole naked and looking so, so fine. She could have been a model, Dre said to himself. She had Mary J. Blige playing softly in the air, "I'm the Only Woman," ringing in Dre's ears and with each step closer towards him the intensity to have her grew. She was the only woman for him and he would have her.

She laid the blanket down on the couch as she helped Dre disrobe, removing his boxers revealing all of his manhood, hard and sleek. As they coupled onto the couch they were like new lovers exploring each other for the first time, like an Adam and Eve.

Tonya massaged his hard velvety dick, stroking it just the way he liked it. Dre returned the favor by laying Tonya on her back and spreading her legs slowly so he could explore her. He spread her pussy lips and tasted her, tasted her juices. He still had a sense of the ice cream on his tongue and the coolness made Tonya quiver. The blending of the ice cream and her cream and the cold and the heat exploded in Dre's mouth. He sucked as if his life depended on it, he couldn't get enough, and all of the sensations at once were almost more than he could take.

Tonya wrapped her legs around Dre's neck, thrusting her hips into his face. His face was drenched with her ecstasy. She was going crazy as Dre gripped her ass even tighter pulling her into him.

"Oh, baby, I'm about to cum," she moaned over and over again, holding Dre's head right where she wanted it so he could swallow every drop of her sweet nectar.

Dre was beyond hard, he was so hard it hurt. He slowly rose from the den of pleasure and turned Tonya around so her ass was pointing in the air. He could smell her loveliness and see her hot pussy inviting him in. He rubbed it ever so gently as if to tell her he was coming home.

He dove into her. As he plunged, her head shot back and up towards the sky, she could feel how deep and big and hard he was, it was making her crazy. She was screaming and yelling uncontrollably. At one moment Dre felt as if he was just along for the ride, almost over whelmed by the emotion and the desires. She was so hot for him and he for her, their noises were hardly audible, almost as if they were speaking in tongues; it was a crescendo of climactic overture. They made sweet music together.

The fire between them smoldered as they lay there in each other's arms trying to catch their breath and believe what had just happened; was it even real, Dre wondered. They lay there still for what seemed like an eternity. Dre moved first.

Dre got up and grabbed a towel from the bathroom, ran it under warm water and wiped himself down before putting his clothes back on. He returned for Tonya, wiping her as well.

She was so beautiful, as Dre slowly went over her body that was glistening from the juices all over her. I'm a lucky man, he thought to himself.

Dre kissed her purposefully and slowly on the forehead and told her he loved her and that same affection was reciprocated by Tonya, only her kiss was warmer. As Dre left her embrace she was covered with a chill of his absence, how she loved being with him. She would miss him.

Chapter 11
It's All About the Benjamin's

Dre and Munchie made it back to Iowa in no time. They exchanged small talk along the way, Dre was focusing on his meditation. He could feel his chest expand with each breath and with each breath he would go deeper and deeper into himself, contemplating where he was, where he had come from and where he was going. Dre was reflecting on his relationship with Tonya, the conversations with Mr. Bone and how he was determined to make his mark; a manifestation of epic proportions- the saga of Dre.

As soon as they walked into the hotel that Dre had rented for the two weeks, they started slicing and dicing. They broke and dug a nice amount of the dope, but didn't really make a dent in the Dog Food. They were seasoned at this, this vocation of theirs.

"I can measure this shit by eye!" bragged Dre as he estimated the proper amounts.

They didn't bring the scale from Claria's place and they didn't want to be dragging the goods all around town, so he guesstimated.

"Cuzo, we don't need to worry about those grams my Dad wanted us to get," remarked Munchie.

Dre was responsive to his cousins' claim, but found it interesting that Munchie was thinking of such a thing at that time. Terry was locked up and Dre was on a mission to blaze his trail.

"Naw'll not now, but we're coming to get cha, straight up," sang Dre in response to the tone of *BG* song "They comin' to get Cha."

When they were done they hurried back to Claria's place and started shaking and bagging the dope with just *Dormins*, a plate and a spoon, they didn't even have a blender. Kind of like *MacGyver* with a rubber band, paper clip and a piece of gum, anything was possible with Dre at the helm.

"Munchie, go ask Claria if she got some playing cards, a fresh deck," emphasized Dre, "it can even be some *UNO* cards for all I care and get me some aluminum foil."

Claria was an introvert; she stayed in her room most of the time and was very polite and supportive. Dre was convinced that she enjoyed the company of two black men staying at her house and that she often fantasized about getting two black dicks at the same time.

"Here you go Cuzo," breaking Dre's fantasy as Munchie handed him a fresh deck of cards.

Dre was working the spoon, smashing the dope and *Dormins* together, as Munchie was stripping and tearing the foil, a talent he learned at his own kitchen table with Terry. Dre was swerving the cards like he's doing a three card Molly. They were so into their process that they didn't even address the coke yet. By the end they had 500 bags that were to go to market at $50 apiece and they still had plenty of the Dog Food left!

After two hours and steady traffic at the *Hy-Vee*, like they were having a year-end blow out sale, Pete was done with the 500 bags. The sun was falling fast now and the later it was getting the hungrier the town seemed to be. Dre and Munchie were infatuated with the prospects that the town held for them!

"They love this baby! We can do this all night!" Pete exclaimed as he handed Munchie another wad of cash.
"Pete, you think it's cool selling here? You sold all this by yourself!" pronounced Munchie.

"This stuff is made so good that other dealers are even shopping! I'm safe, baby, I'm safe!" trumpeted Pete. "It don't get no cooler baby, this is a grocery store parking lot and we got the groceries. Speaking of groceries, I need to check my produce aisle," informed Pete as he nodded into the darkness, "I've got me a couple of workers."

As Munchie was wrapping things up, Pete took some dope that was set aside for his fix and some for his workers.

"Listen Pete, we are going to chill for the rest of the night, but tomorrow we going to take a ride and put this thing in motion right," stated Munchie with confidence and commitment.
"Whatever baby," flung Pete, "ya'll the Captains and I'm just on the Yacht trying to take it all in."

Pete was the middle man and he was punching the clock with a pocket full of money and handful of dope. It was a good day at the office.

Dre turned to Munchie and in a feint of disbelief, "Cuzo, we hardly touched the dope and we are already sittin' on 25 stacks!"
"Yeah, I know, let's go back to the hotel room and put this stuff up, bag up some more dope and talk about our plan for tomorrow," offered Munchie.

It had been a successful day, but a long one and Munchie

needed a break. Dre took it all in and as he did a smile crossed his face, he knew this was only the beginning and he couldn't wait for what was to come.

The next day they were up early and took $10k of the $25k. They made a trip to see a guy who they remembered was selling two *Chevy Brogham's* with the LHS package, one black and one gray. They were one owner vehicles and fully loaded with leather and power everything.

Logistically it was a challenge for them as they still had the van; three vehicles and two people. They paid cash for the sedans and decided to drive one while trailing the van, expecting to return for the other one later.

They also decided that they needed a wardrobe change as well, so they hit the local twenty-first century urban haberdasheries in Waterloo. Dre was adorned in all *Ice Berg* clothing and Munchie was all *Polo,* everything but a horse that is, even a matching pouch.

After shopping they headed back to the hotel still navigating separately. The hotel was quiet and the lights in the parking lot needed to be updated, the dark corners gave the place a rundown feeling. Dre was not interested in drawing attention anyways so the accommodations were fitting for the time being.

"Hey Cuzo, we should get us some new cell phones," expressed Munchie almost like a teenager trying to convince a parent that their idea was a beneficial one for all involved.

"Yeah," replied Dre, "we gotta get up with Pete and shake some more of this shit up, straight up, straight up."

Dre was not taking his eye off the business at hand, he was determined, he was motivated and the quick 25 stacks just influenced him that much more.

"It's still early, let's handle 'bout going to get the other car and taking them both in to get hooked up with sounds when we get the phones," stated Munchie, more in the tone of a question seeking Dre's approval.

They left the hotel in the two different vehicles, Dre in his new wheels and Munchie in the van. Dre had already contacted Pete and informed him that they would be at the Hy-Vee in twenty minutes. Munchie arrived first, spotted Pete, and preceded into the lot and pulled up in front of him and hopped out of the van.

"What's up Pete?" queried Munchie feeling all grand. It was a beautiful day; Munchie had new threads on his back and his pockets were full of money.

"Awe, man, baby I told ya'll that shit was good. We had two peoples OD on that thang last night," admitted Pete with a look of empty concern.

They hopped back into the van as customers were starting to

amass, drawing attention and asking Pete if he was straight. They were hungry for the *Dog Food,* but their shelves were empty. Like any sound businessmen, you want to have product that is in demand in stock for when the customer wants it in order to maintain your reputation. It's all about reputation in this type of business and reputation leads to the Benjamin's.

"Hey, where's your Cuzo Dre?"
"He's on his way," explained Munchie.

Dre pulled up in the clean ass black *Chevy Brogham* LHS, a 1990 box joint with European front head lights. He rolled in like he was on a magic carpet, the king of the new kingdom he was building. He eased out of his ride and jumped into the van as smooth as royalty.
"What's up Pete?" fired Dre.
"Look like you baby, that's a clean ass-fuckin'-Chevy right there and I know you about to hook it up!" exclaimed Pete with envious confidence.
"Yeah, yeah, straight up Joe!" as he gave Pete a pound.
"Cuzo, Pete said some guys OD'd off that thang last night," announced Munchie in an uncertain manner. Having customers OD on your product changed the dynamics of the business as risk management was a key to survival.
"Book smart and Street smart," started Dre, "should've been a chemist, 'cuz I shake smart. I'm the real Dr. Dre!"

The group laughed genuinely, but inside, deep into their consciousness there was an uneasiness; they were not in the death business, they were in the *Dog Food* business.

Pete broke up the moment by getting back to business,

"So, what time we settin' up shop baby?"
"Give us 'bout two hours. We gotta make a run and get some phones and drop the cars off to get done over," boasted Munchie.

Dre and Munchie were doing it all up, Dre with the *R.I.P. Will and Duball* on the headrests and Munchie's with his Mom's name, *R.I.P. Annettee.* Both rides would come with custom four-15 inch *Bose* sub-woofer system with flip TV screens on the visor and back head rests with twenties all around in polished chrome *Assassin* rims.

"Well, ah, let me slide then baby," commented Pete.
"As a matter of fact Pete, you should come with us," invited Munchie.

Munchie jumped into the van as he instructed Pete to get in the drivers' seat as Dre followed in the Chevy.

"Thanks for coming with me Pete. I haven't brought it to Dre yet, but the girl Claria, whose house we at, she goes to work at nine o'clock at night, so we can just use the back of her alley like a spot and keep the packs in the stash spot in the van," disclosed Munchie.

The comment took Pete by surprise as it was out of any context and was information or an idea that he would assume Munchie would clear with or discuss with Dre before sharing it with other people. Pete wasn't sure if it was an effort by Munchie to show some initiative or if it was to demonstrate a deeper trust in Pete.

"That sound like a plan baby, cause everybody talking about that shit!" supported Pete.

"We 'bout to pass out some free blows, whatta you think about that?" asked Munchie.

"I don't really recommend that, it'd be too much traffic baby; they already know ya'll and that you got the bomb with the OD's going down," surmised Pete.

"Slow down right over there Pete," instructed Munchie as he pointed his index finger in the direction and pace he wanted Pete to go; his hand was shaking a little.

As Munchie jumped out of the van Pete hollered.

"Hey Munchie, do you want me to follow?"

"No, you take the van, it's yours now baby," proudly declared Munchie, "and we will meet up with you in a couple hours back at Claria's."

As Pete drove *off* in the van, he could see Munchie in the side view mirror. It looked like Munchie was almost skipping. Pete felt the same inside, a youthful jubilation that he had not felt in years. It was refreshing and inspiring all the same. A smile spread across his face so broad you would think he was the sun shining brightly down on the universe that was made right; made right by the food, *Dog Food.*

Chapter 12
The Master Plan

Like a picture out of a Quentin Tarantino movie, back splashed with some urban grit, Dre, Munchie and Pete sat down to devise the plan, the master plan. Dre had waited his whole life for this. He worked hard on the streets, he meditated on the conversations with Mr. Bone and he felt his destiny taking shape, he would be a master of his fate.

Operating out of Claria's house, Pete would be the runner, with the bundles couriered in the van. They would run in two shifts; the early bird from 6:00 to 9:00a.m. and the second, the graveyard shift, from 9:00 p.m. to 5:00 a.m. They would shake it at Claria's in the morning after the graveyard shift, from 5:00 to 5:45 a.m. Dre always said, the early bird would get the worm, and this was no exception. So, as most of the world was asleep, Dre was already running.

Pete owned the van and Pete hustled the product; as far as the world knew, it was Pete's dope. Other dealers were able to buy product as well. It was good for business to keep other dealers plugged in, because when they got lazy and bought it from them, the better business became. Dre understood the profit margins and dealing in a wholesale capacity put some pressure on the margins, but it also significantly reduced the risk. That was an acceptable risk return ratio to Dre.

The rules were tight and not to be deviated from, whatever was not done by 5:45 would roll into the next business day.

After two weeks of operating like this they had cleared a little over $250,000, cash. That is a quarter of a million dollars for a quarter brick! Their plan was working and it was no surprise to Dre as he was meticulous regarding the timing and execution of things. Dre was a born leader with the necessary business and street savvy required to make it in such an economy. He knew the relationship between supply and demand and how price was a factor for both the product and the consumer and how a shift can modify the model. The one benefit was how extremely inelastic the demand for his product was, it was an addictive substance and as such garnered greater flexibility in pricing as the demand stayed constant or rose due to the addictive nature; a principal Dre would capitalize on.

As the consummate business men, Dre and Munchie thought an addition of real estate to their portfolio would be appropriate. They had Pete put a house in Marion in his name and had it decorated for two up and coming players. The cascading cathedral windows, marble floors, granite counter tops, state of the art appliances and top end electronics to make it all hum.

"Do you believe this Cuzo?" exclaimed Munchie with an adolescent nature.
"I don't believe this at all, straight up, straight up!" replied Dre.

However, deep inside, he did believe it, but out of respect for Munchie, he did not want to sound condescending or arrogant.

As Dre had finished packing more cash in the safe at their Marion crib, he turned to Munchie with that look, the look that showed a beam of appreciation and gratitude, Dre was happy. Munchie was happy. Life was good.

"Cuzo, we've been workin' hard, we deserve a break, let's hit the club," announced Munchie.
"I ain't trying to party with these country ass Nigga's down here," retorted Dre.
"Let's go to the Tycoon," encouraged Munchie ignoring Dre's initial response.
"Aight," conceded Dre, "but we going' to the crib tomorrow, 'cuz we outta dope."
"Let's drive to the old apartment in Vinton and grab those 25 grams that are still there," answered Munchie.

"Yeah, real hustlers don't discriminate nor sleep on no paper!" followed Dre.

Dre was decked out in his Iceberg Jeans with matching shirt and Gucci loafers while Munchie was everything Polo, even his boxers and socks; he should have been paid for all the advertising he was doing for Ralph.

They both had on their Cardi frames, looking like NAS and DMX from Belly, and the aroma of Coolwater Cologne wafted in the air, a smell that always reminded Dre of Will and Duball.

"You sure clean up real nice Cuzo," offered Munchie.
"I see you Mr. GQ," complimented Dre equally. "Check this Cuzo, I don't really want to be riding out to Vinton this late trying to grab a lil' funky ass 25 grams of dope," admitted Dre.
"Ah, c'mon, ain't nothin' gonna happen," assured Munchie.

The drive to Vinton was only twenty minutes, not enough time to reconsider what they were doing. After all, it was only twenty five grams, they knew where it was and they should be in and out, no problems.

When they arrived they could see the padlock was gone and there was just the regular lock and tumbler.
Just as Dre was hunching into an explosive stance however, Munchie reminded him to watch the shoulder as he may need to pick up one of those big girls tonight.

"She better have a big bag of money if she be that heavy!" exclaimed Dre.

Munchie was laughing so hard like he was "falling out" watching Def Comedy Jam as Dre wasted no time. Dre put his shoulder into the door and off the hinges it flew, but interestingly with very little sound and not a wrinkle on his Iceberg. Dre was the master of many things and apparently breaking down doors silently and cleanly needed to be added to his list of accolades.

"Hey Cuzo," instructed Dre, "Go get the dope outta the garbage."
"Cuzo, you grab the dope, I need to get something more important," replied Munchie.

More important, Dre played back in his, *what the hell could be more important than grabbing the 25 grams?* That was the entire reason they made the trip to begin with! As the thought simmered in his mind, Dre began to actually become irritated.

Munchie was losing site of the task at hand, of the business, something Dre would have no tolerance for.
"You can get whatever shit it is some other time, unless you tryin' to get five for breaking and entering," demanded Dre.
"I gotta get our photo album with all my Mama and Grandma pictures," declared Munchie with a tone of plea and confusion that Dre would question him so.

It hit Dre right in the gut, drove right through him like a hot arrow, piercing him in the heart. He loved Munchie and to see the look of what appeared to be desperation and disappointment at the same time and directed at Dre, moved him.

"Oh, my bad Cuzo," sympathetically expressed Dre, trying to comfort Munchie, "Sorry baby, I got you, but hurry up though; straight up straight up."

They made it out of the house with the 25 grams and headed for the highway; another mission for Dre and Munchie successfully completed.

They were reveling in their conquest just as their visions were drowned in the blue light; out of nowhere, all over their bumper and lights flashing, the police.

Dre gripped the steering wheel harder as he pulled to the side of the road while trying to control his breath; shit, he kept saying to himself.

As the officer approached the vehicle Munchie offered some advice.

"Calm down Cuzo and just tell 'em that your name is Terrell Hall."
"Cousin T?"
"Yeah, cousin T," repeated Munchie, "cousin T, he's got licenses."

Dre slowly slid his right hand down from the steering wheel and reached into his pocket to retrieve the 25 grams and covertly pass it to Munchie. If anyone was going to be getting out of the car, Dre thought to himself, it would most likely be him, so better to give the dope to Munchie.

"Good evening Gentleman," began the officer, "license, registration and insurance please," he finished in a commanding voice despite it was phrased as a question.
"Here is my insurance card and registration," promptly replied Dre. "My name is Terrell Hall and this is my uncles' car and I'm here to visit my cousin. The problem is, he is drunk," continued Dre as he looked over at Munchie," and I just wanted to make sure he makes it home safe."
"What's your name?" the officer asked Munchie.
"My name is Johnell Hall," Munchie slurred out of his mouth as his head bobbled from side to side. It was an Oscar moment. "I live just around here" as Munchies finger bounced around in the air trying to find the right direction and was abruptly halted by the belch that ensued. "Oh, excuse me officer," offered Munchie

in perfect timing.

Dre looked at the officer and nodded, confirming that what Munchie had said was true and to see if the officer was buying in too; and he was.

The officer glanced back at the identifications and then at Dre, exhaled slowly and handed them back.

"Ok, guys, have a safe evening and get him home. Have a good night."

As the officer walked away, the sighs that came from Dre and Munchie could have been heard in purgatory.

"Let's get the fuck outta this town!" trumpeted Dre. "Thank you Jesus," Dre said in a whisper. That was a close call, *too close,* he said even louder in his head.

"Cuzo, you like my performance, it's the Cardi frames we got on, feelin' like a movie star acting like a movie star," proudly added Munchie.

Dre wiped the sweat from his brow as he pulled away from the officer, "Damn, we was lucky, I need me a shot of Yak or something!"

"Cuzo," then with a dramatic pause, "we only here once and we gettin' money, got money and we look like money!" Munchie added with a sense of finality and a feeling of being beyond reproach.

They drove out to Cedar Rapids to hit the club "Tycoon"; it was humpin' and bumpin'. There were girls everywhere and every flavor. They were standing out like two shinning diamonds, they were so fresh, like MC Hammer Niggas, *can't touch this!*

"Damn!" exclaimed Dre, "look at these white hoes, lookin' good as shit!"
"I know you ain't lookin' at these girls, Tonya would kill your ass," reminded Munchie.
"Tonya in the CHI," replied Dre not particularly appreciating the reminder," and her ass," he continued, "better be in bed or laying in it with that vibrator playing in that pussy!"

Lil' Troy Baller Shoot Caller is blaring in the air and the white guys and girls are rapping and getting crazy. With drinks in their systems so charged, you can feel the energy rise in the room.

"This how they party down here Cuz?"
"Yeah, I see that look in your eyes," replied Munchie. "I see you ready to fuck something, I can even see it through the Cardis!" continued Munchie as he tilted his head forward and slipped his glasses down just enough to peak up at Dre with an impish grimace.

"I hope these girls are nice like Claria. Check this out Cuzo,

I'm about to go put these 25 grams in the trunk where the spare is. Whatever chick I'm gonna fuck tonight, I'm takin' them to a hotel and you follow us and get a room next to us."

"Bet!" replied Munchie.

Dre departed to stash the dope and when he returned there was a taller white chick staring at him. She was a blond with a sexy face, a full figure, a tongue ring and a tattoo that you could see through her blouse. The revealing nature of her top was alluring, her nipples were almost showing and it turned Dre on.

It was magic when she stepped in front of him blocking his path. Dre could feel his heat bounce off of her, they were as close as two could get without actually touching.

"Excuse me sexy," Dre slid out.

"No, I don't think I will," standing her ground. It was a face off of eroticism.

"What's your name?" she wondered out loud.

"Dre my name and by the looks of you, you must be Mariah Carey," fired back Dre with confidence and a smile that you almost heard a bling when his pearly whites reflected off the club lights. He was smooth; he felt it and so did she.

Stepping close to him and looking into him, "You're close handsome, but it's Mariea not Mariah," as her eyes started to undress him.

Their hands slid together as if to make an acquaintance of a traditional manner, but their body language screaming for more.

"I can see you're not from here," Mariea commented while trying to control her breathing and her palms from perspiring.
"Why you say that?" inquired Dre with a sincere interest.
"Cause how you look, dress and the way you talk. Damn, where your girl at?" she interrogated excitedly.
"I ain't goin to lie baby," admitted Dre, "because I keep it all the way real. My girl, she at her crib."
"See, that's what I'm talking about. Anyone of the lame ass guys around here would've lied about something so simple like that," the end of her comment near a whisper for how loud it was in the place.

She pushed against him harder and squeezed his hands tighter and leaned forward and whispered in his ear.

"Can I go with you tonight?" almost purring.
"As long as you ain't gonna have one of these crazy guys follow us. You driving baby?" followed Dre as he moved his midsection a little to the rhythm in the background as his attention was being stolen away by her growing presence.
"Yeah, I'm driving."
"Well, shit, let's blow this popsicle stand!" exclaimed Dre trying not to get too far ahead of himself.
"I'm following you baby, lead the way," she conceded, like a sheep following the shepherd.
"I've got to get my Cuzo, but meet me outside."

Dre floated through the club, almost literally, or so he thought. He was on one of those highs that follows the heightened arousal of one's manhood in a party scene.

Dre found Munchie talking to some nerdy, preppy black guy.

"Hey Cuzo, we goin," as Dre grabbed him by the arm. "Who was that guy?" Dre shouted back over his shoulder as they were making their way towards the exit.

"That's a friend of mines," answered Munchie. "So, did you find somebody to freak?" inquired Munchie, changing the subject as fast as Dre was trying to get out of the place.
"As a matter of fact yes, as easy as 1, 2, 3 and that is why we are on the move Cuzo," boasted Dre.

As their backs hit the door, *Next*' "Too Close" was thumping in their ears, setting the tone and the mood as they strutted over the threshold. They could feel the eyes of all of the women upon them as they left. They felt a sense of pull to go back inside, but what awaited Dre outside that door was worth leaving the rest of them behind.

As they crossed the street Dre noticed Mariea over by a red Ford Escort peddling some weed. The dim glow from the street light shadowed across her, revealing how voluptuous and full she really was for a white girl. Like a beacon in the night, it grabbed Dre's attention and he zoned in on it like a dog on the hunt.

From behind her Dre articulates clearly and slowly as if he is wearing a badge,

"Hey!" startling and shaking Mariea, causing her to jump. Dre catches her around the waistline, "what are you doin'?"
"You scared me," she pronounces as she playfully slaps him on the arm that is snuggly around her. "I'm just trying to make some money," she finishes.

A thought popped into Dre's mind like a light bulb for a cartoon character, *she could be a valuable asset*, Dre thought to himself, a way to diversify and expand his business model, his empire.

"Look baby girl, what you want to do and where we going to do it at?" rushed Dre.

Taken back by the abruptness and sense of entitlement, Mariea cooled a little by the comment.

"All of that is decided by you," she conceded as Dre's charm outweighed his comment.
"Well...for starters baby, you gotta ride with me because I ain't about to get in that lil' strawberry car like I'm one of the Little's," informed Dre.
"Follow me then," Mariea replied, "I live right off of 15th and Beaver, in the Beaver Apartments."

Smiling inside, *perfect name*, thought Dre, perfect name,

"Alright sexy, alright!"

Dre and Munchie followed her to the Beaver and she went in her apartment and grabbed a night-bag anticipating that pleasures that awaited her. She hopped in the back seat with her bag and all her essence as she fired up a blunt.

"We don't do none of that darlin'," instructed Munchie as he pulled out of the parking lot with one hand on the wheel and one pointing in her direction.
"It's cool," interjected Dre, "in fact, give me a hit of that!"

What the hell is Dre doing, Munchie thought to himself, so much so that he thought he actually said it out loud and sheepishly looked at Dre to see if he had heard him and of course he had not. Nonetheless, Dre did feel Munchie staring at him but excused it as part of the moment and took a hit.

They arrived at the hotel in no time and while Dre and his new found Goldie locks got a room Munchie reserved the adjacent one.

By the time Dre arrived at the room his world was spinning. He sat down on the bed trying to gather himself but realized it had been a long, long time since he had smoked anything, he was feeling like *Goldie off the Mack*.

Mariea could tell that the weed had him flying as his smooth articulation and conjecture was slipping, she didn't want to lose him to the hallucinogen.

"Take your pants off and let me suck your dick," she commanded, bringing Dre to attention in every sense of the word.

"Shit, you ain't said nothin' but a word," remarked Dre. "As a matter of fact, let's just take our clothes off and you keep on your bra and panties."

Dre carefully took his *Cardis* off and placed them gingerly on the night stand beside the bed, between the lamp and the phone.

Dre slid back and took her all in, the vision of her, full bodied and tight. He could tell she had not had any children as she was too firm and her breasts pointed straight out and not down; she was fresh and tight. The nipples protruding through her bra let Dre know that she was as excited as he was and he could feel her sense of urgency.

As she approached the bed at his side he moved his hand upward inside of her thigh and brushed over her love mound watching her wince as he touched her wetness. He slowly slid his fingers into the waistband and helped them to the floor with one full motion; Dre was beyond smooth and this action alone sent her into another dimension.

As her panties hit the floor she stepped out of them like a professional dancer, a ballerina almost of Swan Lake and she simultaneously unhooked her bra. She stood their naked, glimmering in the soft lamp light, dimmed even more by Dre's state of high; all was colorful but more subtle than normal, she looked marvelous.

"Let's sixty-nine," begged Dre but with a sense of control. "Let me taste that sweet pussy while you enjoy this dick," declared Dre as he held out a handful.
"I knew you would have a big fat black dick, too big for my pussy and just right for my mouth," replied Mariea.

Her eyes traced down to his midsection to see the revealing of how excited he was and how so right she was. *Hmmmm,* went through her mind.

The way she said it was full of confidence, admiration and fear all in one. It made Dre start to laugh. The weed was ahold of him now, influencing him and he knew it, but he couldn't change it. So he laughed, it was funny.

Dre took her into his arms and rolled her over on her back, kissing ever so passionately as he turned her on. He was gently inside her as they were turning, but he plunged deep into her as her back found the bed. She gulped for air.

"Oh, yes Dre, fuck me, fuck me hard!" she demanded.

This was enough to put Dre over the top, she was commanding him with some authority and she meant it. It was no plea. It was a direction and one that Dre was eager to obey.

"Roll me over and fuck me like a dog," she barked.

Granting her wish, Dre rolled her over and slid back into her as she gasped again for air throwing her head back and arching her back as her long blond hair fell on him. He was aroused but now he was ready to explode watching her thrust back and forth trying to feel every inch of him. Her hair was flowing and sweeping across her back as his wet glistening dick went in and out.

"Oh baby, this...feels...so...good...," as Dre drove his final assent, exploding in her as she echoed his sentiment and exploded on him, cumming together like they had been with each other before.

Dre didn't know if it was the weed or what it was; all he knew is that he liked it.

"I am so wet!" she exclaimed, "you need a boat for me baby" as their juices were flowing out of her onto the bed.
"I'm your Captain baby and I will drive however you want me to!" boasted Dre as he rubbed his wet stiff dick across her pleasure cove and her full tight ass. *Damn, this white girl got some damn good ass pussy,* he yelled to himself.

They didn't stopped there, they explored one another all night long; slowly and methodically, fast and hard, they traveled the galaxy of eroticism.

Dre knew it was not by chance they met, that it was not coincidence, rather by fate. He had found another partner, one that held a special place in his heart. To her, he wasn't Dre, he was "D," more of a man than she ever thought she could have. They both felt fortunate in a world full of cynicism and corruption; they had found something pure in the world of *Dog Food* and they wanted it to last.

Chapter 13
The Sky's the Limit

"Let's go see my Dad and bring him some whites," urge Munchie.

Dre knew full well that "whites" was dope and he was impressed by how far Munchie had come; the natural usage of metaphors to express himself. The power of communicating allegorically, analogously or metaphorically is imbedded in our culture and here is Munchie, possessing no more than high school equivalency in education and he is a pro!

"Yeah, first let's take these 24 grams to Pete," as Dre did the math in his head by subtracting the one gram to Terry from the 25 they picked up out of the garbage.
"The custoz be goin' crazy without our stuff," exclaimed Dre. "We off to see your Pops for sure, straight up, straight up, after all, this is his dope!"

They had established a routine and strategy for getting Terry his "whites" in addition to making sure there was money on his books. They would bring different "whites" or under clothes for different people on his tier. The recipients were under the impression that Terry was just looking out for them. When they arrived and brought them up however, Terry would swap the new pair with the drugs hidden in them with another new pair he had in his cell. It worked smoothly and most importantly, it kept Terry from the DT's as he was constantly medicated.

Following their visit to see Terry, they shot out to see Pete and to drop off the 24 grams. They also informed him that it should be enough to tide him over until they got back from Chicago and that was that, as in this business you didn't ask more questions than were necessary.

As the two 15 inchers, brought by *Bose*, thumped, Munchie piloted his grey Chevy. His was basically the same vehicle as Dre's but his embroidered head rest read, "Rest in Peace Annette." Keith Sweat was filling the air and Munchie was feeling good. He always felt better when he had a chance to see his Pops despite the dichotomy; he was happy to see him but sad to see him where he was. He was satisfied that he had done all he could do and his conscious gave him a break and allowed him to enjoy things despite the position his father was in.

"What's next?" Munchie triumphantly posed as "I'll Give all My Love to You Baby" hung in the air accompanying Munchie's last note.

"Let's go count this money and figure out whether or not we want to sell this brick whole or just make a profit and we on our way to the CHI on a plane. I'm gonna call Tonya and have her pick us up at the airport, but first I need to give Mama a call," replied Dre.

As Munchie turned the radio down, Dre called Mama.

"Hello?" answered Mama on the other end.
"Hey Mama," expressed Dre with gratification that she had answered, and tinges of satisfaction that he was hearing her voice. "How's my favorite girl in the world doin' and feelin'?"
"I'm fine DeAndre. How are you? Are you o.k.? It has been awhile since you went to Iowa. How is Terry and how is Munchie?" fired Mama at Dre.
"He's right here," interjected Dre before Mama could keep drilling him with more questions.
"Hey Auntie," Munchie yelled into the phone as soon as he heard Dre make a reference to him. "I love you and we on our way home!"
"Well Mama, you heard from Munchie's big mouth where we headed and about Terry, he's cool, we just visited him," informed Dre.
"What time ya'll be here?" asked Mama.
"We taking a plane so it shouldn't take long depending on what time the flight leave," answered Dre.
"Plane? You better make sure this is your first stop. I'm going to cook you a meal. I'll get started now," eagerly committed

Mama.

As Dre hung up the phone he could already feel the warmth of Mama's house and the smells emanating from her kitchen, he didn't know he was hungry until she put the idea in his head. In fact, he couldn't remember the last time he had eaten.

As Dre dialed Tonya a brief flash of Mariea popped into his head and this was coupled with a hint of guilt that he had to force out as the second ring hit his ear.

"Hello," came a sexy voice on the other end only exacerbated with the sounds of her chewing on something, a characteristically adorable habit of hers according to Dre.
"What's up baby, the second woman that makes my life besides the one that gave birth to me," claimed Dre as he was spreading it on extra thick, one part because he loved her and another part to fight the demon of another woman in his mind.
"Hey Hunny Bunny, how are you and where are you?" Tonya asked in a sheepish tone, "I miss you" she said with punctuation.
"I miss you too baby. I'm good and actually on my way home. I'm calling to have you come pick me up at the airport if you not busy," sweet talked Dre into the phone.
"I'm never too busy for my baby, you haven't been down there with none of those white girls have you?" gently posed Tonya.

Dre could not believe his ears. *How did she know, was she having him followed?* The original thoughts he had about Mariea when the phone rang, the guilt he was feeling, and did he say something out loud? All these and more raced through his mind. Dre shook off his paranoia and realized it was a female intuition and she was fishing. All of us have our insecurities and we can imagine what the other person would do relative to what we are capable of or what we can imagine, not necessarily them. Dre didn't know what emotion to react with; seriousness, humbleness, laughter? He chose laughter as a defense mechanism.

"Where all that come from baby?" chuckled Dre, "I'm talkin' about you pickin' me up at the airport, and you talkin' about some white girls? C'mon baby you know me better than that!" exclaimed Dre.

The only problem was, she did know him better and that is what concerned her.

"Tonya, you know he not seeing any white girls around me, I would tell you if he was," blared Munchie into the phone, covering for Dre.

"Tell Munchie he's right and I'm sorry baby," Tonya pleased into the phone. "I'm not sure where that accusin' you came from. Give me a kiss."

Tonya was embarrassed she had gone that far with Dre and actually accused him. She knew better and some things were best left unsaid. She knew Dre and she loved him for who he was and as long as he made her feel like a princess when she was with him that was enough for her.

"I'll be there to pick you up at the airport, what time do you want me to pick you up?" Tonya finished.

"I'll call you with the exact time when we 'bout to get off the plane," directed Dre with a confidence to overshadow any lingering doubts about the "other girl" topic.

As Dre hung up the phone he was compelled to confide in Munchie,

"Cuzo, that's some crazy shit with Tonya ain't it?"
"That girl know you better than you know yourself beside Auntie Sally and she love's your dirty drawers!" pronounced Munchie.

The guilt drove a little deeper into Dre, deep enough for him to hide it and put it away, to repress it from a clinical perspective. He had a good thing with Tonya and what was going on between he and Mariea, he wasn't exactly certain. Dre was hit with a brief moment of confusion, but his street smarts and natural tendency to block things to protect himself kicked in and he was onto the business at hand.

"Let's go back home like Don's," articulated Munchie as he slipped in Marvin Gaye's "Got to Give it Up" and let it bump out the 15's.

Dre smiled on the outside but was feeling something different on the inside. His manner coincided with Munchie's suggested persona and he projected a stigma of royalty and riches.

"Naw'll we leaving like Dons, I'm 'bout to buy me something slick and you too! Fuck these kiddie-ass- Chevy's, Big Boys play with large sums!" declared Dre with a facade of finality.

It was just another way for Dre to push down his present feelings and move on, to survive.

Inside however, he was drowning in thought of how he was deep into two women, his business was expanding and his heart and mind were pushing emotions to the surface that he would otherwise not have and he needed to let go. Dre knew he must stay focused and not let these things get in his way. He was a professional and he needed to act like one and there was no room for interference or uncertainty, in any capacity.

"Cuzo, you really trying to have these Niggas mad and all the hoes throwin' that pussy on you!" shouted Munchie breaking Dre away from his thoughts, like a splash of refreshing water on a hot summer day.

It felt good to Dre to break away from those emotions and get back into his character, Dre the conqueror.
"You like that 'lil white thang, I see when you dropped her off, she kissed you and called you D," accused Munchie .

That was the third white girl Dre had fucked since being

down in Iowa. The first was Claria, as Dre was trying to take care of business because Munchie did not want to. Dre knew nothing was free so he paid in full and even pleasured one of her friends one night, Brittany, an old school friend of Claria's. Dre did not like to be indebted, especially to a woman, so he paid the dues with interest. Munchie owed him.

They headed to the crib in Marion and added all the funds up and Dre decided that they were not going to worry about the book, the key of Coke. Then it occurred to him, an "aha" moment, an epiphany.

"Cuzo," started Dre, "we need to leave this book for Pete to get off."
"Might as well, don't make no sense holding a key of Coke. We already know what happens around here from the first time we had both money and dope on us." explained Munchie.

Dre smiled recalling Munchie's Oscar acting performance and the smile increased as he watched Munchie meticulously pack his all *Polo* attire in his all *Polo luggage.*

"Call Pete and tell him to slide and get this shit," instructed Dre as he packed his *Louie Vuitton* luggage. "We need to catch a plane and plus, we ain't sellin' no more cocaine. We ain't Tony and Mannie, we Dre and Munchie, and they want our product like we Nicky Barnes and Frank Lucas, "before the snitching Joe," reminded Dre.

Pete picked them and the dope up and dropped them off at the airport in Des Moines. They had $150,000 between the two of them and were flying instead of driving. Their life was changing, and the style in which they lived was changing as well. The world was calling them and they were ready, ready to stake their claim and rule their own destinies in this new world; the world of *Dog Food* where the sky was the limit.

Chapter 14
Home in Style

Soaring above the clouds where only the sun and horizon meet, Dre and Munchie found themselves in awe. Neither of them had ever flown before and the mere consciousness of traveling 30,000 feet in the air, if only for a moment, made them realize how many things in life they had yet to do. The economics of their upbringing precluded them from experiencing many things, they committed to themselves, individually and without telling the other, that they would live life to the fullest and not only be participants but also consummate explorers.

"I loved that flight! We gotta do that more often!" shouted Munchie with an adolescent glee like opening up presents on Christmas morning.

"The way we're goin' Cuzo, we going to have our own Helicopter like the big timers cash money Slim and Baby; straight up straight up," added Dre to Munchies already flooded imagination of the things to come.

"We made it here in less than thirty minutes! Now that's flyin' the friendly skies! Ain't it amazing how things are so small out that window?" Munchie flung inquisitively into the air, not necessarily seeking Dre's insight but more of a statement of his experience.

It had never occurred to either of them to contemplate the concept of perspective or objects in motion. They had not been exposed to Newton's laws or positions of Einstein pertaining to movement and objects. Their life had consisted of, until that moment, things that were tangible, things that they could touch and feel, not the intangible, theoretical or philosophical. Such intellectual luxuries were commonly reserved for others they thought. On this day however, they relished in their experience and were as contemplative as any in history, maybe even more so.

"Man, this crazy Cuzo, I remember as a shorty we use to catch the *El-Train* and come down here and break into cars with broken pieces of spark plugs; takin' the stereos, brick phones or whatever we could get our hands on. One time we even broke into an undercover cop car and stole a .357!" reminiscently exclaimed Dre with a new found vigor.

"Cuzo, you were wild" conceded Munchie, "you were wild."

By the time they had reached the luggage return each had replayed the flight in their minds over and over again. The seats in first class were much larger than those in the back of the plane, in "coach" and considering it was their first time on a plane, their decision, or so they surmised, to fly first class was well worth it.

"They better not loosed this $5000 bag," threatened Dre, as he grabbed it off the belt and set it on its wheels as Munchie was following in suit.

Dre could not fight the feeling inside about how their lives were going to change and that this was only the beginning. He had an addictive nature to him, as did Munchie, and things like this they would appreciate and consume, like the pros they were!

Tonya was parked right out front, with hazards flashing and a smile to match despite the cabbie in front of her trying to move her. It had been too long since she had seen her man and no cabbie or anything else was going to keep her from her man a minute longer than needed. She missed him and she didn't realize just how much until she saw him walk out that door. *He looked so fine,* she thought to herself.

When Dre hugged her he could feel the warmth of her body, it was not a sexual one that he commonly felt but more of an adoring one, the type that you feel from a compassionate love. It made Dre feel missed and wanted. *She looked so fine,* he thought to himself.

"How was your trip?" Tonya asked them as Dre pulled away to place his luggage in the car. "I see ya'll with ya'll *Cardis* on!"

"Hey Tonya," replied Munchie, "you lookin' real nice!"

"Damn," interjected Dre before Munchie could say another word. "I was just 'bout to tell my baby that! Since I can't be the first to say that, I will say that you sure smellin' fine!"

Tonya flashed her eyes at Dre wanting more of what she was hearing. She had missed him, she had missed his attention.

"Your hair is lookin' fine and that *Coogi* one-piece-skirt set with the *Gucci* claws and *Chanel* shades! You hurtin' 'em baby! You hurtin' em!" exclaimed Dre as his eyes tracked the curve of her ass as she turned to get in the passenger side.

"So, where are we going?" started Tonya, "are you guys hungry? I gotta a taste for some Chicken; some *Uncle Remes, Kentucky Fried* or *Popeye's?*"

"We will get to that later, baby," softly spoke Dre as he rubbed Tonya's leg gently. "*We* are headin' out to Orland Park first."

"What's out there? We don't have to ride that far out for a good restaurant," stated Tonya with a quizzical tone.

"I want to hit the *Lexus* dealer and get something off the showroom floor," stated Dre with finality as if he had it planned for weeks.

"Are you serious?" posed Tonya with a sheepish excitement.

"Yeah baby, I need one favor from you," Dre slid under her suspicion radar now that she was so excited about the prospect of a new *Lexus.*

"And what is that?" asked Tonya, knowingly and willingly to do anything Dre asked of her.

"I need for you to co-sign or just put it in your name would even be better," Dre asked in a reluctant tone but wanting her to agree.

"If I do this," started Tonya in a serious voice, "*you* gotta promise me that you be careful and watch what you do and the people that you have around you, 'cause I know you not lettin' anyone else drive whatever *Lexus* you get but, Munchie and Ms. Hall!" stipulated Tonya.

That was enough for Dre and the terms were acceptable.

"That's my baby," admitted Dre as he leaned over and kissed her on the cheek. "You know I ain't gonna do anything to hurt my baby."

"How much you wanna put down?"

"We can purchase it," exclaimed Dre.

The Lexus dealership just made you feel wealthy. The atmosphere promoted success and the mannerisms and attitudes of the personnel made you feel like royalty. Dre liked it.

Dre spotted the salesman he wanted to deal with as he walked in. Years on the streets educated Dre and he knew what to look for, a guy who would know the business and would understand the terms that Dre had and it needed to be a decision maker.

As Dre introduced himself, he noticed the title of sales manager on the man's ID, confirming Dre was a good read. This was just the guy he was looking for.

Dre used his charm and way of persuasion to get the "best deal in town" on the new ride. He handled himself with poise and professionalism, a trait that was reciprocated.

Tonya did all the paper work as one of the other managers drove the new jet black GS 400 off the showroom floor. The price was well below anything advertised or discussed openly and Dre calmly handed the manager the cash that was required.

Dre looked sharp next to the Lexus as Tonya walked out of the dealership to join them. She walked straight up to Dre, put her arms around him and stood up on her tip toes so she could whisper into his ear without requiring him to bend down.

"I didn't just sign for a pussy mobile, remember that!" she whispered into his ears and placed a long slow kiss on him as she slid down off her tip toes.
"There you go again baby," laughed out Dre. "Follow me to the *Auto Doctors,* 'cuz I'm gonna get this finished right and then we'll head out to North River Side and get some new *Ice Berg* gear or do you wanna do downtown to Michigan Ave?"
"That's all you wear. Who you think you is, Jay-Z?" trumpeted Munchie who had been quiet the last few hours

just taking it all in.

"Boy you so crazy!" added Tonya. "I'll meet you at the *Auto Doctors,* be safe!" Slapping him on the ass as she walked away.

It was like falling into heaven; the wood grain, the plush leather, the smell so fresh you wanted to inhale it all in at once. The *Auto Doctors* would add the TV's, a set of Twenties, a darker tint and put *Rest in Peace Will and Ball* in the head rest.

The tunes were already bumping as Dre tuned it to WGCI 107.5. Munchie put in Dre Dr. Dre's *Chronic* CD as they were exiting the lot; they were loving the scene, it was fresh and they were all over it!

"We ballin' Cuzo!" yelled Munchie.

"Watch when Slick and dem see this bad mother fucker, they gonna' catch the vapors!" echoed Dre. "Don't even trip Cuzo, you getting' the next ride!"

"I ain't trippen' on none of this. I'm happy to just be with you Cuzo," admitted Munchie.

Munchie struggled fitting in when he was younger and being a part of this, being a part of Dre was empowering and made Munchie feel like he could be somebody, that he could do anything.

"Munchie, I ain't tryin' to get sentimental, but I love you

too Cuzo," admitted Dre as compassionately platonic as he could.

"You better call Auntie Sally and let her know we made it and about to come to dinner," reminded Munchie.

"I almost forgot, thanks Cuzo, that's why I love you!" answered Dre.

'That's right we goin; over there to eat, fuck the restaurant, plus Tonya and Mamma haven't seen each other in a while, straight up!"

Dre reflected as the words came out of his mouth, *he is riding slick with his Cuzo, going' to Mama's for some dinner and his girl is going with.* Life at that moment was perfect for Dre. He wanted to hold on to it for as long as he could. He wanted every day to be like this one. He was overwhelmed with joy as he opened the sun roof.

"Ya'll see me and Munchie, do ya'll see?" Dre yelled out the sunroof. "We handlin' our business Will and Ball, we handlin' our business! Rest in peace!"

They were on the ride of their lifetime, it was luxury, it was comfort, it was decadence, and it was the world of *Dog Food.*

Chapter 15
Evolution

They dropped the *Lexus* off at the "Auto Doctor" with intentions of picking it up that same night as he knew the owner. That was the thing about the streets, while knowing things kept you alive, knowing people kept you advancing. Dre had learned most things the hard way, just as Munchie had, and enjoying the spoils was something they could get used to. How you treated people along the way had a direct correlation to how your journey went; sometimes it was hard and other times it was easy; Dre endeavored to make it as smooth as possible and one way was to be respectful. It was easy to do and paid back in multiples.

The three of them, Dre, Munchie and Tonya decided to hit the mall, *North River Side,* to give Mama Hall time to cook up her feast. The aromas of the mall emanating from the food court made their stomachs turn, they were tasting the food already. No one said anything about it, but you could sense the degree of their appetites as everyone seemed to be concerned about the time revealed in the constant looking at their watches.

"Let's go, I'm starving," announced Dre. *Finer words had never been spoken* though Munchie and Tonya, who nodded and sped up their walk as a testament in support of his idea.

The path up the front walk was so very familiar to Dre and Munchie. With each step towards the door the aroma grew stronger. So many times they had walked that walk levitating towards the solemnest of the warm, loving home. No matter what they were feeling or what they were going through, seeing Mama Sally and spending time with her and sitting down at her table was a reprieve from all of it, a sanctuary in many ways.

"Hey Mama!" yelled Dre as he opened the door," It sure does smell good in here!"
"Hey Ms. Hall, it sure does," echoed Tonya.
"Hey Auntie! My Auntie is the black *Julia Childs!"* Exclaimed Munchie.
"Hey DeAndre," welcomed Mama as their eyes met. "I see you and Munchie made it safe," as she glanced at Munchie with an endearing look.
"And you Ms. Tonya," said Mama Sally while putting her chin to her chest and looking up sheepishly at her, "and when am I going to get my grand baby?"

"Auntie, you know she not tryin' to mess up that shape, you see how that *Coogi* skirt fittin' on her?" interjected Munchie.

"Ooooh child," remarked Mama Sally, "and you Munchie, you just be quiet!"

"How is your family Tonya?"

"Everyone is fine Mama, I can't complain at all and really ain't no one trying to listen if it was something to nag about," admitted Tonya.

"Oh, you can always talk to me baby," offered Dre playfully as he single fisted his chest to demonstrate his steadfastness and commitment to her.

"Boy, if it wasn't for Ms. Hall and me, you probably be in the *Looney Bin!"* retorted Tonya.

The lightness that was already in the air was levitated by the laughter that erupted from everyone. Spirits were high as were the appetites.

"It's just about done, give me another fifteen to twenty minutes," informed Aunt Sally.

"I'll help you Auntie," offered Munchie as Dre and Tonya slipped off to Dre's bedroom.

Not much got by Mama Hall, including this transition; she didn't miss a beat.

"I know what you thinkin' Auntie," offered Munchie.

"And what would that be?" Aunt Sally said with a smile putting Munchie on the spot as she grabbed the last piece of fried chicken out of the pan.

"Let me just get a quickie baby," pleaded Dre as his hands were slowly lifting up her tight fitting skirt.
"I am not about to disrespect your mom like that and go back in there smelling like sex! No!" forcefully articulated Tonya so there would be no misunderstanding.

Dre knew this tone and what it meant when she spoke with clear articulation. She was educated and while she chose to express herself consistent with those in her company, she could express herself with absolute clarity of verse or prose when she needed, something Dre did not mess with.

"Okay, you're right. Then just taste me and I'll go wash up really quick," offered Dre like a little kid trying to get one over.
"Boy, you so nasty, but that is what I love about your black ass. Come over here, but if you grab me by my head it's over."

That was a deal that Dre could live with. He made sure the door was closed and locked as he shuffled over to her as she knelt down. She had to slide her *Coogi* skirt up over her ass revealing her *Victoria Secret* panties and the outline of her pussy. The change in color of the fabric announced how wet she was. She continued to prepare herself to receive him like a baseball catcher taking a position behind home plate. She removed her claw shoes so she would have balance and looked up at Dre giving him the signal that it was ok to approach her.

Dre moved slowly towards her as her hands reached out for him. She unzipped his pants slowly, looking up at him to see his reaction. As the *Iceberg* jeans hit the floor the print of his boxers stuck out at her like a .44 magnum. She pulled it and could see how excited he was as the pre-ejaculatory semen dripped out of the head and made for a natural lubricant as she started to slowly stroke him.

She methodically placed her mouth around the end of his pulsating muscle, throbbing with every heartbeat. She could feel it in her mouth and how the heat coming off him stimulated her mouth and made her tingle. She sucked on him hard while stroking him with perfect synchronicity.

Dre could feel the buildup, growing with each series of stroking and sucking, he was so hard it hurt and he was nearing climax with every breath,

"Oh, yes, baby, oh, Tonya, Tonya, Tonya," whispered Dre as he held his breath approaching his end.

Then she stopped.

"What the?" exclaimed Dre.

"I told you no sex. I said I would taste you, not let you stand there and fuck my mouth and cum in it!" proclaimed Tonya. "I'm trying to be respectful and go downstairs to eat the meal Mama worked so hard on. Anyways, I am going to give you a real buffet later!" claimed Tonya as she stood up pulling her skirt down and patting herself right where Dre would eat from later.

"You know I love it when you talk dirty to me," admitted Dre as he pulled his pants up and carefully zipped in his still hard shaft, trying to tuck it back into his boxers.

"See, you wouldn't be able to do all that if you would've came. So, you can thank me later," foreshadowed Tonya with a grin that made Dre melt.

"Ain't no need doing all of that, my Mama far from a fool and plus you don't have no more lip gloss!" jokingly added Dre.

Tonya turned and looked at herself in the dresser mirror, realizing Dre was right. "Shit! I left my purse in the car. Give me some Vaseline! See what you made me do Dre!" angrily cautioned Tonya.

"Well, at least you got your taste baby!" laughed Dre with a sexist mannerism.

By the time Tonya and Dre got downstairs the room was a smorgasbord of aromas, you didn't know where one started and the other finished. It was a divine. There was macaroni and cheese, fried chicken with Mamas special barbeque sauce, black-eyed peas, potato salad, mustard and turnip greens, corn bread and for dessert, Dre's favorite, German chocolate cake. A feast fit for kings!

Mama loved cooking for her children, especially for DeAndre. She tried to treat all of her children with love and affection, but her and Dre had a special bond. The years they spent together while Mama was in her addiction and fighting it, tightened that bond. They had shared experiences that she had not shared with the others, making their closeness beyond mother and son; their worlds were part of one another's, inseparable souls.

When they were apart for too long their behaviorisms would change and when they were together you could see a spark ignite in each of them. They were good for each other.

"I'm stuffed!" announced Dre as he pushed his plate away from him. "That was delicious!"
"Yeah, Auntie, we need you down in Iowa with us," complimented Munchie.

"Speaking of Iowa, how's your dad?" asked Mama.
"He's Aight, he's seeing what deal they going to bring him or if he is going to trial."
"Yes Ms. Hall," interrupted Tonya, "that meal was delicious. Need to get me some of those recipes for when Dre and I stay together."
"I really enjoyed ya'll company.

"Dre baby, I am so proud of you, not what you are doing, but what you are not doing to your body. You stayin' clean." You could see the tears form in the corner of Mamas eyes. She knew how hard it was to stay away, to stay clean. Her pride was accompanied by all those memories of when she was not strong and it hurt inside.

"I am too," stated Tonya as she reached over and gave Dre a kiss on the cheek.

"Thank you Mama. I am proud of you too, for all of these years of staying clean and thank you honey for the kiss, that means a lot to me," confessed Dre.

"I just take it one day at a time and with the help and strength of Jesus, 'cuz one slip up and this is all gone you know" as she looked around the house and at them. "The first step was admitting to God that I was powerless and that my life had become unmanageable and I had to turn it over to him," reminiscently whispered Mama.

Moved by her, Dre reached into his pocket and pulled out a wad of cash, around ten thousand and handed eight of it to Mama.

"Here Mama, go buy yourself something nice, you deserve it," offered Dre. It was easier for Dre to react in this manner, to offer her money to do something nice for her. He felt compelled to do something, he cared for her so much, and a hug or kiss wouldn't suffice. If he could take away all of her pain he would. For him this was the best way he knew how to express that he hurt when she hurt.

"I'm not going to even ask where this came from, but watch yourself out there on those streets," cautioned Mama while looking at Dre and glancing over at Munchie as well. "You already know there ain't no real friends out there, these your only friends right here in this kitchen. You save some of this for you as all good things come to an end. When the money stops coming in, those so called friends, they scatter like water."

"Mama, you trippen'!" exclaimed Dre.

"What I tell you about tellin' me I'm trippen', I'm like too short I ain't trippen!"

"I'm sorry Mama," answered Dre.

"My nerves just can't take something happening to you DeAndre," expressed Mama as she prayed to herself, *let me stop it Lord, forgive me.*

Tonya and Munchie sat in silence as they witnessed the interaction between Dre and Mama. They could see the reciprocating love they had for one another. It was a spectacle of the bond between a mother and a son. It made both Munchie and Tonya warm inside. It was good.

"Well, you can kiss this eight-thousand goodbye!" exclaimed Mama as she stuffed it in her pocket and smiling.

"In fact Mama," followed Dre, as he reached into his pocket again, "take all of it."

"We need to head out Mama. When do you think you can come down to Iowa?" finished Dre as he handed her the rest of what he had.

"I'm fine in this low income home, baby. My next home is in heaven when He is ready for me," answered Mama as she slowly raised her eyes towards the ceiling.

"That's going to take a lifetime: it's going to take years, years and years," comforted Dre in his best Barry White impression.

"Boy, you sure did miss your calling," joked Mama in return.

"Is there anything I can do for you before I leave, run an errand or anything?" asked Dre.

"No, baby, Mama fine. Oh, by the way, I almost forgot, I got a call the other day from a Mr. Bone. I told him that you weren't here and that was at nine in the morning. When I went to the mailbox around noon, there was a letter in there telling me to pick up five-hundred dollars at Western Union in his name."

"Did you get the check?" inquired Dre hurriedly.

"Boy, you don't even need to ask the question. That was the older guy that you were with in Cook County, right?"

"Yes Mama. Did he leave a number?"

"No. He said he'll call back and to tell you *nice ride.*"

"That's crazy! How he know I gotta new ride?" asked Dre out loud, but reminded himself that he did tell the sales manager that he was a friend of Mr. Bone.

"What new car you have?" asked Mama as she walked to the front of the house to look out the window.

"It's in the shop getting detailed," proclaimed Dre.

"He's getting all those sounds Auntie," added Munchie.

"Yeah, and TV's and rims and all the works," Tonya also added. With each comment you could tell the pride each of them had in it. It was more than a car, it symbolized that they were moving up, they were going places and Dre was their leader.

Mama gave her hugs and kisses, her solemn goodbyes.

Even though Dre had to go, he was sad to do it. He knew he couldn't stay there with her forever, but the comfort and safety he felt was without compare.

As they pulled out of the drive Mama looked up to the sky through the window, closed her eyes so tight that they hurt, and said a prayer. She gave thanks that she no longer led the life she once led and that her boy, her angel DeAndre, would be safe. Mama knew that life was hard to begin with, but it was even harder in the world of *Dog Food*.

"Oh, protect us heavenly Father, for that which we have done and that which is left undone."

Chapter 16
High Roller

As Tonya dropped Dre and Munchie off at the *Auto Doctor's,* she couldn't help but reflect on what they had been through together. Memories flashed through her mind like a whirlwind, however, certain moments would stand still, the images frozen in time, even though long ago, they felt just like yesterday.

"You boys be good now and be safe, I love you baby," offered Tonya as she began to pull away. It had been a long day and she needed to work in the morning, so this is where they would part she thought. She loved the man and seldom wanted to leave his side, but she knew that they would be doing their "guy stuff' and she needed to be fresh the next day.

Dre gave her the smile she loved, nodded and blew her a kiss, something he seldom did, it made her feel warm and safe inside. He really did love her she thought, even if he was seeing other women at times, she figured it was something he would grow out of and what she didn't know wouldn't hurt her, or so she rationalized.

"Hey Dre," said a voice that came out of one of the offices. "I've got you right over here, let's take the cover off. I didn't want anyone to see it but you," said the voice with pride and anxiousness.

"Mr. John," replied Dre, "I feel like I am at an art gallery and we are about to unveil a work of art, a Picasso or Rembrandt."

Dre went silent as did Munchie. Then without a cue, Munchie started to jump up and down like he had just won the lottery.

"Cuzo, look at that, I can't believe it!" exalted Munchie.

"This is me, those *Giovanna* rims are going to be flicking'!" punctuated Dre.

"I wanted to call you about that, I thought the nineteens' would look better ran flat," admitted Mr. John.

"Mr. John, the only thing I know how to do to a car is put gas in it," admitted Dre with a smirk.

Dre jumped in and started it up to be met with what reminded him of what a cockpit on a fighter jet would look like, accompanied by the pulsating waves of the four twelve inch subs in the trunk. You couldn't miss a beat as Slick Rick's, *The Art of Storytelling,* "Go Get the Hump Out Cha Back Now" featuring *Outkast* spilled out all over the shop room.

"Oh, one of the workers must have left that in, sorry about that," apologized Mr. John.

"Naw'll, it's cool," answered Dre. "Is the stash spot here too?"

Mr. John nodded with satisfaction, cuing Dre to inspect the work.

Dre admired the elegant stitching of "R.I.P. Will and Ball," the inlayed TV's, the dark tint and the stash spot. The tint was so dark you almost needed a flash light, dark and low just how Dre liked it.

"Is it to your liking?" inquired Mr. John with a tone of confidence awaiting a positive reply.

Dre sensed it and so he hesitated, providing a dramatic effect, that caused Mr. John to hold his breath, literally.

"More than to my liking' Dre confessed. "You put everything I asked for and then some! I love it, straight up, straight up!" exclaimed Dre. "If you need a flick of me in front of the *Lex,* showing off your work, just let me know, straight up."

"I am pleased that you are pleased," replied Mr. John, like a serf to a lord.

"Munchie, pay the man," instructed Dre.

No sooner had Munchie withdrew the funds from his Polo pouch and they were on their way down Lake Street, cruising in their black chariot, feeling like kings. The lights of the boulevard reflected off the el-train and bounced off the store fronts, highlighting the nineteen inch chrome *Giovanna's* as they gleamed in the dark.

"Cuzo, this *Lex's* like a space ship with all these lights and gadgets and the leather is so plush and so soft," offered Munchie as he took it all in.
"We like a couple of pilots in the first class cockpit!" announced Dre.

They both laughed and recalled their recent flight, also a first.

"Where we headed Cuzo?"
"Let's go over on Central Park and holler at Slick," informed Dre with a sense of arrogance.

They pulled up to the corner where a group was playing dice. You could tell by the rides that it was Slick and a posse, heavy security with tunes flowing and girls loitering on the peripheral in front of their whips.

"Look at these Nigga's Cuzo. Should I pull right up on them, right up their ass and stunt?" asked Dre but with a sense that he had already answered the question himself.

"Yeah, it's your summer baby! Creep real slow and hold on," instructed Munchie as he reached into the arm rest, grabbed a CD exchanging it for Slick Rick.

As they crept up on them, the sleek black snake, slithered across the asphalt as onlookers gawked. *Dr. Dre's Chronic,* "Dre Day," overpowered all of the other sounds. It was like the soundtrack to a movie and the scene was rolling up on them like a predator would its prey, a prowler, all in black and tinted.

All heads turned in their direction in unison and to the beat of the tunes, a choreographed musical of sorts, with not a word from a single person, only the expressions on their faces, awe and wonderment.

They could feel the road coming up from underneath them as the nineteen's punched a hole in the night.

Slowly the window came down as the tint turned to light to reveal the master, the wizard behind the curtain, Dre.

"Hey Slick, what up?" through Dre out the window
"Oh shit, just look at my Nigga!" exclaimed Slick as he jumped up from the game, leaving his cash on the ground. "A Lexus GS, you ain't bullshittin' Joe," sighed Slick with an admiration and conceit.

Just as Slick was heading for the car he was intercepted by a man handing him some cash. Slick looked at and shook his head and handed it back to the figure.

"Whatcha you in, the manufacturing business? You feedin' me some packaged up bullshit with this short paper?" threateningly questioned Slick with little regard to discretion.

Dre knew that you didn't handle business openly like that, even when you catch someone trying to screw you. You didn't make your business everyone else's business. Granted, you handled business decisively, but you also handled it more discretely.

This was Slicks arena so Dre didn't say anything as that would be too disrespectful, moreover, Dre didn't need the drama.

"What's up baby?" slid Dre as he closed the door behind him and nodded at Slick as they both walked away from the crowd.
"Man, we outta here, look at those rims! I've got two hoes for us up North on Sunny Side, we fuckin' as soon as they see the *Lex,"* promised Slick. "I see that paper come back triple when you outta town Joe!"
"Hey you just gonna donate this money or come watch your fade Nigga?" was shouted from the crowd around the dice.
"Dre, let me get this Nigga' money real quick," whispered Slick to Dre as he walked back towards the group. "Oh, and those hoes I was tellin' you about? They ain't no rats either, they good college girls," jokingly admitted Slick with a smile.

Both men were laughing from this comment as they approached the group.

"Dre, you want some of this free money from the dice game?" asked one of the players in the huddle.

"Naw'll, I'm shittin' money Nigga and I don't want to bend these *Gucci* loafers!" shouted Dre back at the group. Dre could sense the eyes on him.

"Yeah, you probably still sniffing all your money, Nigga!" echoed the voice.

This hit a nerve with Dre on two dimensions, one, the man was right, it is something he used to do, but second, Dre was a new man, a leader in the streets and he was above that, making it an insult. Both accounts affected him emotionally, the first hurt his feelings as he was driven back in time to when things were so and it made him angry. The second was offensive and it made him angry. Either way the behavioral result was anger.

Dre was steaming as he stepped towards the car, but feeling all eyes on him he knew that he must demonstrate restraint and maturity, he needed to act like a leader and not like some street rookie looking to fight every time someone talked smart. He was above such comments therefore he was above such reproach.

"Who dice is it? I'll buy the dice for a hundred!" offered Dre and as fast as the words were out of his mouth the guy handed him his dice. "Aight big mouth, one hundred I hit and one hundred fade," bet Dre as he rolled the dice in between his hands, rolling them in unison with his verbiage."

"Seven, eleven, y'all," announced Dre as he rolled a seven. "Same bet Nigga?" egged on Dre.

The man bet. Dre rolled an eleven.

"Same bet Nigga?" encouraged Dre. "You asked for this shit so it's coming like a storm!"

Dre rolled a four.

"Two hundred on the ten to four," bet the man sitting across From Dre.
"It's a bet, it's down!" confirmed Dre.
"Short roll a 4 from Coconut Grove!" announced Dre as he hit a three and one.
"You want some more of this or you wanna tap out?" challenged Dre.
"You might want to make it light on yourself," recommended the man.
"Aight, you shoot a stack, you bet a stack," *damn big mouth,* Dre thought to himself as he shuffled the dice in hands.

Dre passed ten times, as he was talking slick, snapping his fingers and bending those *Gucci* Loafers. The man was sick.

"You know," announced Dre," my uncle Al Skinner showed me this!" taunted Dre. "Bet a stack?"

Seeing his bank roll diminish before his eyes, they guy offered,

"Let's shoot back to a hundred like we started."
"Naw'll I'm straight Playboy."
"Yeah, dope fiends get lucky too," commented the voice with a hint of sarcasm under his breath.
"Yep, that they do, but they ain't ridin' no *Lexus* like me and out scuffing up some *Gucci* loafers and wrinkling an *Iceberg* suit, are they," retorted Dre with an arrogant confidence.

Dre stood up to walk away and as began to turn, he turned back to the man's attention,

"Oh, by the way, thanks for the whole hook up. Now your ass broke like a dope fiend. Here, take this Nigga" as Dre tossed a hundred down at him with a look of victory in his eyes as those looking back at him showed nothing but defeat.

Not willing to concede and in an attempt to save face, as Dre just roasted him, his retort hit home like he knew it would,

"Fuck you, bitch!"

Dre rushed at him, but Slick and the rest of the group was there to intervene.

"Hey man, you making my spot hot and disrespecting my

partner!" shouted Slick at the man. "Get the fuck on, before it won't be Dre you worryin' about, but me putting those shorty's down there on the corner on your ass sore loser!"

The guy realized he was being called out and was smart enough to know how that would end for him, so he jumped into his Regal Sport and took off, hitting the gas like the accelerator was though the floor.

"That sucker ass Nigga had his goofy turned to the max Joe," admitted Slick.
"Yeah, he was about to get his as whooped!" supported Dre as he was stuffing the wad of hundreds in his pocket.
"You strap?" asked Slick. "Naw'll," answered Dre.
"I know you had Mr. John to put you a spot in there. I'm about to go upstairs and get us two thumpers," enticed Slick.
"That's cool, I'll be in the ride."

Slick returned with a *Pelle Pelle* leather jacket on and hollered something to one of his runners and then proceeded to jump in the back seat of the *Lexus*.

"Hey Munchie, what up Joe? I forgot you were on the scene," admitted Slick with a slight surprise in his voice.
"Good, what up Slick?"
"Here Dre put these thumpers in the spot!" instructed Slick.
"Just give 'em to Munchie," answered Dre.

As they headed from the scene, Slick handed Munchie a

Ruquer 9mm and Desert Eagle with a diamond on it bigger than the Diamondback Razors baseball field. All eyes were on them as they slowly drifted away, including a pair that they hadn't seen before.

"Man this mother Slick, just like my name," admired Slick as he lounged comfortably in the back firing up a blunt."

"Slick, this a brand new ride, you just going to take the new scent away doing that!" cautioned Munchie, seeking some approval from Dre as well.

"It's cool Cuzo, after what that sucka ass Nigga tried to pull, I can sha'll use me a hit!" admitted Dre.

"C'mon Cuzo, that's twice in one week," pleaded Munchie.

"I gotta hit it baby," demanded Dre as he grabbed it from Slick.

They all sat back in the plush luxury of the ride, each one in their own heads, miles away from where they actually were.

"Cuzo, I'm startin' to really feel this shit, I'm 'bout to pull over at the next gas station and let you drive," mentioned Dre in an airy off-track tone.

"All right, let me push the *Lex!*" accepted Munchie.

They pulled into the *Shells* on Roosevelt and Western and Dre and Munchie changed places.

"Hey Munchie, I got the Munchies!" joked Slick.

The comment found a cold stare from Munchie. He didn't

appreciate the influence Slick had on Dre and he certainly didn't appreciate Slick making jokes at his expense.

"I'm kinda hungry too Cuzo," sheepishly voted Dre.
"Well, ain't too many restaurants open; you want me to turn around and go to *Cicero Street* to *Hody's?*" asked Munchie with a sense of curtness.
"We straight," replied Dre and Slick.
"We might find the wrong Niggas up in there," followed Dre.
"Let's ride on Canal to Lawrence Fisher's," instructively offered Slick.

They took Western to Cermack, following Cermack to Canal and took Canal all the way there. Two hundred dollars later, full of shrimp, fish and chips and frog legs they were content.

*D*re and Slick were engulfed by the comforting upholstery, the soft gentle contours of the engineering was proving to be worth every penny.

"Hey guys, this van behind us, it seems like it's been trailing me since we left Lawrence," announced Munchie with curiosity and alarm.
"Dre hit the stash spot," yelled Slick with an impatience and panic as he fought coming down from his high.
"I think those punk mother fuckers' is on us!" exclaimed Dre as he and Slick peered out the windows trying to

determine if they were being followed. There was a fine line between paranoia and astute observation, the drugs made the deductive reasoning no easier.

"It is time to see what this thing is made of, to see what's under the hood!" challenged Slick.

"Run the next red light Munchie," instructed Dre," and if they still behind us, punch this bitch to the expressway!"

Munchie was already on it. Terry had him as a driver since he could remember; he even taught Dre how to drive, so swirlin' and twirlin' the *Lex* was nothing for him.

As Munchie ran the light, the van was still on their bumper. Any intention of being unnoticed had vanished and now whatever game was afoot it was upon them. Munchie punched it and all three found themselves pressed against the back of their seats. It was no performance sedan but Toyota gave it some low end torque allowing them to create a distance from the pursuing van as they made their way onto the expressway at the Cermack ramp.

Munchie took the next exit and re-entered the expressway and repeated this pattern a few more times. The van stayed with them with each maneuver.

"Next time stay off the expressway and hit the nearest parking lot, do a 360 and let Slick and I jump out and handle this business!" emphatically instructed Dre.

Munchie took the next exit as instructed, hit the parking lot adjacent to his right and pulled a 360 in the open lot, spinning like a washing machine then coming to an abrupt halt.

Dre and Slick hopped out like firemen to a blazing fire. It was like a slow motion scene from a western gun fight; their cannons were out and cocked as Dre and Slick walked towards the approaching van, each with a swagger as the sweeping illumination of a falling June sun gave a backdrop of cinematic proportions.

"Dre, Dre!" is yelled from the van, "what's up?"

Noticing the man, Dre quickly put his hammer into the front of his pants and motioned to Slick to do the same.

"Man, what the fuck yo crazy ass on?" questioned Dre in a threatening, irritated tone.
"Damn Dre, I didn't know it was you, shining all bright like that! I'm working baby, I'm tryin' to catch me one of these Nigga's slippin' and ridin' with a bitch. You know the drill, baby," quickly informed the man as he wiped the drain from his nose. His eyes were hallow and his skin fading, he was in need of a fix.

"Damn man, you almost got this diamond in your ass!" warned Dre. Dre had a history with the guys' cousin and had spent some time with the cousin in county jail.
"What's up with your Cuzo?" asked Dre as he was suddenly

reminded of why he didn't like his cousin. "The guy said Fuck that Nigga and he didn't even come to bond me out. I should've stuck his ass up!"

As the sun vanished off the man's face Dre could see the eyes, the uneasiness, the emptiness that accompanies coming down off too many highs.

"Here you go man," as Dre reached into his pocket, "how many of yaw' ll in the van?"
"Three the hard way," he answered.

Dre handed the man three hundred, "go get yourselves medicated and tells those Nigga's in the van they almost got lit up and nobody would've been blowing on shit!"

Dre knew that good public relations went a long ways, if not for his business directly but at least for the products that his business dealt in. Giving the man money to go buy product from a competitor maintained the demand for the product produced; an economic element that Dre depended on. Better to give a man another dealers' dope and keep the addiction alive so as to serve the man repeatedly in the future.

"Good lookin' out man. You know how it is, you'll beg, steal, kill, rob, the whole nine yards just to get a fix on," admitted the character that stood wilting in front of Dre. "You sure ridin' slick and I'll tell my Cuzo I seen ya," he announced as Dre and Slick hopped back into the *Lex*.

As they drove off, Dre couldn't help but consider what would have happened if they had just opened fire on the van.

Moreover, why would the guys in the van be following them? The windows were tinted and as a result they could have been anyone. Dre just shook his head in disbelief. The things people will do in this world, this world driven by *Dog Food*.

Chapter 17
Living the Dream

A clear warm June sunrise always made Dre feel better. This morning was no exception as he, Munchie and Slick headed to Iowa to size up the economic potential and try to ascertain how much money Dre could clock. It was by Slick's convincing.

Slick brought another three-quarter of a brick that he retrieved from the stash spot where the two pistols from yesterdays near 'OK Corral' incident still resided.

When they made it into Iowa, Dre phoned Pete to let him know they were on their way. Dre never really wanted to let people know when or where he was precisely and he especially did not care to let people know well in advance. In the time it takes a friend to become a snitch is faster than that *Lexus* would ride.

"Slick, you Aight?" asked Dre from the back seat.

"Yeah Man, I'm just not use to seeing this kinda shit. When I see trees like this I am usually on my way to the joint," admitted Slick in a melancholy manner.

The openness of the topography appealed to them. They may not admit it, but the silence that accompanied the last twenty minutes of the ride and the sense of contentment within the cabin of the *Lexus* was enough to paint a picture of their appreciation of the scenery.

The open fields and rolling hills were lined with trees as far as the eye could see. It portrayed a sense of freedom, a vastness that contradicted a restrictive 7 by 10 cell with bars. It was a dichotomy for Slick as it represented a freedom that could not be verbally expressed, but at the same time, the only other moments when he would appreciate them was when his freedom was challenged, as he sat in custody on the way to one facility or another. The deals he would make with himself on those rides; appreciating every branch of every tree that blew freely in the winds, just as he wanted to be, free again. No matter the convincing of himself, shortly after he was out, he was right back into the game. The memory of how he vowed to be different quickly faded.

Tupac," All Eyes On Me" played softly in the background as Dre picked up the phone to call Pete again to let him know they were almost there.

As the phone began to ring Dre lost himself in the moment,

he sat back in the plush reclining leather of the backseat with the remote in his hand and his Cuzo as the captain; things were good.

"What's up baby?" announced Dre at the first sound in a smooth comfortable tone that made you think of big money.

"Man," began Pete," we had a small lil' problem."

"What kind of problem?" asked Dre as he hit the ATT on the system.

"I wanted to wait until you made it here, that's why I didn't call ya. We got rob for a lil' shit," admitted Pete with anger and embarrassment in his voice.

"Man, we on this phone. Meet me at the crib in about twenty minutes. Later!" urged Dre into the phone as he hung up. The scenery began to shrink as Dre was hit with the news. The once vast terrain now closed in on him, reminding him that you are never free like you want to be as he shares the news with Munchie and Slick.

"This the shit I like Joe, I'm right on time!" brags Slick reinforcing a belief that he would have Dre's back.

"I'll be damn these slow country ass Nigga's wanna try me?" Dre asked the universe as he rubbed his chin slowly and chanting to himself, *okay, okay,* as he bobbed his head back and forth in unison with the rhythm of his words.

"You sho it ain't your runner pulling a wool over your eyes?" asked Slick.'

"Naw'll he one hundred man, I treat him good. He like family and he fuck with that thang, he like that *Dog Food,*" convinced Dre.

"I can't never knock what he doing, cause shit, when you was out there bad, you'll fuck over a Nigga quick, whoop packs on him giving him Dormin and Actifed, but you never played your boy. Now, just look at my Nigga!" summarized Slick.

"Yeah, I'll get really silky, like a worm on a Nigga. How you knew I was givin' Nigga Actifed Whoop?" inquisitively inquired Dre.

"Remember I caught Yo ass in the drug store before, shit, I gave you the money for them!" trumpeted Slick.

They all laughed, breaking the tension of the situation, giving a rebirth of attitude towards the situation, they were ready to roll now. It didn't take much in their world to turn the tides of attitude, a simple comment, a simple word or a simple look was sometimes all it took. Life was fast and it could be hard so you needed to be able to cope with all the emotions that were never shown or discussed, and humor was always a nice way out.

Dre sat back and turned up the volume of the tunes and reflected on his past and how he had always been held accountable for things that he had done. He recalled one time in particular when he took some shit off some Nigga and when they caught up with him, he paid. Payback was just that, a pay back!

They pulled up to the crib and all three exited the vehicle

and walked to the door without saying a word. The place was nice, really nice and it was common to keep the words low when the crib was so high.

"This is a bad mother fucker right here!" announced Slick breaking the silence.

"Like you told me about your crib, this ain't shit! I'm gonna get one overlooking the water like you," fantastically claimed Dre as he watched Slicks' eyes scan from the floor all the way up to the high cathedral ceilings. Dre was proud of the place but he was genuinely committed to a bigger place on the water.

Munchie ran the stuff upstairs as Dre showed Slick around a little, kicked back on the leather black pit sofa and hit a blunt.

The doorbell rang and both Dre and Slick got up to answer it. They knew it was Pete and as they walked to the door Dre was hit with a slight wonderment; *why did Slick get up too?"* He deduced it was merely a polite gesture of respect and thought nothing more of it.

"You know Tone and Wee?" began Pete immediately as he entered the place. "Well, they caught me leaving McDonald's getting the workers some breakfast."

"How much did they get us foe?" asked Dre.

"A couple stacks. They ass was so nervous and thirsty, they skipped over the ten stack I had in the glove compartment," informed Pete almost as if it was rehearsed.

"They caught you in the van?" followed Dre with a sense of disbelief.

"Yeah, they jumped in while I put the bags in the passenger side and was about to go in on the drivers' side."

"You lucky they didn't take the whole van," interjected Slick.

"I'm glad it wasn't started up," added Pete.

"You cool?" asked Dre.

"Yeah, I'm good. Here the rest of the paper," sheepishly squeaked Pete as he handed Dre the remaining fifteen thousand hoping it was would ease some of the pain that the news brought. "I got a chopper in the van too."

"Those Niggas still fuck with those twins in *Alexander Apartments* on First, don't they?" Inquired Dre with a tone of plotting.

"Aight, I gotta lil' surprise for them," announced Dre quietly as he returned to rubbing his chin again in a slow methodical manner.

By eight o'clock that evening, just prior to the evening shift, they had the plan. *Payback was going to be a bitch,* Dre thought to himself.

Slick and Dre were in the van, followed by Munchie and Pete in the black Chevy. They were constantly chirpin' at one another as they scoured the area looking for Tone and Wee.

At the red light on 16th Ave SW Dre spots Wee and Tone in the Cutlass like a cobra stalking two baby birds in a nest.

"There go those two mother fuckers we looking for right there," chirps Dre to Munchie and Pete while pointing at them for Slick to see.

"I see ya'll at the stop light," confirmed Munchie like a sergeant in the battle field.

"When this motherfucker turn green, get ahead of me because they just made a left on 1st!" instructed Dre.

"I'm on their bumper like a high speed chase!" announced Munchie.

"Don't let them make it to the inside of the parking lot, cause they got speed bumps inside, we going to fire that bitch up!" commanded Dre as he nodded at slick and whispered, "you ready?"

"Yeah, I'm ready!" hammered Slick as he hopped in the back and put on his black gloves. Slick lived for this kind of shit, it was his thing. Some kids liked to hit a ball with a bat, Slick liked to hit punks with his fist!

While Dre instructed Munchie to fall back he punched the accelerator and let Tone and Wee know they were there. Seeing this, the Cutlass tried to put distance between them and having anticipated this, Dre already had the accelerator to the floor.

"These Nigga's on some bullshit," mentioned Tone to Wee. "We almost at the apartment, keep going!"

They could not have been more wrong. As they

approached the first speed bump and slowed down, Dre was there. He had slid the van behind them sideways so the side door matched with their bumper.

"Perfect!" hollered Dre, "now handle your business!"

Slick opened the side door and opened up an all carbon SKS- fold-away-stock-chopper filling the cutlass with holes. The long shells were jumping out of the weapon like a pack of *Jumping Jacks* on the Fourth of July.

Slick turned a half ton of steel into rat cheese in a matter of seconds and if Wee and Tone weren't dead they would have enough holes in them to wish they were. They lit that bitch up!

The side door was still open as they pulled away and as they created a distance from the apartments Slick closed it, fell back into the seat and reached for a blunt; a little smoke after the smoke.

They dropped the van off so Pete could get rid of the SKS and round up all of the workers. Then they headed to Claries' to drop off the chopper to shake some dope later.

Slick and Dre headed back to Marion in the Chevy to grab some dope, some clean clothes, to put some money up and do some accounting. Munchie took off in the other Chevy as he had some other business to attend to.

Dre and Slick returned to Clarie's in the *Lex*. They shook the dope and started the shift only thirty minutes late. Dre and Slick sat back in the *Lex* in the shadows on 15 overlooking the alley.

"Man, these white folks spending this bread!" exclaimed Slick.

"Just picture all them custoz you seein' spendin' a hundred or better up until five o'clock in the morning!" expressed Dre. "Then, I shut this bitch down!"

"Man, you need to let me come down, we do six to six shift; I do day and you do nights and we rotate," offered Slick.

"I ain't got my feet wet just yet," cautioned Dre.

"Man, you've been back to cop three times, you in too deep," responded Slick.

"Anyways, you know who got some good weed around here?" asked Slick, conceding the discussion for now regarding Dre coming down and playing a part on a more permanent basis.

"I got a lil' white bitch I'm fuckin' on that sell weed, with some good ole pussy. Matter of fact, let me give her a call," informed Dre as he began to dial her number.

"Hello?" said the gentle voice on the other end of the line.

"Hey! What's poppin'?" thumped Dre with a debonair confidence knowing that it wasn't Mariea's voice. "Let me speak to Mariea."

"I can't hardly hear you, you want to turn that music

down!" yelled Dre into the phone as her voice was barely audible.

"Hey D, I was wondering when you were calling, what's up?" replied Mariea with a freshness and newness that Dre appreciated. He liked her and her personality; she was fun and outgoing and just hearing her voice ease his mind.

"You what's up baby! I see you're partyin'!" claimed Dre.

"No, it's just one of my girls over and we are drinking."

"What ya'll waiting on ya'll boyfriends to come over so you can all start fuckin?" asked Dre playfully hoping to compel a response of an erotic nature.

"No. So how about you coming over here and fucking both of us? I told my girl about you and how you got dick for days and enough for us to share," replied Mariea without a hesitation.

They were sweet words to Dre's ears. It was the type of response he was soliciting.

"Damn girl, you getting' my dick harder than a Chinese arithmetic!" admitted Dre in an eager hungry fashion. "I'm on my way, but I got a partner with me. Maybe your girlfriend can give him a shot of that wet pussy?"

"I can arrange that. I really didn't want to share that big fat dick of yours anyways. How long you going to take because I'm ready to suck on that dick right now!"

Dre could hear the hunger in her voice. He could already imagine how her lips would feel wrapped around his long, thick hard shaft.

"Slow down baby, you're going to be the reason I have an accident!" laughed Dre. "By the way, you still got some of that shit I seen you with at the club?"

"Yeah, we can talk about that while Im jagging that dick and getting it super hard for my mouth," enticed Mariea.

"Give me ten minutes baby," answered Dre and hung up the phone.

"Man, I got these white bitches, pussy hotter than a microwave and they need a fire extinguished like yesterday!" announced Dre.

"You don't even have to tell me twice Joe," confessed Slick as he felt his heart beat a little faster.

Dre and Slick headed towards Mariea's place. With a full day of business behind them they looked forward to the comforting venture that awaited them. This was only one brief chapter in the saga of the dream they were living in; the one in the world of *Dog Food*.

Chapter 18
Revelations

It took Dre all of nine minutes to make it to the doorstep of Mariea's house. That which makes young men so eager to concur, flowed impress, so eager play, so eager to concur, flowed through Dre's veins and motivated him at many turns in his life and this was no exception.

As the door slowly opened Dre's heart beat faster and he felt a dryness in his throat as he tried to speak, but her voice beat him to it.

"Hey D!" exclaimed Mariea as her smile opened up even further when their eyes met. She could already began to feel her stomach move and her pulse quicken as well. Her breath was heavy and hot and she could feel it on her tongue, she was on fire.

"What's up baby? This my main man Slick," introduced

Dre as he nodded towards Slick and then back again at Mariea as he passed her in the threshold.

"Well, hey Slick," politely greeted Mariea, "and this is my girl Molly," she added, nodding in the direction of the other woman sitting on the couch.

"Is that your *Lexus* out there?" inquired Mariea as she caught a glimpse of the ride as she closed the door behind Slick.

"Naw'll if you with the PoPo's," sarcastically responded Dre.

"Don't play with me D," responded Mariea.

"I can't play with you baby. I'm sorry I forgot how sensitive you white girls can get," comforted Dre as he turned back towards her and embraced her with a full-bodied hug.

"Yeah Daddy, I'm very sensitive and spoiled. How about my pacifier?" questioned Mariea as she looked up at him while her hand found his package and stroked the outside of his pants slowly with a sinister smile that almost put Dre through the roof.

"Hey, slow down baby, we going to get to that. Let me get what I asked you for first; give me a dub sack."

"I need to go in the back to get it. Molly, come with me," instructed Mariea.

As the girls headed to the back to get what Dre had asked for, they engaged in the ever *so* typical conversation of boy meets girl and what do you think. Molly was honest that Slick would do, but she really wanted a piece of Dre. The honesty made Mariea feel good but at the same time a little unnerving that she could be so forthright about another woman's man. *Dre is a fine chocolate thing, I bet he got a huge dick on him,*

Molly thought to herself.

"Here D," announced Mariea as she tossed the bag to Dre when they returned to the living room.

"What's this, a five dollar bag?" asked Dre.

"Sorry honey, but that's an eighth of weed and we sell it for twenty," informed Mariea.

"Here," said Dre as he reached into his pocket to pull out a wad of cash, "I'm going to buy this, but were going to do something about this."

"Like what?" asked Mariea with a hint of sarcasm and curiosity.

"I'm going to let you know. When I tell you, just be ready to ride, Aight," divulged Dre with a seriousness that she hadn't seen in him very often. It made her feel important that he would confide in her; feeling such a degree of respect made her even more aroused.

Dre and Slick rolled the weed while Molly and Mariea hit the shots. The music was playing in the background, slow and easy went the rhythms, as each of them became more comfortable with one another.

While Dre sat back and took it all in he couldn't help but think how trusting and trustworthy Mariea was and he began to formulate how he could exploit that for his benefit.

Dre's contemplation was abruptly interrupted by Molly challenging Dre to a bout of *Truth and Dare*.

"Let's play a game, Truth or Dare," egged on Molly with a sense of mischievousness. "So, is it true then Dre, that you have a big black dick?" she questioned in such a manner as to be looking for a truth in the form of a dare.

Dre not being one bit shy of his endowment, stood up slowly, undid his pants and pulled out one of the fullest shafts Molly had ever seen, it even glistened in the lights.

The saliva increased in the girls' mouths, each of them wanted a taste of his candy, wanting to feel it pulsate on their tongue. While Molly was getting wet, Mariea was now flooding and she could hardly bare the pressure that was building up inside her.

In an effort to avoid eye contact, Slick turned his head, but not in time for Molly to call him on it.

"Are you packin' a fire hose like that one too?" interrogated Molly with her eyes slowly dropping to Slick's midsection and running her tongue across her lips.

"Come over here and check your temperature with this thermometer," announced Slick as he pulled out an equally impressive tool.

Molly walked over, got on her knees, gently took him in her hands and slowly pulled him near her. Slick could feel her breath on his tip right before it entered the coven of her wet warm mouth.

This was an invitation for Mariea to follow suit. She walked towards Dre not taking her eyes off of his, here is the man that but a minute ago respected her with a confidence and now she would take him in her and repay the compliment with all she had.

At first the moment was awkward for Dre and Slick, but that moment quickly subsided as they were taken away by the sweetness wrapped around them, they both put their heads back and enjoyed the moment.

Their clothes found the ground as each member hit a point of arousal that prohibited turning back and a mood that removed all apprehensions. The orgiastic scene was right off the pages of *Forum,* each one of them giving and taking in turn, willing to satisfy one another to their fullest. The entire night consisted of exploration and sexual indulgences that most only dream about. The thick black shafts of Dre and Slick plunging into the warm wet pink pussy's was accompanied by the bouncing of their full breasts in every direction as they were taken around the world.

The moaning gave way to gasps of air as their pussy's were methodically massaged and penetrated slowly and softly, followed by hard thrusts and deep penetration sending each person to new heights.

"Oh, yes, yes, yes, don't stop, fill me up, give it to me!" each girl screamed, or a variation thereof, as if competing with the other. This only drove the men to drive harder and harder; sweat everywhere, cum everywhere. The noise of them slapping hard up against their asses as they bent them over was like the drumming of a symphony leading to a crescendo of crashing symbols as each man left every ounce they had left in them. All four passed out in exhaustion.

Dre and Slick rose early to get Slick back to CHI as there was much business to be done and only so much could get done in his absence. It was a beautiful June morning as they drove into the rising sun that shaded the early yellow sky with hints of orange and red as the blue began to sweep the landscape before them.

"That girl had some good pussy on her!" announced Dre with an admiration and appreciation.
"Man, she tried to wear a Nigga out Joe," admitted Slick. "I heard you in the other room pounding the fuck outa Mariea!"
"Hey man, I got the equipment and the stamina, just like Barry White, straight-up!" bragged Dre.
"Dre, I dig it Joe, you having way too much fun down here. You fuckin' these white hoes at will, getting a shit load of paper and riding like the president!" summarized Slick with a sense of envy pushing towards a jealousy.
"Man, this ain't my doing at all," claimed Dre as he looked up to the sky through the sun roof as if implying that it was divine intervention.

"You know I already got one foot in the grave and the other in a jail cell and my hands are either shakin' dope or one step from snorting it," admitted Dre with a sense of pride and remorse at the same time.

They both began a laugh that was maintained and fueled by the comment, each other, the events that occurred the evening last and the prospects of more moments to come.

"Hey, let me ride and check on Pete and grab a lil' paper from him, get a change of clothes and check in on Munchie and then we can jet like Uncle Tom bring your saddle on home," recommended Dre.

They drove by the spot Pete was pumping to witness how smoothly things were flowing, and it was only thirty minutes into the early bird shift. The customers knew that the window would close in three hours and not open up again until the evening. If they missed their chance, they would have to deal with the other dealers whose stuff was not as good as Dre's.

That was one of the keys to Dre's success; he kept the mixture right because the addicts knew the difference. The hustlers paid more attention to how much they could cut into it and this over the long-term was bad for business. In this game most thought short-term, so the one with the long-term perspective and with the proper plan would capture more and more market share. This was proving true in this area as well, as the dealers bought Dre's stuff from Pete and stepped on it, creating a different experience for the consumer. Dre was on top of the food chain and his responsibility was to see that his product made its way into Iowa and Pete would handle it from there.

As Dre road up on Pete as he sat in the van surveying the operation, Dre could not help but get butterflies as a reaction to a sense of pride. To see his plans taking shape and working so smoothly would make any CEO of any fortune 500 company equally proud.

"Hey baby, good morning. What's the business?"
"Everything lovely this morning as is making money," replied Pete as he tossed a brown paper bag at Dre. "I see ya'll up with the birds," as he nodded at Slick and then back again at Dre.

Slick nodded back at Pete sluggishly as Dre just flashed a smile.

"Ya'll must've plucked on some chicken heads last night. What time it is?" finished Pete.
"Yeah, that's what you on Pete?" replied Dre. "Check this out, I'm on my way to the city to take Slick back and pick up Munchie and I'll be back tonight. You have enough shit, right?"
"Yeah, we good baby," confirmed Pete.
"Aight, I see this mother fucker pumping this morning Dr.

Pete. Oh, one more thing, when you close this shift down I need for you to go and see Terry or at least take him some white for me Joe."

"Say no more Dre, I got cha. As a matter of fact, I can go start on that right now. After what happened to Wee and Tone, you can't pay a mother fucker to even come liter around this spot! Word of mouth travels swiftly baby!" exclaimed Pete.

As Dre and Slick pulled away they were laughing at Pete and his juxtaposition. They made small talk the remainder of the ride, each floating in and out of their own thoughts and ending where they had started in the conversation by the time they reached Dre's place.

Dre put some money up in the safe but kept some to cop and go shopping with. He checked in on Munchie and found his room empty. The room had a staleness that no one had been there in a while. Then it occurred to him that his car was not in the driveway either; *where's Munchie* Dre thought to himself repeatedly.

Then it hit Dre, he was with that nerdy looking guy they met at the club the other night, *it had to be and now I gotta drive to the city all by myself,* concluded Dre.

Not wanting to drive by himself Dre pulled out his cell phone and tried Munchie just in case.

"Hello?" answered the half asleep voice on the other end.

"Wake your ass up Cuzo!" trumpeted Dre into the receiver.

"Oh, hey Cuzo, what's up?" replied Munchie in an ever increasing coherency.

"I see you are sleeping good. I need you to make a run with me," answered Dre.

"Cuzo, I'm as tired as I don't know what. Get Pete to ride with you and I'll open up the spot on the next shift," offered Munchie as a consolation.

"Naw'll I'm cool, I'll just slide down there and slide back," determined Dre.

"Won't you take that lil white girl down there," suggested Munchie.

Suddenly Dre was filled with insights on how he could utilize Mariea in his enterprising. "Cuzo, that is not a bad idea, not a bad idea at all. Let me jump off the line so I can call her. Hey, I also told Pete to take your dad some whites."

"Cool, I'm going to see him lil" later," conceded Munchie. "Aight Cuzo, I'm out, holler at ya later love!"

"Love back and be careful and you betta not let Tonya see you with that white girl!" cautioned Munchie as he hung up the phone.

Dre grabbed all he needed and he and Slick were back on the road in no time.

"You goin' to pick up Munchie?" asked Slick.

"Naw'll he over at some Nigga's crib," informed Dre.

"Yeah, whatcha you think 'bout all dat?"

"Whatcha ya mean, what I think?" defensively responded Dre. "I can't decide on the gender he chooses. That's my Cuzo, I love him and regardless if he starts smoking crack and better not no mother fucker fuck with him or we going to have a serious problem. Munchie a grown boy and if he likes boys that his prerogative, like Bobby Brown'! Straight-up!"

"I guess you right Joe. I love him like my Cuzo too and I feel the same way. You just know how some of these Nigga's get," admitted Slick.

For years Dre had tried to avoid the reality of Munchie's decisions when it came to gender preference. He never judged Munchie but at the same time he never openly supported it either. Dre had not entirely dealt with his feelings on the subject, so, when the topic came up he became aggressively defensive. The aggression was not so much directed at Slick, but an attempt to shatter the consciously apparent imbedded archetypes from society. Those that would categorize Munchie as something less than a man, something less than the Cuzo he had come to cherish and love and Dre wouldn't have it.

"Man, fuck these Nigga's! Half of these Nigga's who be scream in' all that tough Tony shit, they be in the closet with that shit themselves. I've seen so many of them type in the County, straight-up!" continued Dre.

Sensing the angst building in Dre, "Hey man, I dig it, but

let's chop it up on something else," offered Slick.

"What? You startin' to feel a lil' uncomfortable Slick?" followed Dre abruptly.

"Naw'll, ain't no question about my masculinity Joe," replied Slick confidently.

Dre wasn't ready to confide in Slick or have a conversation pertaining to the behavioral and cognitive aspects associated with the interpersonal dynamics of his relationship with Munchie. Dre didn't challenge Slicks' sexual orientation as his reply implied, rather he was challenging Slick's opinion of Munchie and of himself for loving Munchie. Accordingly, Dre let it slide so as to avoid further discussion of the issue.

"O.K. talk to me then," encouraged Dre with a sense of concession in his voice while a look of frustration still hung on his brow.

Completely breaking the topic, Dre picked up his phone and began to dial as it was back to business and they were headed towards Cedar Rapids, "I'm gonna call Mariea so she can ride with me."

Dre looked out across the horizon and the future that always seemed so clear to him began to get muddled. He had Tonya and now he also had Mariea. He had never taken the time to think about what he was doing with both of them and how the multiple relationships affected him as well as them. He and Munchie were always so tight and now Munchie was not around as much and he was feeling forced to confront Munchies' sexual orientation and to defend him in a cynical world. On top of all of that, he hadn't talked to or seen Mama in a while. Dre felt a little lost. His business was booming but he still felt empty and he couldn't put his finger on it despite the transparency or obviousness of the situation. Sometimes the solutions evades the individual when the rest of the world can see it. That is not uncommon in a world of fiction that is not uncommon in the world of *Dog Food.*

Chapter 19
Dog Catchers

At roll call the Narcotics Task Force in Cedar Rapids carried a different tone.

The topic centered on the recent overdoses in the area as it hit the family of one of their very own. There was an emphasis on apprehending who was ever behind it. Pure heroin was a poison that no town wanted and now that it found its way onto the streets of Cedar Rapids and into their homes, the attitude was one of a desperate seriousness.

"Good Morning!" announced the older gentleman with the tight haircut. He carried himself with an authority that was absent of a pride that seemed to have been drained from him over the years. His stature and the lines on his face told stories of the hard ridden life he had led to this point, but still unwilling to concede to the forces of nature.

"I wanted to bring the current events to your attention, those that have impacted my family directly. I am certain that you have all been briefed on the overdoses resulting from the pure heroin that has found its way onto our streets, but I am not sure if you knew that one of those victims was my brother," concluded the Captain as his chin fell to his chest on the last word; "brother."

Solemnness overtook the room. Many stared at the floor while others stared off in another direction trying not to make eye contact with the Captain. The sea of faces depicted a Picasso, as a blur of varying emotional images occupied the room. The Captain could not look away from his brethren; he needed to see something in their eyes that showed him he was not alone in this fight. As he stared into their faces he could see it burning within them, a fire whose flame would not soon dissipate.

"I see in your faces the grief that this brings. I see in your eyes the pain this causes you and I respectfully thank you for your caring and condolences. With that however, I need to ask you for something more. I need a promise that we will not stop until we find the bastard responsible for this travesty. My brother has left us too early and while the pain may not subside for years to come, I implore you to join with me to bring justice to...to bring justice..justice to...," exhaustively conceded the Captain as they were the only remaining sounds he could get out. He began to fold inward from the shoulders, shaking as the tears rolled down his face. He brought his hands to his face and wept into himself.

The Lieutenant had to step to the podium to relieve the Captain, but in his effort to continue the meeting he was overcome with a shared grief, and instead, turned to the captain and embraced him as a brother. The lieutenant had a deep respect for and a profound loyalty to the Captain, so as he saw the man before him so broken, he too felt the anguish.

The lieutenant leaned into the Captain and in a stolid whisper, "Don't worry my friend, we are going to get the son-of-a-bitch and whoever he is connected to, no matter what it takes!"

Captain Boot looked up from his palms to meet the eyes of the Lieutenant. He stared into them, searching for the commitment behind such words and found more than that, he found a friend holding him and comforting him in his greatest time of need.

"Adjourn the meeting my friend," he gently mentioned to the Lieutenant as he turned and exited the room.
"Before we adjourn, remember to work your leads. We cannot let any trails get cold on this one. You know as well as I do, once the word hits the streets that the Captains' brother was hit, those responsible will go into hiding and they will seek cover making it harder to dig up their bones! Meeting adjourned. Let's go hunting!" exclaimed the lieutenant.

As the room emptied the lieutenant sat by himself contemplating what was happening, he was filled with so many emotions. *They didn't teach you this stuff at the Academy,* he thought to himself and in all his years of service, he had been fortunate to not lose someone close to him. To see his Captain so distraught pained him. He was about to cry when a strong hand found his shoulder. He looked up and saw the Captain looking down on him.

"It will be ok, son, it will be ok," said the stoic leader before him.

Here, not but a few minutes ago the lieutenant was supporting him and now the Captain stood over him reciprocating such a gesture and act.

"Oh, Captain, I cannot begin to pretend what you are going through," conceded the Lieutenant. "I have some of the best informants out there and I will get cleared for some marked bills and initiate some hand to hand transactions until we work our way through the chain if we have to!" excitedly expressed the lieutenant in his eagerness to devise a plan to capture the perpetrators and demonstrate to his leader that he was truly sorry for what had occurred.

"Thank you for your eagerness, assertiveness, and commitment. I will assist in whatever capacity I can," the Captain assured the lieutenant.

"This issue goes beyond me...you ....my brother. It is about our streets becoming infected with a disease that is incurable and if we don't stop it, it can become an epidemic. We need to do whatever it takes," expressed the Captain in a desperately serious tone as he gripped the shoulders of the lieutenant to the point it hurt.

The lieutenant rose to meet the Captain face to face, they looked at each other for a moment without saying a word. They nodded in unison confirming the understanding between them, and as the tears dried on their faces, they turned and walked out of the room determined to bring it down, to bring it all crashing down; the whole world, the world of Dog Food.

Chapter 20
Another Girl, Another Town

By 8:30 Dre and Slick were well on their way back to Cedar Rapids. The Eastern sun hung in the sky forcing daylight to emerge across the flat terrain. The openness was such a contrast to CHI and Dre was beginning to appreciate it. His thoughts were stolen by the remembrance of his need to call Mariea.

"Hello, Good Morning!" welcomed the professional voice on the other end.

"Hey baby, it's me! I don't need to say good morning 'cuz we spent last night together," replied Dre with a teasing confidence.

"Hey D, I was just thinking about you while I was in the shower letting the water hit this warm pussy of yours," reciprocated Mariea.

"What I tell you about all that freaky talkin', you must

want me to tear some shit up on this highway, straight-up, straight-up," announced Dre with an innocent frustration and seriousness.

"No D, I would never want to be the reason behind anything like that, I wouldn't be able to live with myself if I had," admitted Mariea in a sensitive measure that caught Dre off guard as Mariea was typically more erotic with her words than caring and nurturing.

Making Dre uncomfortable he cut her off, "That's just a joke baby, remember what I told you yesterday besides how much I love your wet warm pussy that I love fucking all night long like *SWV Song?*"

"What D? You always know the right things to say to me," embarrassingly confessed Mariea. Mariea knew that Dre was a man of few words when it came to serious feelings so when he made such erotic remarks she knew it was his way of expressing himself. After all, she started it with the tantalizing offer as she shared with Dre her shower experience. Dre was simply following fashion but expressing himself at the same time, regardless of the vulgarity that is commonly associated with such a vernacular.

"You ready to ride, baby?"
"To where D?"
"Don't ask so many questions, it ain't the moon, so you don't need to worry about wearing your astronaut outfit," joked Dre.
"But look sexy like you know how to do."

"Molly is still here, can she ride with?"

"Naw'll not this time, I wanna take care some things for you and the less people is the less problems," instructed Dre.

"Okay D, I was on my way to the gym so I need to put something else on. What time you picking me up?"

"That's cool. What you have on is fine and I'm coming up off the interstate right now so I'll be there in about ten tops. I will blow the horn and just come out."

"Alright D, I'll see you shortly," finished Mariea in a gentle soft endearing voice that made Dre melt.

"Aight baby," replied Dre as he hung up the phone and signaled as he exited the ramp.

Mariea looked absolutely delicious when she came walking out of her place. She had on a *Baby Phat* sweat suit that was fitting all the white girl curves with a matching baseball cap with a pony tail coming out the back. She hopped in the back of the *Lex* joining Dre and Slick. The feminine aroma heightened Dre and Slick's awareness. The beautiful smell of a woman was something they both appreciated and Mariea smelled fresh and sweet, definitely the compliments of *VictoriaSecret* perfume; they took it all in.

Mariea was a little surprised to see Slick as Dre did not mention him, but she remembered how adamant Dre was about not asking too many questions, so she bit her lip and jumped in and shared her normal jolly demeanor with a side of sexuality.

They made it to CHI a little after 12:00 and the sun hung high overhead and beat down on the arid streets of Independence and Central Park. Slick's spot was running fine as usual and there was an inordinate amount of traffic; so much so that even Mariea was a little overwhelmed by the density of people. Plus, she was the only white person she could see. She took comfort that Dre and Slick were with her so she let go of her fear and enjoyed seeing all of the people and activity.

Slick knew better than to talk business in front of Mariea so he kept the dialogue to innocent observations.

"Slick, I see your weed spot still acting a fool," riddled Dre.
"Yeah, my bags a lil' bit bigger than the ones your girl was selling," Slick replied with a smile as he slowly turned his head towards the back seat and gave Mariea a kiddingly sarcastic look.
"Since my bag was so small, how much do you mind selling me a quarter pound for," followed Mariea without missing a beat.

This impressed Dre and reinforced his already gaining confidence in her and it gave Slick reason to do the same. *She got it together,* Slick thought.

This was exactly what Dre and Slick were discussing at one of the rest stops on their way out to the CHI. They planned on just giving her weed to make her think it was all about her and to be cautious while driving.

"You probably need to ask your man about that," directed Slick. "Well D, how much?" asked Mariea.

Dre saw this as an opportunity to test her wit and for him to engage in an intellectual exercise. His dad always taught him to never give a woman what she wanted right away. Dre knew that she had some weed on her already and something else as well, only she didn't know it yet. He contemplated his response briefly and decided to play this little game.

"I don't know about that weed baby, you gotta be extra careful driving," answered Dre.
"I'll drive careful baby, please," begged Mariea in a desperate measure that gave Dre the feeling that she caved too easily. He was hoping for more intestinal fortitude than that.
"Aight, check this out baby; we'll pick up a whole pound when we ready to get on the highway," as he cocked his head to look at Mariea as he made the offer.

Mariea was not as duped as Dre thought, she hadn't just risen with this morning's sun, she had been around some and while she was giving the impression that she was crumbling she was playing her own hand.

"So, D, tell me, how much?" in a more serious tone with a splash of sexy in her voice. She was a woman with endowments that she could use when the time called for it, but she also had a brain, something that allowed her to go further in many circumstances than her physical features would have allowed.

"Don't worry about it baby, it's nothing, just think about it the next time those pussy lip muscles are flexin' on this big fat dick! Straight-up!" delivered Dre as if it were a punch line.

"Is there somewhere I can show you right now?" challenged Mariea.

"Well, you heard the lady," interrupted Slick sheepishly, "just chirp me when you ready. Later Dre, Later Mariea."

"Oh, tell your girl Molly to get at me," reminded Slick as he stepped out of the car to retrieve his belongings in the trunk.

Dre jumped out as well to holler at Slick and instructed Mariea to get in the front seat. Dre watched his surroundings, he observed the onlookers as they hawked the Lex and noticed as their eyes grew larger as she stepped from the car; an attractive white girl with an ass like a sister. She drew attention and Dre liked the attention as it reflected back on him.

"Slick, I need you to give me a whole brick of that thang," mentioned Dre as they walked back to the trunk together.

"Man, it is hotter than a bullpen full of snitches!" exclaimed Dre.

"I hear that and I got cha Joe," granted Slick as he returned the smile that shown across Dre's face from the *bullpen* comment.

"Put it in a custom book with the insides half cut, that work like Mexican' *Hurricane* style," instructed Dre.

"Aight Joe, what about the pound of weed?" reminded Slick.

"I'll put that in the spot and I don't want her to know about the other stain, she just thinks I'm getting' weed for her. I'll go get her a couple of outfits and pick you up a pair of new shoes and have the money in the shoe box. I also need to take me a couple of these coffee cans with the false bottoms," summarized Dre for his sake and Slicks so they were on the same page.

"I'll try to have you some of those. Let me go see what Regina got counted up as I fill her up as well. She gets a little nervous when she goes too long without some of me," bragged Slick. "Those thumpers still in the stash spot too."

"Yeah, no doubt. Straight-up," offered Dre as they gave each other a pound followed by a shake and an embrace. Slick headed towards his ghetto palace and Dre to his Lex.

"Who is Will and Ball?" Mariea asked Dre as he got back in the car.

"Those my two hearts that's resting in peace. They ride with me everywhere I go," solemnly confessed Dre with a quiet humbleness and respect.

Mariea saw another side of Dre at that moment. His face was almost innocent and a fondness spread across him that caused him to miss a breath and have to catch up. Mariea could see the impact the memory of them had on Dre and her feelings for him grew stronger at that very moment. He was a man with principle and with compassion; he was more than what was on the surface and she yearned to find more.

They pulled away from Slick's place to the bumping of *R-Kelly's,* "Get Up On A Room" and Dre was feeling untouchable as if the hands of Will and Ball were upon him. He was back on his streets, in his neighborhood and was riding slick with the *Lex* and fresh with the *Iceberg Gear* and smelling fresh like the *Cool Water* Cologne he always wore. It had been years since he saw Slick's uncle ride up on him when he was just a boy. Today, he entered the kingdom as the new king and everybody was pointing, just hoping he would stop so they could pay homage.

"Mariea," announced Dre, "we are about to ride over to my Mom's."
"I'll love to meet your mom. Your mom isn't going to get upset that you are bringing a white girl home, will she?" cautiously inquired Mariea looking for support and acceptance.

Dre came to the calling and his best "white" impression, "Why, of course not, why would you think that my Mariea?"

It made Mariea laugh and make her feel more comfortable inside. It was one thing to meet the mother but knowing that Dre's world did not include many white people, she was still a little apprehensive.

"D! You are so crazy" replied Mariea as she hit him playfully on the arm.

There was a connection made at that moment when her fist found his arm; her reliance on his protection and his reliance on her dedication. They were giving each other something they normally didn't give someone else. They were not afraid of it, it was enlightening, but at the same time it was new and they were not sure what it meant in entirety.

Just as Dre was turning off Roosevelt onto Cicero he got a chirp from Slick.

"Dre?" frantically asked the voice on the other end. "What up Slick?" Dre fired back.
"Where you at Joe?" rushed Slick into the phone.
"On Roosevelt and Cicero," informed Dre.
"The Boppers just pulled me over and I'm dirty than a motherfucker Joe! They running my plates now. I'm on sixteenth and Drake in the *Nav,* I need you to come through and make some noise," conducted Slick.
"Don't even trip, I'm turning around now," comforted Dre.

Dre made a U-turn on Roosevelt and was at Central Park heading towards sixteenth in a flash. *My boys in need and I won't let him down,* Dre thought to himself. Dre could see the Nav pulled over on the side of the road so he rode in the alley adjacent. He hit the stash spot retrieving the 9mm and shot five into the air and slowly pulled away as the smoke wafted away from them leaving a faint residue in the air, a smell that was new to Mariea. She didn't like it, but the thrill of what was happening gripped her and showed her a reality that she was unaware of.

Less than a minute later Slick chirped again, letting Dre know that it worked as the men in blue were pulling away. *It was a close one,* Slick thought to himself as did Dre. Life in the fast lane was inches and ounces, timing was essential and being lucky had its advantages. You never knew what tomorrow would bring, so you lived for the day, it was the only way in the world of *Dog Food.*

Chapter 21
Found Humanity

Dre and Mariea found the ride back to Cedar Rapids relaxing. She had her pound of weed, bags full of new clothes that she anxiously awaited to adorn and her man at her side. Similarly, Dre had his brick stashed in the hollowed out books, he had his own bags of clothes and he even had a new outfit for Munchie's birthday that was fast approaching. Each one was so into their own thoughts that the music was inaudible but clearly just as it should be. They were lost in themselves but enjoying one another's company, sharing the moments that drew them closer.

"Thank you baby for the clothes and everything," calmly offered Mariea as she grasped Dre's hand and squeezed it tight, looking at him with adoration and love.

"I told you once before it's nothing," replied Dre. "When we get to the gas station by the interstate you're going to grab the wheel and bring it home."

The reaction confused and hurt Mariea. Here she had just provided an opening for them to have a moment and he dismissed it as no big deal and immediately addressed a logistical issue of who was to drive. She could tell that something was on his mind, but she knew better than to pry. No matter how much she wanted to know him, wanted to share things, wanted to be there for him, wanted to show him how much she cared, she understood that there were certain places you didn't go with Dre unless he brought you there himself.

"Okay, baby, I told you before that I'll drive," responded Mariea obediently.

You could see the tiredness in Dre's face, not the kind that comes from a lack of sleep, rather the kind that accompanies deep contemplation. Dre pulled away from the red light a little faster than normal with thoughts filling his mind. *Screeeeeech* went the brakes as Dre and Mariea were both thrown forward in the car with their heads falling back on the headrest. Dre's quick reaction prevented them from hitting another car or driving off the road as the little pup stood there frozen in place looking up at them.

Dre and Mariea stared at the puppy sitting in the middle of the road too terrified to even move.

"He wants you to get out and help him," encouraged Mariea as Dre sat there thinking to himself; *Damn, I am happy I didn't hit that lil' fella.*

Reacting naturally, prompted by Mariea, Dre got out of the vehicle to tend to the pup, thinking, *I'm ridin' way too dirty to be playing dog patrol.* He gracefully swooped the pup with one hand and cradled it gingerly. He returned to the vehicle and put the puppy in the backseat, quickly jumped back into the *Lex* trying to minimize the traffic congestion. Mariea immediately began to play with the pup and while it had no dog tag on his collar and was so clean it was no stray.

"This is that lil' rascal's lucky day, he now rollin' with big Dre!" exclaimed Dre with a sense of pride and comfort.

Dre had a little gleam in his eye. He had never been a father, but seeing this pup and Mariea getting along so playfully, it gave him a feeling of family. Seeing this side of Dre made Mariea melt, he *was a man of many dimensions and this one suited him well,* she thought.

The gas station was only a few blocks down and when they pulled in there were two young kids waiting to see if they could pump the gas. Dre remembered hustling the same thing when he was kid, making a dollar or two with each customer. The station attendant didn't seem to mind as long as the kids were respectful and these kids were.

"You kids still in school and ya'll stayin' out of trouble?" asked Dre.

In unison they replied, "Yeah" as if it were a musical and not just an affirmative.

Seeing himself even more in them as they looked eagerly at him, he reached into his pocket and handed each boy a crisp hundred dollar bill. Their eyes were the size of plates.

"Now, you two are done pumpin' gas for the day. You need to buy your families a good meal and stay out of trouble, you hear me?" Dre instructed like the father figure he wanted to be.

The two boys shook their heads in agreement as they were both still staring down at the crisp bills and rubbing it between their fingers as if testing them to see if they were real.

"Thanks a lot mister!" both boys shouted as they turned and sped away as fast as their feet would carry them hooting and hollering until they were out of sight.

Dre smiled as he grabbed the pump handle and started to pump his own gas. Mariea looked on in admiration; *what a man he is.*

Dre returned with a bag of snacks and found the passenger seat welcoming. Dre forget how tired he was until his back settled into the plush leather. He looked at the pup lying contently on the towel that he had laid across the backseat. No sounds, no fussing, just looking up at Dre *with the eyes of an angel* Dre thought.

"I gotta give this lil' fella a name" announced Dre not wasting any time in assuming possession and responsibility for the pup.
"Name him Dre or D," suggested Mariea.
"Naw'll, I'll name him *Dusty* since he's brown and I picked him up off the streets, just like when I was a kid and we found two dogs and named one *Snowball* and the other *Dusty,*" confessed Dre.
"That sounds like a perfect name," confirmed Mariea.

The remainder of the trip became all about Dusty. At each rest stop they would pull over so he could relieve himself and they would feed him and give him something to drink.

At the beginning of the trip they were so content in one another's company and with their bags of clothes and drugs. Now, this new addition made all of those things pale in comparison. The addition of another living thing meant more to them than any of the clothes in the bags or drugs in their stash, a revelation of humanity for both of them. The caring they shared for one another they now shared with this pup, a reflection of compassion and care. In their world of fast talking and hustles full of agendas, they found the epitome of something pure, a pup in need of love and attention. There was no agenda and no hustle, only the desire to be wanted and cared for just like those that found him on their path of destiny in the world of *Dog Food*.

Chapter 22
Out of Place

They left as two and returned as three; Dre, Mariea and Dusty. As they pulled into Cedar Rapids, Mariea was overwhelmed with joy, with a sense of peace, almost tranquility. She felt the bond that had formed between her and Dre and the addition of Dusty made it feel like a family. If she only knew what else was in the car with them.

"Well D baby, thank you for everything. I really enjoyed being with you; the shopping and the smokes, and just, everything!" she exclaimed as she leaned over and kissed him hard and purposefully. As she pulled away she noticed Dusty observing them with an absolute innocence and wonderment.

"Yeah baby, that's my lil'man back there. I enjoyed having you for the ride, but you know the real party is goin' to start later on," replied Dre.

"I know what type of party you talking about," sheepishly

admitted Mariea, "the kind where I am in my birthday suit."

"You got dat right!" confirmed Dre. "I gotta make a couple of stops and check in on Munchie though, but I'll holla at cha later."

"Okay," responded Mariea, hanging on his every word.

"Let me grab that weed outta the spot for you. If you don't mind, hold the shopping bags except the two custom outfits," instructed Dre.

Dre gave her the weed and helped with her bags, bringing them inside. Dre considered that she wouldn't ramble through his things and the average person would have thought he had purchased new books anyways.

Dre jumped back in the *Lex*, closed the door and looked at Dusty in the rearview mirror. As his voice started, Dusty's eyes looked at him, as if he understood that he was being talked to.

"That girl got a whole brick of my *Dog Food* and she don't even know it, $80,000 worth," admitted Dre in a low tone that bordered on concern and confidence.

Dusty barked twice at Dre as if to comfort him and slumped back down as if the effort was too much for just a puppy.

Dre smiled and look forward out the window, looking ahead into his future; *this was all part of the game,* he reminded himself as he pulled away from Mariea's.

When Dre hit the spot where Pete was, everything looked copacetic. Pete approach the *Lex* nonchalantly and jumped in when Dre came to a stop.

"What's the word, tell me something good," started Dre.

"We doing great as usual and what do we have here?" asked Pete as he eyed Dusty lazily lounging in the back seat.

"That's Dusty, the newest family member," Dre presented in confidence as he patted him on his head and gave him a scratch behind the ears.

"They say, dog is mans' best friend," claimed Pete.

"Yeah, cause I don't have to worry about him speaking, but he understands. Ain't that right Dusty?" replied Dre.

Dusty let out two sharp barks and looked at both men intently. They fell out laughing.

"Pete, you tryin' to do the 24 hour shop, *Dunkin Donut* Style?" asked Dre, breaking into a more serious conversation, now that the introduction had been made.

"Whatever needs to be done to bring the money in Captain!" Declared Pete. "Speaking of money, I gave Munchie a nice amount last night and again this morning. He came by with some guy in the Chevy. The guy looked like some lil' sissy."

"Hey Pete, 'member that's my Cuz, so let's leave that 'sissy' word out of the sentences," cautioned Dre with a warning.

"Okay, Dre, I got you, he was just smacking his lips and batting his eyes everywhere is all," explained Pete.

"If that's what Cuz like, than I support it, even though I don't

100% condone it. Who am I to judge anyone? I love him regardless," admitted Dre.

"Blood is thicker than Mud baby! I love Munchie too," offered Pete as a consolation so Dre knew he meant no disrespect towards Munchie.

"So!" exclaimed Dre, again moving on to business. "So, check this out, I got some more shit we gonna shake up. Let me go get up with Munchie and I'm going to slide back on ya later. You got enough for now?"

"Yeah, we cool 'til later," answered Pete.

"Aight Pete, you need anything, let me know. Hey, who's that guy over there with the prosthetic arm that's shopping and steady lookin' round like he the police?" inquisitively and observationally conjectured Dre.

"Ah, baby, he lookin' for me. Sometimes he have a hard times putting his works together with that hook on the end of his arm, but he's been bringing me lots of business. Let me go holla at him. I'll see you and Dusty when you ready to go to the shake table," expressed Pete as he exited the *Lex*.

Dre pulled away leaving behind a stigma of doubt. He was certain that there was something more to the guy than just one less arm. He also thought he saw another guy, a white motherfucker, taking pictures? As Dre replayed the scene in his mind's eye, something didn't fit, something was wrong.

I've known Pete for a minute and now a new guy comes on the scene, one that Pete speaks of as a premier customer, has loads of money and yet cannot even do his own dope at times. It didn't fit, something was out of place, Dre thought to himself, but he couldn't put his finger on it.

Just then Dusty barked three times getting Dre's attention. As Dre looked at Dusty in the rearview mirror he admitted, "You're right pal, I gotta keep my eyes open."

The stakes were too high to be blind, to be non-assertive. Dre needed to stay focused and treat situations with skepticism, not a proletariat indifference. This was a tough world, one that could turn on you at any minute and Dre needed to stay ahead of the game, he needed to stay out front in this world of his, this world of *Dog Food.*

Chapter 23
Cuzo Lost

Dre picked up the phone and Dialed Munchie. As he listened to the phone ring, it occurred to him that his life seemed to be shifting; it started with Terry and Munchie just a few months ago and now it was a different world, one with different people. Dre felt like the same person but he felt a little out of place, especially as he heard the voice on the other end.

"Hey Cuzo," resonated the familiar voice.

A warmth passed through Dre and whatever apprehensions he felt listening to the ring tone was abruptly squashed by the tone of Munchie's voice.

"What up Cuz?" asked Dre.
"How was your trip? I went by Pete's twice while you were gone," replied Munchie, completely ignoring Dre's question.

Both men, so eager to talk to the other, were more concerned on the common pleasantries of how the other one was. Neither took the opportunity to directly answer the other's questions.

"Pete told me that. Where you at, I need to holler at cha," announced Dre.

"I'm out in Hiawatha at my friend Jason's house. Want me to meet you at the crib?" replied Munchie, holding his breath, not certain which prompt he would take, the fact he was at Jason's or to meet him back at the crib.

"Just give me the address of where you're at and I'll come and pick the both of you up and we can go get somethin' to eat," answered Dre.

The reply made Munchie feel good. Not only did Dre not judge him, he invited Jason along. Munchie knew that Dre loved him no matter what and it was little gestures like this that reminded him that it was true.

Munchie provided the address and Dre and Dusty were off like Batman and Robin. Dre thought through the preferences of Munchie and tried to make sense of it all, but in the end he was unsuccessful. He loved Munchie and that would have to be the beginning and the end of his internal debate.

Dre would do anything for his Cuzo and he actually respected him. It was not always easy for Munchie and Dre knew this. Munchie was comfortable with whom he was and that made it easier for Dre. Munchie was not a pretender, like so many looking for attention. Munchie kept it real and Dre could honor and defend that. It was a sign of character, and there weren't many in his world that had demonstrated such a personal integrity. Dre was proud to call him family, he was proud to call him friend.

They pulled up to the house and Dre tapped the horn, summoning Munchie and Jason. It was a nice crib, causing Dre to consider; *who is this Jason?* They came out to the car, Munchie with Jason in tow, and Dre recognized Jason from the *Tycoon* the last time they went out. *What is he, some dope boy?* Dre thought to himself, as he noticed how Jason's attire complimented his crib.

"This my cousin Dre," introduced Munchie as the two of them jumped into the *Lex*. "The one I have been telling you so much about" Munchie mentioned to Jason. Hey Dre, where did this dog come from?" continued an excited Munchie, causing him to keep firing questions.

Dre could tell Munchie was nervous and he wanted to assure Munchie that he was not being judged and that Dre would support his decisions.

"Hey, what's up Jason?" politely asked Dre hoping to ease some of Munchie's anxiety by showing an interest in Jason.
"And Cuzo, that's Dusty back there. Our paths just kinda crossed. He's *Toto* and I was like *Dorothy* on my way from home and he just landed on the *yellow brick road* in front of me," finished Dre with a sincere smile on his face, and a look in

his eyes that confirmed his belief that fate stepped in and put them in each other's way.

"I've heard a lot about you Dre," stated Jason with an obvious effort trying to make his voice masculine.

"Well, I hope it was all good," joked Dre. "But hey, Jason, you can be real with me and use your real voice. I'm not here to judge anyone."

"I'm so glad," appreciatively expressed Jason in a much higher pitched feminine voice. "I thought I was going to have to use that voice all day long."

"So, Cuzo, this is where you have been?" accused Dre as if Munchie was *absent without leave.* "Jason, this is a nice crib, what type of business you in, if you don't mind me asking that is?"

"I am an investor in the markets. My uncle introduced me to it in '96 and I have been doing it ever since. My first investment, was in *Viagra,* well actually in the company that makes it, *Pfizer.* It did so well that I kept pursuing investments. I also dabble in numismatics and other investments that offer a potential for return," answered Jason thoroughly and distinctly.

Dre nodded his head, confirming he was listening and if there was more he was willing to entertain it. Jason took the opportunity.

"Like I was telling Munchie, I don't want to get all up in your business Dre, but I know that this fine ride and the big house with the cathedral ceilings was not the result of selling *Icee* cups and *Penny* candy. I can show you how to wash your dirty money clean," continued Jason.

"I see you picked you a good one; he's far from a fool," complimented Dre. "Ya'll hungry? Let's go to Applebee's, I gotta a taste for some steak and shrimp. I want to think about this cleaning money thing on a full stomach," offered Dre with a smile.

"You know we can't take Dusty in there. Did you take him to the vet to get his shots?" followed Munchie, the consummate care giver.

"Not yet," admitted Dre. "I'll drop him over to Mariea's house while we go eat. I got somethin' in the trunk too Cuzo. I know your birthday is right around the corner," informed Dre with a suspenseful charge.

"What is it Cuzo, what is it?" asked Munchie with a youthful exuberance.

"It's a surprise. If I tell you what it is, it will spoil it. Straight-up, straight-up!"

"He right," corroborated Jason," Dre right."

Dropping Dusty off at Mariea's house was more than a responsible dog owner act, Dre wanted to check on his investment as well. He had left the $80,000 to $100,000 unattended and he was eager to make sure it was still alive. It was.

Dre was developing more and more confidence in Mariea and was becoming accustomed to the conveniences she presented there in Cedar Rapids.

As the three of them headed off to *Applebee's* Dre

couldn't help but feel his fortune; friends, money, and family, but not exactly in that order. These aspects of his life shifted in consideration of and depending on the situation. The world he was in was fluid, very dynamic and to rest your laurels on one aspect could reveal a weakness if somebody wanted or needed something from you. In his world, he was surrounded by all types of addicts. He needed to be careful, he needed to be prudent and he needed to be aware. But above all, he needed his family and friends close in the ever changing world of *Dog Food*.

Chapter 24
Dog Catcher II

The dim sun dusted room was filled with a concoction of odors emanating from; off the shelf cologne, sweat and old wood furniture with a hint of the lemon Pledge. The blinds were drawn and as daybreak attempted to peak in, it cast a shadow across the room highlighting the Italian leather wrapped chairs and a deep red oak desk that occupied the room. The walls and bookshelf, functioning as backdrops, played host to memorabilia, pictures and accolades.

"Captain, sir, the last time we spoke, I informed you that I would be working diligently to find any leads on the case regarding David," announced the lieutenant as he shuffled manila folders in his arms.

As the word *David* fell from his mouth, his ears couldn't believe what they had just heard. To say his name was not so much eerie as it was fearful; a fear to hurt the Captain's feelings or to speak of the dead, the Lieutenant couldn't identify specifically what it was, but it just felt wrong saying his name.

"Okay, lieutenant, what do you have for me?" replied the Captain in a professional tone that seemed indifferent to hearing his brother's name.

"Well, all my informants and staff conducted surveillance and logged the foot and vehicle traffic that ultimate lead to an alley on *Fifteenth* and *Sixth Street.* A location that is known for drugs," updated the lieutenant, still a little sheepish from the David comment a moment ago.

"Is it a specific house we are talking about here? One that we can target, pick up the trash on, or try to obtain a search warrant?" Inquired the Captain eagerly.

"Our trail is cold in that respect sir, but we strongly believe that there is a connection with a blue van that is hovering around the areas we are concentrating on. We believe it to be dropping dope around," advised the lieutenant as he pulled a picture from one of the manila folders and handed it to the Captain.

Just then a light knock was heard on the door. Considering the blinds were drawn and the door was closed, the Captain knew it had to be important.

"Come in!" ordered the Captain," come in."

As the door opened, Captain Boots recognized the familiar face.

"Ah, Captain Rivera, and to what do I owe this honor?" asked Captain Boots with a type of equivalent rank chiding.

"How are you John?" started Captain Rivera. "I am so sorry for your loss and that I haven't called you. That is why I wanted to stop in; to offer my condolences personally and to see if there is anything I can do to assist you in any capacity."

"Not a problem at all Jerry. In fact, I was just wrapping up with the Lieutenant," replied Captain Boots as he set the folder down on his desk. "Lieutenant, I will look through your briefings here and get back with you. You are excused."

As the lieutenant left the room, Captain Rivera felt it odd that he was not introduced to the Lieutenant, but considered it a matter of respect or unnecessary under the present circumstances.

"Oh, and lieutenant," summoned Captain Boots," it's ok to use his name; it gives me comfort to know that he is not easily forgotten."

As the Lieutenant left the room is was amazed at the composer of the Captain. He was overwhelmed that the Captain could read it on his face and take the time and effort to console him and it was the Captain who had suffered a great loss. *What a great man,* the Lieutenant thought to himself, *what a great man.*

"Jerry," started Captain Boots with a serious and direct tone,

"I'm not going to lie to you. It's been hard on me, but I know he is in a better place. I am committed to getting the bastard responsible and we are hoping for a break in the case; a lead that will help to expedite the apprehension," ended Captain Boots with a hopefully finality.

"What do you have here in the file, may I?" asked Captain Rivera as he reached for the file that Captain Boots had just set down. Captain Boots nodded in approval. He knew Captain Rivera's reputation and the progress he had made over in Vinton and he welcomed any insight.

"I've seen this van," claimed Captain Rivera as he fingered the pictures. "I cannot place it, but I know I have seen it," articulated Captain Rivera with a conviction of certainty.

"I'll see that I get the info sent over to you. Let me know as soon as you can place the identity. It appears there are no plates on it and there is an orange tag in the back window," instructed Captain Boots with a formality accustomed to men in their positions.

"I will, John, I will. All my best and again let me know if there is anything else I can do. We will see what we can work on our end and I will keep you posted if we uncover anything. Good day my friend," solemnly offered Captain Rivera as he embraced Captain Boots, leaving as promptly as he arrived.

Every Captain feared the infusion of this type of drug in their neighborhood, the type of destruction it can cause. They needed to get a step up on the ring and do it fast before more were lost, lost to the world, lost to the world of *Dog Food*.

Chapter 25
The Duality of Reality

To say, "Business was good," would be an understatement. The money was pouring in and their client base had been growing exponentially as their reputation for great product at a great price spread. It was a basic economic principle, one that Dre understood and they were exploiting it as much as possible; they were maximizing utility.

The addition of Jason and Mariea to the operation was paying dividends at a rate beyond Dre's expectations. They brought a nice diversification of customers to their target market and balanced out the team personally and professionally.

Dre, Munchie, Mariea and Jason had plans to head to Iowa City for an evening of fun and celebration; it was Munchie's birthday.

"Get up!" demanded Dre as he entered Munchie's room,

threw off the comforter and opened the blinds.

"Happy Birthday Cuzo! I got you a present outside! And you know how special the month of June is, with it being your birthday, Ball's birthday, 2 Pac's and the memorial of Will. So, get up!" repeated Dre.

"Cuzo, what you got me?" asked Munchie in a low sleep ridden tone.

"You need to get up and see for yourself!" replied Dre.

"Dusty, knock it off!" complained Munchie as Dusty jumped up on to the bed to give him a happy birthday wish as well. "You need to knock it off," grumbled Munchie as he scrubbed behind Dusty's ears, sending his tail into a frenzy.

"C'mon, let's go," encouraged Dre, slapping his leg to get Dusty's attention and staring down Munchie to get his.

When they walked outside Munchie thought he heard trumpets blare and saw the heaven's open. He had an idea of what Dre might have done, but this was more than he had imagined. A brand new Silver Tahoe with matching *Jet Skis* and trailer in tow!

"I love you Cuzo!" Munchie kept repeating as he jumped up and down, jumping higher with each attempt.

"That ain't all, look in the glove compartment," teased Dre.

Hurriedly Munchie approached the passenger side and opened the door. Dre had it all done up right including the TV's and four 15 inch sub-woofers with a *Bose* system. Dre waited on the rims because he knew what happens when you flickin' rims; the *jackboys always in your rearview mirror!*

As Munchie was scurrying in the glove compartment, Dre slowly put his hand into his own pocket and slid a watch over his wrist.

Munchie was speechless. There in the glove compartment, Munchie found a treasure, a gold *Rolex*. He quickly put it on, held up in the morning sun to see the flicker of the brilliance and ran to Dre.

Dre met him with arm raised showing him a reflection of what he had on his wrist.

"We got matchin' *Rollys!* Your boy Jason got me the hook-up. Straight Up!" triumphantly announced Dre.

No sooner had the word Jason escaped Dre's lips and he pulled into the drive in his *Chrysler Sebring*.

"Happy Birthday, bitch!" exclaimed Jason as he exited the car and walked towards Munchie.
"What did I tell you'll 'bout using that b-word like that around me?" reminded Dre in an irritated tone.
"Okay, Daddy Dre," apologetically replied Jason as he spun on his heels to retrieve the camera from his car.
"Dre's cool, so leave the 'Daddy' for your own sweet daddy!" remarked Dre as he looked at Munchie for some support and confirmation.

Munchie missed the look Dre gave him as he was so intent on getting in the truck. Jason followed with the camera in hand taking photos of Munchie and his new ride.

"C'mon Cuzo, come get in a flick with me," pleaded Munchie to Dre.
"You just woke up, you still have sleep in your eyes!" commented Dre in a declination.
"You the one who woke me up, so you best get over here boy! Bring Dusty too!" demanded Munchie in a lovingly excited manner.

Jason continued to take all sort of pictures including them sitting on the *Jet Ski's* while on the trailer. As the sun was rising over the roof tops out of the east, the day was suggesting it was going to be a beautiful one. Considering how it was starting, how could it end any other way.

"Dre, I gotta see my dad today," announced Munchie, breaking the light hearted mood to one more mixed with melancholy.
The drive over to the County jail was without event as Munchie was torn with emotion, he was so happy about his gifts, about it being his day, but at the same time he would not able to spend it with his dad the way he wanted to, in the flesh.

"Dent visit!" the officer yelled as Terry emerged through the sliding doors in his orange jumpsuit. He picked up the phone, sat down and looked into the mirror; *we look so much alike,* he thought to himself as a smiled formed across his face.

"Hey Dad! How are you holding up?" asked Munchie with a type of impatience and concern that only a loved one can express.

"Happy Birthday son!" declared Terry with a pride seldom found in his voice. "I can't complain about a thang, I'm still breathin'."

"How's the case looking?"

"These some bullshit charges they got on me, they just wanna Nigga to cop out to twenty!" exclaimed Terry.

"Aw, Dad, that messed up," replied Munchie with a sadness and desperation in his voice.

Terry could sense the pain in his son and it made him uneasy. He wasn't proud of where he was and for his son to see him like this, but he also knew that he needed to be strong; strong for Munchie and strong for himself.

"Don't you worry, I ain't going! We going to that motherfuckin' box! I'll rather let a jury of twelve decide my fate, than a fat man in a robe with a gavel in his hand!" preached Terry.

"Dad. Let's just say you lose at trial, what's the worst that could happen?" inquired Munchie in such a manner as to give Terry pause. Munchie was concerned about losing his father to the system and Munchie had learned enough to know that being *full of an ego* was not always the best tact.

"We ain't lookin' that mother fuckin' far, but they say thirty years to life!" admitted Terry adamantly.

"Dad," said Munchie with a seriousness Terry had never seen

in his son's face before, "take the twenty."

"Son," replied Terry with the same seriousness. "Sometimes in life you gotta stand up for something you believe in whether what's the outcome, and I'm strongly standing behind this. I gotta go down fighting! I gotta go down fighting!"

"Dad. I miss you and I need you out here with me," pleaded Munchie as the tears gently rolled down his face. "We can get you a lawyer for whatever the cost!" urged Munchie.

"I ain't going to waste ya'll money. These FED's play a viscous game, but they ain't got shit on me!" proclaimed Terry with a steadfastness resembling more of an ignorant stubbornness.

"Dad, you was the last real person I had out in these streets. Back when Mama use to tell me I wasn't shit and never going to amount to nothing but a black faggot mother fucker; it was you who came and got me from all of that! I still love her to death, but now everybody gone and this shit...well...Dad...it really hurts," choked out Munchie with tears steadily flowing down his face.

"I'm still here," reminded Terry. "I ain't goin; nowhere and you got Dre too! Speakin' of which, where is he?"

"He is still downstairs in the car. I told him I wanted to visit you by myself today. He dropped you off some whites though" answered Munchie.

Terry paused for a moment and sat forward in his chair staring intently into Munchie's eyes.

"Wipe your eyes son. It is your day today and we ain't gonna spend one more minute cryin' over something we can't change right now. Hey, what's that on your wrist?" asked Terry as the bling almost blinded him when Munchie raised his arms to wipe away the tears.

"Yeah, Dre got this for me today!"

"I see ya'll takin' real good care of ya'll selves. Tell Dre to keep his eyes open, I be hearing a lot of shit about him in here, Nigga's be hatin' you know!" cautioned Terry.

"Yeah, they goin' to do that," admitted Munchie with a concession to the reality of it, but not of the fear of it.

"Well son, I'm 'bout to make the lunch move. I'll keep you posted on what's going on and thank you for everything, and hey, Happy Birthday!"

"Thank you dad, thank you. I love you."

"I love you too son, I love you too."

Those words echoed in Munchies head as he walked out of the County jail; *I love you too son.* The day had kept up its end of the bargain and let the sun shine bright. The sun was warm on his face but his heart was cold; it was the duality of the reality that he struggled with inside.

He was bitter at the world for what it had done to him; how it had taken so much of his childhood and now it was threatening to take his father. A world he never asked to be in, but was thrown into and forced to survive in; a world without remorse, a world without compassion, a world without mercy, the world of *Dog Food.*

Chapter 26
Asphalt Cowboys

The ride to Iowa City was a blur of lights and anticipation of Munchie's birthday celebration. Munchie was feeling grand behind the wheel of his new Tahoe, Jason was sitting shot-gun and Dre and Mariea riding up each other all in the back. *Jay-Z's,* "can I get a, what, what, fuck you", lyrics are monopolizing the cabin as the beat goes on.

"Cuzo, you want me to get you two a room?" hollered Munchie over the chorus of *Jay-Z.*
"You know I'm not going to disrespect your leather interior like that," promptly answered Dre as he continued to grope Mariea as a foretaste of what was to come.
"I wish you would," Jason stated under his breath. "I wish you would. I'll love to see that banana and coconuts in that monkey!"

Munchie could not contain himself. He meant no disrespect towards Dre or Mariea, but that was funny. This allowed for Jason to follow suit; both men laughing hysterically.

"What the hell is so funny up there?" shouted Dre.

"Nothin' Cuzo! We're almost there, where do you want to go; *Gabe's* or the *Green Room?*"

Images of the *Green Room* flew through Dre's head and he tightly squeezed Mariea's hand. "It's your day Munchie, so wherever you land your truck, it's cool with us," replied Dre.

Munchie pulled into the next parking lot and they walked to *Gabe's*. The line was around the corner so Dre took them all to the back door. Dre had connections there. In fact, Dre had connections at most of the hot spots in town. He provided most of the *Dog Food* to the college guys that worked the doors or the floors.

Dre and Munchie walked through the door like *Nino Brown* and *G-Money* off "New Jack City" with their medallion bling swinging side to side in unison. Jason and Mariea flanked them as if an entourage. They looked like money and garnered attention.

"I'm going to grab me a seat," instructed Dre as the other three headed towards the bar.

Sisqo's "The Thong Song", filled the air as Dre sat and enjoyed his Cranberry juice and watched as the girls went crazy on the floor, including Jason. Mariea tried her best but she always seemed to be a little off rhythm, but she could still shake it. Dre smiled.

Look at my baby, Dre thought to himself. *I gotta give her a lil' R&B, a little rhythm and soul. She's definitely on beat while she throwing that hot pink pussy on me. She's fittin' those jeans especially nice for a white girl even if that ass is not big like Tonya's,* he observed.

By the time Munchie left the dance floor and headed back to Dre he could feel the liquor in him.

"Hey Cuzo, let's take some flicks! Just check out the spray paint backdrop they got with the Chicago skyline. That's our city west side baby!" exclaimed Munchie with an excitement and pride as if he were a part of the permanent scenery.

"Westside! So that's why this liquor wasn't always legal!" Dre joked in return.

Dre and Munchie proceeded to the camera booth and started taking pictures. The moment of just the two of them was abruptly bothered by several of the ladies in their sight. The bling, the *fee* and the *Cable* around their necks shouted out to the ladies! The new *Rollys* they were flossing acting like beacons in the night as they reflected the brilliant light thrown from the dance floor.

Dre took advantage of the situation and palmed some asses while pictures were being taken and prior to the arrival of Jason and Mariea.

"Move around bitches, ain't no pictures needed with ya'll in them," instructed Jason in a protective tone for his sake and Mariea's.

Dre had on his *Iceberg* outfit while Munchie and Jason were sporting *Polo* and *Nautica*. Mariea completed the commercial while wearing a cute *Hilfiger* outfit with a belly shirt. They were all into the moment, the music, the lights, the feelings. Their experience only heightened by the weed Mariea had brought with. All four of them on a cloud, thumpin' and bumpin'; they were on a ride.

The ring of Dre's phone startled them even though it was barely heard over all of the noise. It was more Dre's face than the sound of the ring that seemed to startle them.

"What's up? Speak on it Pete!" Dre rushed into the phone as he cleared around the corner of the restroom where it was not so loud.
"We got some more drama baby!"
"What you mean drama? Police or Nigga?" inquired Dre distinctly.
"Nigga's some clowns from Detroit told me to shut this shit

down and that our reign was over. One way or the hard way," carefully articulated Pete.

"Who the fuck these Nigga's think they is; *Willie Lloyd* or *Pierre?* I'm on my way, gone and close shop. Everything accounted for right?"

"Yeah Dre, everything accounted," promptly answered Pete.

"Give me about forty-five minutes or an hour. Meet me at the crib and saddle up the horses," instructed Dre.

As Dre stormed out of the restroom like a dragon; there was fire in his eyes and his jaws were tight. Anyone in his path knew to stand clear.

"Munchie, give me the keys, get Mariea and Jason and meet me at the truck," demanded Dre in a fast serious tone that took the wind out of Munchie immediately. He knew something was wrong.

"What happened Cuzo?"

"Nothin' we can't handle," comforted Dre, "just some more drama on the spot that needs to be addressed."

"Let me get Mariea and Jason and we'll meet you at the truck," conceded Munchie as he reached into his pocket and handed Dre his keys.

You could feel the tension in the truck. No one said a word until the unsaid vow of silence was broken by Dre.

"We got some drama. These punk mother fuckin' Niggas from Detroit tryin' to take some food outta my mouth. They tellin' Pete to shut it down and that our reign is over one way or the hard way! Well, just like Hall and Oats, 'I can't go for that!"

"Who they think they is, *Willie Lloyd*?" echoed Munchie. "No can do, baby, no can do!"

"That's the same thing I said to Pete' offered Dre.

"They must not know where we come from. The county of Cook; where Niggas dress up like ladies and hit 'em with burning 380's!" exclaimed Munchie with a seriousness not often seen.

This gave Dre an idea. Another one of his epiphanies, this time it was about putting the end to something as opposed to building something.

"Cuzo, let's bake these Niggas a cake! Jason, we about to go over to your house!" announced Dre.

"What ya'll need, some heavy artillery?"

"That too, but first I need you and Munchie to do something. I need you to do it up right, all sexy with wigs and short shorts with ya'll ass all out the back and make sure it ain't a stubble of hair on ya'll face," Dre instructed with clarity and vision.

"Now, this is my specialty!" bragged Jason. "Plus, hair doesn't grow on my face."

"It doesn't grow on my face either Cuzo," reminded Munchie.

"Mariea, I need you to do the same thing baby, some short sexy stuff too."

By the time they arrived at Dre's crib, Munchie and Jason were looking like too hot chicks as the wigs fit their facial structures and they relished in playing the part. Mariea rounded out the trio as her ass was all out, her shorts wearing up her crack and cleavage spilling out begging to be touched.

When Pete saw them he did a double take and smiled.

"Okay, we got two AK 47's, Pete has on the vest and so do I, and all these *Desert Eagle* glocks got red beams on them. I hope there insurance policies are paid up, 'cuz they ain't about to stop us from eating, so the least they can do is leave something for someone else!" announced Dre with a passion and conviction that left no doubt as to the expected outcome.

Dre carefully and methodically went back over the plan with the group. This was no playing, if there was a mistake it meant blood and the only blood they were interested was the kind that came from Detroit. Mariea, Munchie and Jason would take the *Lexus* and Pete and Dre would take the new *Tahoe* and all of the gear. The Chevy was not an option as the chrome rims would not only bring attention by the authorities but most likely be noticed by the Detroit gang as well.

Dre and Pete parked a few blocks up from the spot with binoculars to watch the scene where Jason, Munchie and Mariea would be acting out their roles. Pete took the opportunity to tell Dre everything he could remember about the guys, the type and color of their car and so on.

Mariea, Jason and Munchie strutted up and down on 15th and 6th, the spot that was usually hopping. However, when cars would come by and see three chicks sitting in the Lexus they would keep going; pussy was pussy, but dog food was *Dog Food*. They would get the occasional thirsty stupid mother fucker that would pull up on them anyways and Mariea would simply ask them if they wanted to buy some pussy or a blow job. That would be enough to send them on their way, leaving Munchie, Jason and Mariea all laughing hysterically.

As time wore on Mariea wondered if the plan would work. Dre, a few blocks away, shared a similar sentiment. Both of their doubts were shattered by the next approaching vehicle; blue Michigan plates. It rolled up on the Lexus as if to make a challenge. Mariea could see the plate in the side view mirror so she was ready when they pulled up. She took a deep breath and slowly released it and told the guys to get ready.

Dre had them on the scope within a two block radius, waiting for them to take the bait. Dre noticed the plates at precisely the same time Mariea did, exhaling in a similar fashion as Mariea as well. Dre could tell by the way they pulled up on them that it was the same pompous, arrogant motherfuckers that threatened Pete; he could feel it with every fiber of his being. It was time.

Showtime, Mariea whispered to herself as she got out of the car to talk to them.

"I was wondering what took ya'll so long. I need 10 grams, 5 for me and five for my sorority sisters," faked Mariea as she turned around pointing at the *Lexus,* revealing her *coochie-cutters* with her ass hanging out of the edges.

More often than not, those that have the pussy want the dope and those that have the dope want the pussy. This was no exception. They could not resist the temptation of Mariea and what sat in the Lexus. Their imaginations taking them to places no amount of acting could induce. Mariea had done her job and done it well.

"Hey sexy, you gotta follow us. We didn't expect anyone wantin' 10 grams. We right over at the *Red Roof* Inn on 33rd Street. Better yet, why don't you and your sisters jump in with us and we'll all cum, I mean, go together!" instructed the driver with an impatience that hormones bring.

They were losing sight of their job, losing site of the rules, something Dre was counting on.

"I don't know about that," offered Mariea as she leaned in to show them her full breasts and give them a whiff of her perfume and her personal pheromones that were secreting their own sexual potion. "You might try to rob us," she continued trying to get a sense of what they were about.

Mariea was educated in street activity but she felt she might be getting in over her head and was trying to buy some time to get her bearings.

In response to the challenge, the man reached under his seat and pulled out a rack of hundred dollar bills.

"I wipe my ass with that kinda money!" bragged the figure now partly revealed by the streetlight as he leaned towards Mariea.

She did not recognize him and her attention was soon diverted as the other guys in the car started to laugh about his comment.

Mariea smiled innocently.

"Okay, hold on, let me go ask my girls what they want to do."

Mariea hopped into the Lex and hit Dre on the speed dial. Her heart raced and her back hurt for some reason. The tension was mounting for her and she needed to keep it together. Munchie and Jason sat impatiently awaiting instructions.

"Dre? Baby, they want us to ride with them to 33rd, The *Red Roof Inn*," informed Mariea trying to create a brave voice to match the brave face she was putting on.
"Perfect, this gonna be easier than I thought!" replied Dre. "We'll be right behind you, no worries baby, we got you, we will take the Lex, just keep the keys in it," comforted Dre.

Jason was meant for the job, playing the role of "Melody". His articulation was a close second to an ejaculation as he stroked one of the members and licked his red lips excessively. Munchie, playing the role of "Janet" was making small talk and Mariea sat in the passenger side with "CEO," flicking her eyes at him and making sure he kept an eye full of her. The guy thought he was the hippest thing since the *twist* and Mariea would use that egotistical persona to her advantage and feed it.

Dre and Pete followed in the shadows, Pete in the *Tahoe* and Dre in the *Lex,* and pulled into the *Red Roof Inn* minutes after the other car filled with Mariea, Jason, Munchie and the group from Michigan. Dre wanted everyone to get settled and if that meant some kisses needed to be given out to buy them some time, so be it. A small price to pay for what was about to happen; a .small price to pay to protect their world, to protect their business, to protect one another.

The Michigan ride was parked outside a room on the lower level away from the lobby. This was convenient for the guys from Michigan but prophetic for Dre and his plan. One less thing to worry about; they didn't need any witnesses, not tonight, not for this.

Dre and Pete exited their vehicles, decked out and packing heat; including bullet proof vests and Desert Eagle glocks with the redline to make sure they didn't miss! Dre could feel his own heart beat and knew that Pete was feeling the same. No words were shared between the two men only the look that each one knew what needed to be done and they were prepared to do it. Dre was feeling like *Jimmy* from the "*Kings of New York*", sporting the twin glocks in the shoulder holster; *all gangster like.*

"Pete, walk around the spot and see how the cameras are facing the building and our exit," instructed Dre wanting to leave nothing to chance.

"Let's just kick the door in and chop some shit down baby! My AK is tuned and ready to be played!" exclaimed Pete all charged up.

"Naw'll, we don't need to draw no extra attention, our glocks are tough enough. I'm gonna peek in threw the curtains first. I will wait for you to come around before I make a move. These *Cain* and *Abel's* going to do the trick too," replied Dre as he snuggled the shooters against his chest.

With each step towards the unit, Dre gripped his hammers and twisted his hands around them. He could hear Pete's footsteps in the other direction. Just then the door next to the room they wanted opened. *Oh shit,* Dre said to himself.

"What's up Mona?" were the only words that Dre could think of at a time like that. The last time he saw her, she was flat on her back, moaning as he pleasured her pink cove of delight.

"Hey Dre, what you doin' over here, getting a room for us?" she replied wittedly.

"Not really. Come walk over to the car with me for a sec," instructed Dre.

"Ain't nobody in the room. You can lay me down on the bed and fuck and suck this pussy. I want to be comfortable for you baby," Mona teased, not knowing that Dre was not coming onto her, rather needing her out of the way. *Wait, maybe in the way,* he thought to himself.

"On second thought, you're right. I need you to do something for me. I need you to get this nigga to open up his door and then for you to get out of the way. Can you do that for me?" asked Dre with a sense of confidence and a lofty feeling of nefarious behavior, a sense that turned Mona on.

As Mona thought too much on the question, Dre intervened to make it simple,

"I have 10 grams of Dog Food and more of this dick if you do it for me!"

"You promise?" she asked.

Dre was almost laughing as to her playing "Ms. Negotiator" when he is about to make Swiss cheese next door.

"Have I ever lied to you baby?" retorted Dre.

By the time Pete returned to them he had scoped out the cameras and grabbed a couple more clips and handed Dre a mask and another set of black gloves matching the ones he had on. Mona now understood what was going on. *Oh shit,* she said to herself.

Mona knocked on the door as both men flanked each side; Dre on the left and Pete on the right.

"Hey is Julie in there?" Mona yelled, using the first name that came to her mind. She knew a Julie once and didn't like her, so why not use it now she thought.

Before the door could come completely open Pete busted through, almost knocking Mona down in the process and blocking Dre's entrance. Pete's glock found the face of the man that opened the door, followed shortly thereafter by Dre's, as he now felt left out considering he came a little late to the party and wanted to make up for it.

The blood splattered across the door like a spiders' web and Mona screamed as the man fell on her and doused her with a red stain. She could feel each of the man's heartbeat's as he lay against her, the blood flowing excessively, covering Mona more and more by the second.

The other guy lay spread eagle on the bed as Jason pleasured him orally. The look on his face was a mixture of ecstasy and fear, he was frozen in motion.

Munchie and Mariea sat on the adjacent couch and yelled,

"There's another one in the bathroom!"

Just as the bathroom door flew open, a 9mm started throwing slugs in Dre's direction, hitting him and knocking him backwards just before Pete filled the man with holes; Bang! Bang! Bang!

The room smelled like sex, blood and smoking steel. The smoke that circled in the air was broken by Dre's body as he fell to the ground with Munchie and Mariea yelling his name, "Dre!"

Just as Dre hit the ground the man who they hit at the door was up and out of his shell-toe *Adidas* trying to run away from the door.

Pete swung around and fired two quick shots trying to at least wing him; Bang! Bang! Resonated off the walls. The man was too quick, Pete missed.

As Pete's head cleared the threshold he turned in the direction the man was running to see him flee up the outside stairwell towards another room. No sooner had the man opened another door then it rained fire down on Pete. Pete could feel the heat of the moment as the rounds flew past him at an alarming rate, shattering everything around him.

The man must have a "street sweeper" Dre thought to himself as he heard the loud shelling outside the motel room.

Dre's adrenaline was redlined and allowing him to regain composer. He walked over to the man on the bed; his pants were still down around his ankles, condom still in place and had one hand on his face and the other on his dick.

"I hope you enjoyed that," swaggered out Dre with tone and mannerisms between John Wayne and Clint Eastwood," cause that is the last one you ever going to get! Jason, take your wig off!" demanded Dre.

The man's eyes said it all, absolute confusion and disbelief as the reality quickly sank in as he stared at Jason kneeling before him with a wig in his hands. The man blinked and his eyes grew even bigger as he replayed the other words in his head, *this is the last one.*

"You hear me, your last!" annunciated Dre with a sense of finality driven by revenge.

Dre looked in the man's eyes, piercing the veil of ignorance as if looking into the man's soul.

"Just to let you know," calmly instructed Dre as he came closer to the man, "when you're in hell, watch out of whose coming after you!"

Dre saw the red light, emanating from his glock, come to rest on the man's forehead. Without hesitation, Dre pulled the trigger. *Sploosh!* went the man's head as it fell back onto the pillow revealing the blood stain on the headboard behind him. The bedcover quickly soaked up the blood and brain matter oozing out the back of his head. Dre thought the glock would be cleaner than that.

The sounds outside of the shoot-out between Pete and the man that escaped quickly reminded Dre the fight wasn't over. He knew he was probably losing blood as the sting he felt a minute ago was now returning, a reminder that he was wounded.

Dre told them to get to the Lex as he joined Pete in the fight. The man was tearing up the world, as the automatic weapon ripped apart the scene. The man was not a good shot, but he could keep a finger on the trigger.

Dre was ducking behind a car hoping the man did not see him, but hoping to get a glimpse or a shot at the guy. Munchie and Jason hit the stash spot in the *Lex* and retrieved the *Rugger* 9mm and another Desert Eagle. They approached sternly, making it a four on one fight that they were determined to win.

This son-of-a-bitch need to eat some metal! Dre said to himself.

The man desperately ran to his car and jumped in, with every intention of getting away. The man was aiming right for Dre, Dre's bullets wouldn't stop the car as he couldn't make the proper angle unless he completely revealed himself. He had no choice. Dre stood up and faced the approaching vehicle. Dre aimed at the driver side and pulled the trigger. The vehicle kept coming at an increasing rate. Dre fell to his knees and exhaled slowly. He felt the pain of the shot and the fact he was losing life as the blood drained out of him. Dre considered this might be his last stand; he closed his eyes and smiled as he pulled the trigger, ready to accept the fate of the gods.

Bam, Bam! Was all Dre heard as the *Lexus* smashed into the side of the man's car. It was Mariea. She sacrificed all for her 'D'. She looked up from the steering wheel with her hair in her face, trying to catch a glimpse of Dre. She could see his image as he sat on his knees hunched over, motionless.

Pete ran to the man's vehicle, shot the window and pulled the trigger again and again, exploding the man's head against the head rest.

"Mariea, are you o.k.?" yelled Pete. "Munchie and Jason, get Dre out of here! Take the vest off him and get him to the hospital! He is losing too much blood!" continued Pete in a frantic yet decisive tone.

"Give me all the guns and straps," continued Pete, "I'll put everything up in the spot and get the Lex outta here before the boppers roll up."

The group complied immediately and handed over all of their weapons, including the AK 47's still in the truck. There was a melancholy to each of their movements even though they were moving quickly. Each of them coming off of the adrenaline rush and reality was setting in; Dre was in trouble.

They made haste and took Dre in the truck to Mercy Hospital. Jason had an acquaintance there, *an acquaintance of reciprocating pleasures,* as Jason flippantly described it. Dealing directly with the doctor allowed for Dre to avoid any unnecessary questions, and most importantly, no police.

As Dre began to grow colder he could not help but dwell on the metallic taste in his mouth. He refused to shiver, he refused to give in; he refused to taste the taste of death.

The bullet went right through and missed any significant artery or vein cluster. Some pain, along with some stitches and a sling like Tony Montana and Dre was out. The scar, that would one day replace the stitched wound and act as a reminder, lay directly above the tombstones of *Will* and *Ball*.

Dre smiled and bowed his head whispering to himself; *thanks for putting in a good word for me to the big man, thanks Will, thanks Ball.*

In all it was a success, less the Lexus that is. No one reveled in death, but in the fact they were all living; it was their victory and not the others defeat that compelled them to enjoy the moment.

"That Lex, look at my car and say, oh brother, I throw it in the gutta and go buy me anotha!" trumpeted Dre, plagiarizing the words of *Easy-E,* "Boyz in the Hood". He was down playing the loss after Mariea told him about the condition of the *Lex*. It wasn't completely totaled, but there was significant damage. In his mind though, there was an entirely different discussion going on; the one with Tonya. He was hoping she would not be too upset with him.

All the group knew at the moment they left the hospital is that they were hungry. They had an insatiable appetite that called for food, and plenty of it. Denny's seemed to be the answer, it was convenient, had a decent variety on the menu and they could see the Denny's sign as they pulled out of the hospital parking lot.

Images of the events rushed through their minds. Each of them now seeded with new disturbing visions to deal with; new demons to conquer. How long it would take for them to forget the events of the day, no one could say for sure, possibly, most likely, never.

It was nothing like the movies. At the movies you have two dimensions, sight and sound. You can't feel the burning of flesh as the bullets rip through or the adrenaline as it rushes through your veins or the odors so pungent and the blood so red. You can't smell the metallic smoke or the certain death around you, and you can't taste the sweat or the blood as it drips into your mouth. Fiction is nothing like the sensational experience of reality.

Munchie looked at Dre with a sense of compassion and Dre returned the expression with one of gratitude, Dre was thankful for the friend, for the confidant, that he had in Munchie.

"Sorry your birthday ended this way Cuzo, I was hoping to really party it up!" confessed Dre to an attentive Munchie.

"It's Aight, Cuzo, I wouldn't have had it any other way. We partied at the club and then we partied on the pavement, what more could one want?" replied Munchie with a smile that confirmed the sinccrity in his claim.

"Straight up, Cuzo!" responded Dre with a distant look as if contemplating all of the tomorrows, "I just don't want you to ever get hurt on my account."

"Straight up," echoed Munchie as he observed the concern on Dre's face. As a small tear ran down Dre's face, Munchie pretended not to notice, but inside he was filled with a wonderment of being loved and he felt indefinitely protected. It felt good and Munchie would hold onto that feeling for as long as he could.

This was as real as it gets. They almost lost their leader. They almost lost the one that tied them all together; the soul of the group, the heart of the family. It all happened so fast, but in retrospect it played out in slow motion and the events would stay with them forever; just another token from the world, the world of *Dog Food.*

Chapter 27
The Dream of Poets

It had been three weeks since the eventful day that left three men dead and Dre's arm still stiff as a remembrance. The papers and the talk on the street revealed no leads and business was back as usual. The last quarter brick of dope was running low, but scaling back a little and slowing things down was determined apropos considering the heat that murders bring to the streets.

Jason was proving to be a vital advisor for diversifying Dre's interests. Dre had invested in an old vacant department store and had turned it into a car wash, beauty shop, record store and restaurant all-in-one type set up. The final stages of construction were under way and things were coming together nicely.

Dre had decided to go the route of a *Ford Excursion* to replace the *Lexus* and purposefully opted for no special effects.

No sound, no tint, no chrome rims, only the headrest stitching that read; *R.l.P. Will and Ball.*

The shot in the arm was as proverbial as it was literal, it changed him. It was a wakeup call for Dre. Not so much for his livelihood but for those around him, for those that he loved, those that he cared for. Dre felt responsible for their futures, whatever that might be.

Mariea and Dre's relationship blossomed as they spent a considerable amount of time together at the house in Marion as Munchie and Pete ran the street business and Jason ran the legitimate business. Dre was in a good place and he was thankful for what he had and vowed not to take it for granted again.

"Dre, your bath is ready!" announced Mariea, as she swirled her hand to feel the temperature of the water and to stir the bubble bath that filled the large corner Jacuzzi tub.

"Thank you baby," politely replied Dre as he walked into the bathroom allowing his bathrobe to fall to the ground, revealing the scar from the wound.

As Dre grabbed his arm and rubbed it gingerly, "my arm is still giving me pain baby, I think I need you to foam me down," stated Dre as more of a solicitation than an offer.

"Well, my patient, do you need me to foam you down or fuck you down?" replied Mariea with a bedside manner that any man would notice. "Plus, I have been waiting to show you this new trick I can do with this new tongue ring I got yesterday," teased Mariea.

"I love the sound of that, let's do the both!" exclaimed Dre with a boyish smile as he flexed his abs, sending Mariea into a sensual whirlwind. She loved his body.

The heated tiles beneath their feet were only the beginning of the heat that was dwelling within them. Mariea put on *Sade,* "By Your Side" as Dre slowly entered the bath.

Mariea floated across the room in nothing but her panties and erect nipples. She moved her body methodically and rhythmically to the feeling of the sound, moving to the soul of the song, "Think I let you down while on your knees, I wouldn't do that," mimed Mariea as she pointed at Dre.

Dre stood up, randomly covered by the bubble bath, revealing portions of his naked sleek body, glistening from the water and his tight skin shining in the light.

"Come here baby," seductively demands Dre.

Mariea goes to him as if in a trance, and Dre awaits her with the same. Each entranced in the others passion and desires, both wanted to give to the other, but willing to receive just as well.

"How I miss that tongue baby, teach me baby, practice what

you preach, but I'll do the honors today," offered Dre in a little more than a whisper.

As their bodies touched, the heat shot through them, exiting out of them as if the two bodies exploded into one. The passion between them was heightened as their personal relationship had grown closer. They no longer needed to pretend; they wanted each other, they desired each other, they needed each other.

Dre gently slid her panties off and helped her into the tub, setting her on the ledge with her pussy resting just above the water line. Dre stared intently into her eyes as if to passionately warn of her of what he was about to do. Mariea moaned.

As Dre's dick hardened from the sensuality of her moan, he knelt down in the tub and began to caress her pussy with his lips. Mariea threw her head back and grabbed his head and held it firmly in her hands, the heat that was emanating off the water had made her moist, seeing his rock hard dick made her wet and now feeling his tongue tantalizing her made her want to cum.

Dre continued to suck the sweet nectar from her honey blossom. The smooth, pink flower that smelled like roses, accepted Dre as he drove his tongue in and all around her.

"Oh, D. you feel so good, I love you so much, don't ever leave me, you are my world," passionately declared Mariea.

The words caught Dre off-guard but they didn't scare him.

In the alternative, they made him feel something inside like he had never felt before. It drove him to want her more, he wanted to suck and suck and suck on her until she couldn't stand it. He wanted to give and give to her until she couldn't move. It was all about him pleasing her and not her pleasing him as he had become accustomed to through all his conquering's.

"Oh, D. don't stop, please don't stop!" begged Mariea.

Dre wanted to show her how much he cared by pleasing her so he had no intention of stopping. Dre slid his hands under her ass cheeks and lifted her slightly off the ledge, plunging his face into her as he gripped her ass in his hands firmly.

Mariea started to buck like a wild bull, wanting Dre to take all of her in him, every ounce, every part of her, body, mind and soul. She was building up and she couldn't stand it. The heat was making her light headed, his pleasuring made her feel like she was floating, she was being overcome by so many emotions and feelings she didn't know where she was or where she was going, only that she loved where she was; in his arms, in him, in love.

Dre stopped as he sensed her willingness and eagerness and slowly turned her around so her ass was bent in the air inviting Dre to enter her. He mounted her like a bull in heat, compassion now drowned by passion being challenged by pure animal desire. Their emotional closeness now pushed them to higher animalistic heights sexually, a contradiction that they could not explain.

Dre rode her hard, filling her with every inch of him as her hair swayed back and forth caressing the crack of her ass, as he ran his fingers along her sides.

Dre grabbed her hair and lifted it off her back as if reins on a bronco.

"Whose pussy is this; whose pussy is this?" Dre repeated over and over again as he inhaled the sweet fragrance of *Red Dior*.
"It's yours D, it's yours. We were meant to be lovers!" Mariea declared in one full voice. "Oh, your dick feels so fucking good!"
"Not as good as your wet, warm, tight pussy." Dre whispered as he bent forward.

Mariea couldn't take it anymore, she thrust herself against him wanting to fill him feel her up inside.

"Cum in your pussy, do whatever you want with your pussy, I'm....about....to....cum!" Mariea forced out of her with each breath she had left.

It was a contest of who could cum first, who could hold on the longest, back and forth, stuck in the moment between orgasm and climax, a moment all lovers wish they could hold in place.

"Oh D!" was followed by, "Oh, Mariea!" as both yelled each other's name out over and over again until you couldn't tell who was saying whose.

They both began to shake causing them to drive harder towards one another, wanting to feel safe, hoping the other would catch them if they were to fall.

They exploded inside each other, leaving a part of them in the other, rendering them full not empty. The emptiness they felt as individuals was filed by the union of their partnership, by the love and passion they shared. They both collapsed into the water.

Dre fell into the tub, splashing water off the back, feeling the warm sensation of the water on his neck and the sensation on his skin as the hot water cleansed him; he was intoxicated on love.

Mariea could feel her heart beat as if it were to shoot out of her chest; she had to make an effort to control her breathing. She could feel the remains of Dre drip out of her and the numbness she felt as her body was absorbed by the hot water. She thought she was dreaming and she felt safe. For the first time in her life she genuinely felt safe.

They gently foamed one another down, speaking only with their hands as they gently massaged each inch of one another. They were physically exhausted, but refreshed emotionally and nourished spiritually. This was something that felt so right, something the poets only dream of, one of the blessings that they found each other on such a path, on the path of *Dog Food.*

Chapter 28
Million Dollar Scheme

Dre and Mariea enjoyed each other's company that day as time was no matter, with one moment flowing into the next. To feel so close to someone gave them both comfort, their relationship had evolved beyond the physical intercourses and now encompassed the emotional. They didn't feel like they needed to pretend around each other to gain acceptance and that made them feel safe and genuinely desired. They found a *tranquility* amidst the chaos; it was peaceful.

As comforting as their company was to one another, business needed to go on. By 4:30 the following morning, Dre, Munchie and Dusty were at it like thieves in the night. They were in the *Excursion* back to CHI having already dropped Mariea off.

Pete had enough Dog Food to last until they returned, but other matters laid heavily on Dre's mind.

He knew it was about time to bring Mama down to Iowa, but he also felt it was time to bring down Tonya. It was like a door that Dre walked through or a switch that could somehow be turned off or on. He had just felt so close to someone and now, just out of her presence, he has concerns for another? Was it a concern for their relationship or more of a concern of hurting her? Was it a guilt that drove Dre towards Tonya or was it something more? He didn't know and today he would not answer it.

Munchie was behind the wheel causing Dre to laugh inside to see this little stature of a man controlling such a big ride like the *Excursion.*

"Cuzo, I can't believe how big this thing is, it's like a RV camper almost!" excitedly exclaimed Munchie.
"Yeah Cuzo, big trucks for big Niggas like us, straight up, straight up!" responded Dre.
"Jason asked how long we were going to be down here and I told him a couple of days," asked Munchie in the form of a statement.
"That's cool," replied Dre, "cause even though we been doin' good business, I'm still like Nino, 'I don't trust a mother fucker but you' Munchie money."

An hour or so into the trip the sun started to fill the horizon, shooting rays of red, orange and yellow in every direction. It was a sight to behold as Munchie stared into the magic blend of hues as Dre and Dusty slept. Munchie would find himself lost in thought, absorbed by the warm colors on his face and the smell of a fresh new day emanating off the fields as he sped past.

The shoulder ruts would wake him occasionally from his stupor and remind him he was driving, a sobering experience.

"You cool Cuzo, you want me to take over" inquired Dre as the bumps had awaken him as well.
"I'm alright Cuzo, I just went in deep thought about somethin'," conceded Munchie.
"Aight, we got a truck full of cash in here, close to a half-mill based on Mariea's count, so let's keep it all smooth," reminded Dre.

By 7:30 they were to the CHI exiting the Independence ramp heading towards Central Park. They needed to holler at Slick and Dre needed to put his bid in for his re-up on that *Dog Food.*

When they arrived, it was like a ghost town. Something Dre had never seen. Slick was always hustling, always open for business, *twenty-four hours a day, come sleet, rain or snow, you could always count on Slick for some blow*, Dre thought to himself. Today, there was nothing. Something was obviously amiss.

"Damn! What the fuck going on over here! Pull over and let me go holla at Regina and see what's the business," exclaimed Dre in a concerning yet irritated tone.

As Munchie pulled over to let Dre out he was filled with all kinds of thoughts, none of them good.

Dre knocked on the door, sensing his impatience growing only to be met with a half-naked Regina in just a *Camisole.*

"Put on a robe," commanded Dre as he let himself in.

"It's too early, this is how I sleep. Next time I will just answer the door completely naked," cheekily replied Regina.

This ain't nothin; but a little hoe, Dre thought to himself, trying to concentrate on the matter at hand as her full breasts and ass were looking good, almost too good to resist.

"Where's Slick?" raced out of Dre's mouth before thoughts of Regina took up too much of his mind.

"He's in jail. They arrested him and five other guys last night. He hasn't called me yet, but I'll give you a call when he calls me," offered Regina trying to comfort Dre.

"Aight lil' mama, keep me posted on him," Dre answered hurriedly as he walked back out the door just as abruptly as he walked in it.

Dre jumped back into the truck, his voice was silent but his mannerisms and facial expressions were speaking volumes.

"What's up Cuzo, you got a curious look on," observantly commented Munchie.

"Man, Slick locked up," Dre admitted with an emptiness.

"For what?"

"Regina said they arrested Slick and five other Niggas last night and he hasn't called her yet. This, while she was trying to throw her pussy on me, so I didn't stand around and wait for anymore," replied Dre with multiple frustration and irritation precipitated by Regina's actions considering the circumstances.

"Snoop said it best on the *Chronic,* 'Bitches Ain't Shit'!" exclaimed Munchie with a sense of pride.

"Yeah, who am I going to spend this money to cop with?" Dre asked the nothingness between them. "I never knew his connect."

"Man Cuzo, I had to get outta there before my dick started doin' the thinking; but you swing at bees they'll sting you that bitch was campaigning hard"

The words hung in the air, neither not sure what to say. It was certainly not a move in the positive direction for their business, but at the same time, Dre was envisioning a change. He was not sure what the change was going to be, but it would have been on his terms. This was simply a catalyst towards change; an element that is not only essential in building a successful business, but necessary. The world evolves and so too should your business. Dre was ready, he just wasn't too comfortable with how this part was going down.

Before Dre could play it out in his head Munchie pulled up to Mama's house. The quietness and serenity of her comfortable home, and the memories that resided within, always gave Dre a sense of ease, something he needed at this moment.

When Dre and Munchie walked into the kitchen and found Mama sitting meditatively over a cup of coffee. Dre broke her trance with a clearing of his throat and when Mama looked up at Dre, she lifted her head towards the clock, it was 8:30.

"I was just sitting here thinking about my four babies, but you most of all DeAndre and here you are standing in front of me. Thanks be to the heavens. Now come over here and give your Mama a hug and a kiss."

Dre sheepishly walked over to Mama with his head down just slightly and as he approached he lifted his head so their eyes could meet, he could see the love in her for him. He had missed her too, only he didn't know how much until that moment when he hugged her. Dre felt a lonely tear fall down his face.

"Hey, Mama," whispered Dre into his mother's ear, "I have missed you and I love you."
"Oh, how I have missed you, love you and I am so happy to see you!" exclaimed Mama.

Mama looked years younger from when they first saw her sitting there. How she brightened up when Dre was around her, it was amazing. It was like a type of fountain of youth for her and it showed.

"Mama is going to work," she announced as an afterthought.
"Mama, let me take you," insisted Dre.

"I'm fine taking the *El-Train*. I will see you when I get off if you're still here," Mama replied with equal stubbornness as she grabbed her bag and headed out the door giving Munchie a hug and kiss as well.

Dre and Munchie took the opportunity to get some rest while Dusty roamed in the back yard. Each one of them content with where they were; Munchie was with his best friend and Cuzo, Dre was in his Mama's house and Dusty was free to roam.

Dre was awakened by the constant intrusive ringing of Mama's phone, *Ring, Ring, Ring!*

"Hello?" Dre was able to get out in hopes of making the ringing go away.

"You have a collect call from Edward Bone, do you accept the charges," methodically inquired the operator on the other end of the line.
"Yes, yes," replied Dre with equal frankness.
"Hey Dre, what's up?" started Mr. Bone.
"Mr. Bone, how, how are you?" politely asked Dre with a sense of caution and anxiousness in his voice.
"Well, despite my circumstances, I'm at peace," answered Mr. Bone with a confidence that came with so many years of learning and insight.
"I have been watching you all the way through your junior and senior times, but are you ready for the pros?" asked Mr. Bone with a sense of pride.

"What you talkin' about Mr. Bone?" asked Dre with an ever growing anxiousness and curiosity.

"I don't do that much talking on these phones. I've been getting real good reports on you and I brought a scout to bring you to the big leagues. You know her well and she has a couple big surprises for you too. Look out your window. I will call you later."

Then he was gone.

Dre looked out the window and there she sat in a cherry red *Benz* all tinted out, but Dre could feel her peering out, staring at Dre.

Miss Mindy? Dre thought to himself. *Could it be? What would she be doing here?*

Dre hung up the phone and almost as if in a trance, walked outside to the vehicle and tried to look inside, but it was too dark to definitively tell who occupied the ride. He heard the unlocking of the doors and immediately hopped to the passenger side and got in.

The smell hit him first; luxury and perfume emanating from the vehicle, filling him with even more anxiousness. When he heard the pop of the gum, it was confirmed. When he turned and looked into those hazel, welcoming eyes, his heart skip.

"Hey Ms. Mindy!" exclaimed Dre.

"Are you surprised to see me?" she flirtatiously asked Dre.

"Yeah I am, straight-up, straight-up!" Dre replied without a moment of hesitation.

"I see you have been a real busy man, movin' from Cedar Rapids to CHI Town and back again."

"How you know that?" asked Dre as a child asking a magician about his trick.

"I know a lot of stuff that you don't know I know. I need to update you on some things that you don't know about" she replied with a tone of espionage right out of a movie.

"Like what?"

"First of all, Edward is ready to give you the world and I'm having your world," she stated in a calm proud way as she rubbed her stomach gently and stared intently into Dre.

Now he knew why it seemed like she was glowing, but the moment between the realization and the articulation was too laggardly.

"What are you talking about Ms. Mindy?" asked Dre in a fog between a reality of denial and a fiction of acceptance.

"Dre, I'm pregnant, it is your child and I am having it whether you want me to or not," she replied as if she had rehearsed this moment over and over.

"How do you know that's my baby?" asked Dre reactively as he looked down at her stomach.

"I wasn't the only Nigga you were giving that pussy to in the County," continued Dre in an adolescent reply driven by fear and uncertainty of having a child, but knowing inside that she was telling him the truth.

"Dre, Niggas can call me a lot of things, but a hoe I'm not! After the first time we had sex, this pussy didn't come out the cage for no Nigga!" Ms. Mindy declared with a sense of confidence and yearning to be believed and supported.

"What about Mr. Bone?" asked Dre.
"What about him? I work for him. That is why I am over here on my day off!"

Dre sat there motionless, his mind was running faster than he liked. He couldn't put all the pieces together right then and there as he was accustomed to. It was unnerving to the point of a little frightening for him; to be a father.

"Whatcha worried about that brown skinned girl with the Halle Berry hair-do I seen you with at the hotel?" threatened Ms. Mindy.
"How do you know about her and how did you see us at the hotel?" shot back Dre with intention and purpose.

Any fear he had vanished in a moment with the challenge before him.

"I was doing what I'm doing right now! Working for Edward and his interests!" exclaimed Ms. Mindy.
"You'll looked kinda cute if you ask me," mumbled Ms. Mindy as if to give a compliment but not too much of one as

she did have feelings for Dre behind the bedroom.

"Enough wit the small talk and surprises, what brings you here and the call from Mr. Bone?" interjected Dre to steer away from the topic and the acceptance, contemplation and internalizing of the prospect of becoming a father.

As they drove down the expressway heading towards Michigan Avenue, Ms. Mindy explained everything to Dre. As they pulled into the parking lot of the Amber Inn, one owned by Mr. Bone, Dre was still rustling with the possibility of fatherhood as the notion fought for attention over the idea of Mr. Bone wanting Dre for something more.

As they headed toward the Suite, Dre gazed at Ms. Mindy's sexy walk and stared at that ass that he had had so many times in his hands, as he rode her pussy back in County. He reminisced, methodically in his mind how he would pleasure her and how she would pleasure him.

Damn, this just might be my baby, Dre conceded to himself.

Once inside the suite, the phone rang just as if programmed, timely and efficient. It was Mr. Bone.

Mr. Bone proceeded to explain to Dre that he had eyes and ears everywhere, a valuable resource that he learned so many years ago, information and location was paramount to Mr. Bone. He confided in Dre that he knew that his connect was locked-up and that when he received the first half of the key of *Coke* for

$3,000, that was a test. Mr. Bone also included his disclosure of how he set Dre up with the full key for $17,000 as well. When his Uncle went to jail with his half, continued Mr. Bone, and that Dre came up from that, Mr. Bone instructed Slick to give him all the plays.

Mr. Bone had effectuated everything, or so it seemed to this point. So much so, that Dre wasn't sure what part he had earned and what part he had been given.

"Give me twenty-four hours and you'll be taking a blizzard with you in the summer time," expressed Mr. Bone with the voice of conviction and sincerity.
"Ms. Mindy will give you a phone to carry and we'll call periodically for the deposit," Mr. Bone instructed.

Visions flashed through Dre's mind like a tornado across the field, ripping apart anything in its way, any previous notion of who he was, who he was to become and what he was about, was now coming to fruition; Dre was meeting his destiny.

"Are you ready Dre?" asked Mr. Bone.

Before all the words were out of Mr. Bones' mouth, Dre replied, "More than you know, Mr. Bone, more than you know."

Ms. Mindy and Dre found their way to the elevator and out the Lobby immediately following the conclusion of Dre's conversation with Mr. Bone. Ms. Mindy did not ask him what the call was about and Dre did not offer. The walk was silently but purposeful.

While they waited for the Valet to bring their car around, Dre's attention was captured by a blue *Puegot* parked in front of the hotel, so much so that he walked around it to take a closer look.

"I like this car. Its low key, but sporty on the luxury side," observed Dre.
"That's a *Peugeot.* You probably can't even pronounce it, it's from France, named after a cat that looks like a lion. It's a nice sedan and I see that you like it. By the way, it's Edward's. Take it for a spin," instructed Ms. Mindy with a sense of pride and soft authority.
"I'll take you up on that offer," replied Dre as he stalked the vehicle, appreciating the emerald cat on the grill and the blue leather interior.
"You right daddy. I'll give you a call," answered Ms. Mindy as if to denote a conclusion to their meeting.

"Hey, wait, you haven't given me a phone so you can call me," interjected Dre hurriedly.
"I'll call you Dre," she replied as she jumped into her Benz and pulled away. Just like that, she was gone.

Dre shook his head in wonderment and hopped in the car. As he pulled out of the Lobby area, the phone in the car rang. On the dashboard, above the steering wheel was an indicator informing Dre that there was an incoming phone call. Dre pushed the little phone icon on the steering wheel.

"Hello?" asked Dre sheepishly.

"I knew that you would have liked that ride!" immediately announced the voice on the other end.

"How you know that?" curtly replied Dre with a smile.

"You and I, we have very similar tastes. That is one of my reasons for recruiting you," replied Mr. Bone.

"I like this car, yes I do! So, the twenty-four hours, does that start now or later?" anxiously inquired Dre.

"Twenty-four hours started when you cranked that engine. So, drive carefully because there is a false bottom in the trunk, under the spare where you will find all you need and more. You will also find a phone. Hit the number that is taped on it when you are ready."

"Good looking, Mr. Bone. I won't drop the ball!" avowed Dre with a sense of conviction and commitment.

"That's why you are on my court. You say you want to be a controller and not the customer, well, here is your chance. So, the ball is in your court. Keep your eyes open. Later Dre," provided Mr. Bone, like a Magi to a student.

There was a mystical aura about the events, one that Dre couldn't put his finger on. Dre was aware of his station, cognizant of the events that had unfolded, but to what ends or measures he knew not. It was a fast ride to the top and Dre was ready for control. He felt he had earned it and that he deserved it, but the world would show him all of that which he inherited so quickly in this rewarding yet treacherous world; the world of *Dog Food.*

Chapter 29
Dog Catcher I I I

The lieutenant under Captain Boot's authority was determined to make good on his promise; I swear I am going to find *the people* behind *the* drugs *that* killed *the Captain's brother,* he said to himself routinely; a self-motivating mechanism.

So far he had one of his informants grab the VIN number from under the hood of the suspect van and ran a search on the title and came up with a name; *Terry Dent.*

In addition, he uncovered that Mr. Dent was presently being held on other charges in the Linn County jail. Considering the jail was only a few blocks from the department, the Lieutenant decided to walk there personally and pay Mr. Dent a little visit.

Mr. Dent was sitting back on the *Max Block* playing *spades,* talking shit and as high as the sky off *that Dog Food;* nay a concern in the world despite his plight.

"What did Rodney King get beat with?" trumpeted Terry as he slammed his cards on the table.

"Clubs! Clubs mother fucker! This new spade in town! See, I told ya'll young Nigga's it's more than one way to skin a cat and I got them for days! For days!" bragged Terry as he continued to unload his hand full of clubs. His partner was quick to pick up the "books" and count their winnings as Terry finished his demonstration with a long rub of his nose as snot ran out of it.

"Dent, Dent, you have a visitor," came crashing through the PA system causing Terry to pause for a moment as it caught him off guard. *Who the fuck can be visitin' me?* He thought to himself.

"I don't know why my lawyer want to see me. Shit, he working against me instead of working for me, the racist bastard," commented Terry to the rest of the table.

The group went up in a roar. Terry always kept them laughing and even when things were not funny, they kept laughing because Terry scared the shit out of them.

Terry slowly rose, pulled his jump suit all the way up and meandered towards the open gate as the officer escorted him down the hallway to a meeting room.

Terry's face was more stoic than when he played cards as

he walked into the room and looked into the unknown eyes of the gentleman seated across the table from him. *Who the fuck is this guy?* he shouted to himself.

The man stood up as Terry approached, extended his hand and in a confident respectful tone recited, "Hi, my name is lieutenant Dukin."

Before the man's last breath pushed out the words, Terry responded definitively,

"What the fuck going on here? What you think I'm about to rat on a motherfucker? Get me outta here! I wish I had a good lawyer to call. Shit, he probably your brother for all I know. I ain't got shit to talk about on my case!" exhaustively articulated Terry with great emphasis.

Terry did not extend a hand reciprocating the Lieutenants' common gesture of pleasantry.

"I'm not here about your case. Mr. Dent," replied the Lieutenant with equal frankness, but maintaining an element of professionalism as he slowly withdrew the hand he had extended.

That always pissed Terry *off,* how guys like this could stay so calm when underneath they were lying or had a hidden agenda. Terry was not naive to the streets and he could play the game as good as anybody.So, he did.

"Well, shit! You want to fill me in on why you taking me away from my good ass *spade* game I'm playin' for candy bars?" inquired Terry with a grin and flare bordering on obnoxious.

"I didn't mean to disturb your game Mr. Dent," replied the Lieutenant while trying not to laugh or smirk at Terry's dry sense of humor.

"Does this van belong to you Mr. Dent?" followed up the Lieutenant as he slid a picture across the table for Terry to look at.

Terry didn't blink. He sat back and slowly put his feet on the table.

"These the only *Vans* that belongs to me," answered Terry with a sense of pride in his witticism as he nodded at the shoes on his feet.

"This what the fuck you came to holler at me about? I don't know who the fuck owns that van. I'm probably gonna get life. Hell, I'm goin' to trial in a couple days," confided Terry with a sense of urgency, coupled with an underlying pleading that had unconsciously surfaced.

The Lieutenant sat quietly waiting for Terry to finish.

"That's you and Shaggy's van right off *Scooby* Doo! *Scooby, Scooby Doo* where are you mother fucker, where are you?" mimicked Terry as he pointed at the Lieutenant.

Terry held the long "O" until it vanished into the air and was absorbed by the rage in the lieutenant.

"Officer! Take this man back to his block, in max, A-block!" commanded the Lieutenant, "We have had enough fun for today," as he slowly slid the picture back into the manila folder and shook his head in disappointment.

This did not go as the Lieutenant had planned. He wanted so badly to tie the van to someone, to something, and this Mr. Dent was no help at all. Both men knew that Terry was lying, but it didn't matter, that's how the game was played. The lieutenant was confident in his hand; he was relying on the deck he could stack against Terry.

There were not many rules in the jungle and there were fewer on the streets. Terry knew this and so did Lieutenant Dukin. However, you called it, Terry won the moment, but did very little to save the day. Life is fickle and you play the best hand you can with the cards that are dealt to you, and a Royal Flush was not always the best hand in the world of *Dog Food*.

Chapter 30
Pete's Way

To the West things were still wild. While Pete waited on Dre to re-up, he was selling only bags, no real weight. He had to work harder than usual but he was contented by the fact that he was in charge of a million-dollar operation. *Where else can a junkie find such a vocation?* He thought to himself.

Pete no longer had that drawn-out-dirty look that he had carried with him for so many years. He stood more upright now and was outfitted with a new platinum *FUBU* outfit trimmed with the latest *Air Max's*. He looked the part and he felt the part, he had been transformed; he was a new man.

Pete had always had a knack for numbers and every dollar that ended up in Dre's or Munchie's pocket, Pete had counted. Pete would sit back and let the numbers fly as a square hung at the corner of his mouth.

It came easy to Pete and he liked doing something that he was good at, that not everyone else was. It would make him feel good about himself and allow him to suppress the reminders of the so many short-comings he had experienced in his life. Pete would even think to himself from time to time, *hell I coulda been a mathematician.*

Pete also knew that while he could count, he could just as easily spend. He loved to trick off and smoke cocaine. He was a functioning addict and as long as he always had a fix he would be just fine. So, as he was proficient in accounting he was just as weak in the concept of saving; a dichotomy that he never seemed to overcome.

"Hey mother fucker, is this all right baby?" asked Pete as he counted out five grand in a flash as the worker who had just handed him the pile turned around.

Pete was sitting in the van overlooking the spot as he usually did, and having his people bring him the money to the van made it efficient and effective for Pete. Pete continued to count the stacks of money on his lap as he listened to *Curtis Mayfield,* "Think".

Pete would often reflect on his journey to this point. He would reminisce over all those years of using, so much so that his veins were now collapsed and his hands were not as big as boxing gloves from the years of abuse caused by all of the Heroin.

I might as well leave the past just where it is, in the past, Pete concluded to himself as he walked to the back of the van to get him a fix. The walk down memory lane for Pete was not one filled with sunshine and roses. As he would remember certain events of his past, he would be struck with regret and remorse. He would frequently end with wishful thinking that he could have been someone different, he could have been better, a better man than he was. This hurt too much so he needed an out; he needed an escape from the pain.

Without Munchie and Dre around, he answered to no one and he liked that. His mannerism revealed a certain arrogance in their absence as he often referred to himself as the "under boss".

Pete methodically broke his *works* out and kicked his shoes and socks off. There was not much there any longer to choose from. The vision flashed through his mind of the time he resorted to finding a large vein in his dick. *Not today though,* he thought to himself, *please not today.*

By the time the Dog Food was heated, Pete had his ankle tied up. He tapped on the most visible vein anticipating the surging through his body and then it hit him like a warm rising sun on his face. The warmth traveled throughout his body, sending jovial release to his face like *Scatter* off "Superfly," right before an overdose. He was in paradise as the sound track played in his ears and his head did the *yo-yo bounce.*

Pete was addicted to the drug, but he was more addicted to the feelings that he would escape from. His life had not been easy and as he wrestled with his demons he tried to cope. His only friend, the one that never let him down, the one that always made him feel better, and always made him feel safe was the gracious food, the pure giving of *Dog Food*. While Pete laid back and realized he was an addict, he felt comfortable with his friend there by his side, he took everything from it he could and he was unaware of what it was taking from him.

Chapter 31
Blue Prints

Dre pulled up to the front of Mama's house full of thoughts, one in particular kept reappearing; *why didn't Slick tell him that Mr. Bones was his connect?*

Dre followed Mr. Bones' directions, heading straight back to Mama's keeping a low profile. He did not bother to check out how much dope he had in the trunk, as he rested confidently in Mr. Bones' indication and concluded that he was on easy street. Life was good and he conceded that, *not everything in life needed to be explained.*

"Cuzo? Cuzo" yelled Dre as he walked into Mama's house.

"What's up Cuzo?" answered Munchie with a concerned look on his face as he ran down the stairs to meet Dre.

Dre started laughing at the look on Munchie's face.

"My bad Cuzo, we more than all right. I just hollered at one of my partners that gave me enough dope that we don't have to come back down here to cop until Christmas!" declared Dre with a sense of accomplishment.

"Get outta here! Are you serious?" replied Munchie.

"Yes, Cuzo, I am serious," replied Dre with a sense of ease and a prelude to something more that he needed to say.

Dre told Munchie everything. He summarized the history of the preceding months as he now understood them. He told him about Mr. Bones, the time they spent together in county jail and how he was Slick's connect. He highlighted his moments of fucking Ms. Mindy, how she worked for Mr. Bones and he even mentioned the blue *Peugeot*. He told him everything.

"Cuzo," steadily addressed Dre, "let's get our bags and the cash and we out!"

"How are we taking two cars?" inquired Munchie immediately following the instruction.

"You and Dusty is driving in the truck and hopefully me, Mamma and Tonya driving the *Peugeot*," explained Dre with a hint of hesitation and hopefulness.

"You taking Tonya? What about those girls in Iowa? You know Tonya going to read all that!" cautioned Munchie.

Dre nodded as he walked away from Munchie towards the truck to go to Tonya's house. He decided it was best to leave the *Peugeot* parked in front of Mama's house where Munchie could keep an eye on it.

Tonya came out of the house looking fine as usual. She was

sporting a nice blazer with a pair of jeans and *LV* slippers. Her hair was sexy as always and the smell of her perfume that filled the cab when she entered could have woke and man from the dead.

"Hey hunny-bunny!" Tonya greeted Dre with a brilliant smile and enthusiasm to match. "When did you get this ride?"

"A couple of weeks ago," replied Dre curtly. "Where's the Lex?"

"Oh, I had a minor accident," answered Dre while focusing on keeping a straight face when he answered.

"Dre! That car was in my name. I hope didn't nobody get hurt or anything," Tonya sympathetically complained while fishing for more of the story.

"Baby, calm down. It wasn't my fault at all. Some guys hit it while I had it parked trying to get away from the police," offered Dre as a completion of the story, hoping it would suffice.

"My bad baby," reacted Tonya, "I'm so sorry not thinking you're responsible. Here, give me a kiss. I miss you," finished Tonya.

It worked. That was enough to pacify her curiosity. *It was almost too easy,* Dre thought, but he didn't have the interest or inclination to pursue such a course of conversation or thought as to why that was enough. He had other plans that took precedent.

"Listen, baby, I need you to take your vacation days and go with me to Iowa," informed Dre.

"When, baby?"

"Like, yesterday," answered Dre.

"Why didn't you let me know ahead of time? I'll try, but I hate lying to people or putting them in a tough spot." As Tonya took out her cell phone to call her boss a thought occurred to her; *one's lack of planning should not necessitate an emergency on another's.* The words almost came out of her mouth, but she bit her tongue knowing that Dre may not appreciate her candor.

Tonya's boss bought the story, believing her convincing version of it anyways and they were off to Iowa. However, Mamma was not going to make it, *but one out of two ain't bad,* Dre thought to himself. *Plus, he had just given her a large stack,* he rationalized.

The ride to Marion was peaceful. Dre opted not to divulge to Tonya what was in the trunk. He figured it would make her worried and he wanted to enjoy the time together. Dre always appreciated the scenery, so did Munchie as he followed behind in the truck with Dusty.

Tonya had driven the path many times before when visiting her brother in Minnesota or when she made the twenty-hour trek to see her aunt in Florida. She had seen the road in every direction so she did not appreciate it as much as Dre and Munchie.

The couple looked like they owned the road. They had on their shades, dressed sharp and the truck in tow made them feel like they were being escorted. They fit the role.

They made it to Marion safely and dropped Tonya off at the house along with Dusty and Munchie jumped in with Dre.

"Munchie, were about to go over here down the street by the *Hy-Vee* and get a storage spot to put all this dope in," informed Dre.

Dre was always thinking about his product. He needed to keep it safe but he needed it accessible. A storage garage or space would work best he thought.

They rented unit number 1227, a unit so spacious they drove the Peugeot into it. In the abruptness of the plan, as it were, neither man had a lock, so they had to make a trip back to the office to purchase one. On the way, Dre made a note of the security cameras.

Once inside they turned the lights on and opened the trunk. They removed the spare tire and unloaded the items from the false bottom revealing ten whole bricks of pure heroin. They were now the official *Pet-Smart* of *Dog Food*.

"I told you we was on like a light," remarked Dre.
"We on like Buzz-Light Year!" echoed Munchie.
"Hey, Cuzo, let's put the load back into the trunk. Shit, here's a shopping bag. Let's put one brick in here and we will call Pete and have him pick us up in front of the *Hy-Vee,*"

offered Dre.

Dre proceeded to pop the hood, take the car key off his key ring and place it carefully on the battery. He locked the door behind them with the padlock.

The walk to the *Hy-Vee* was full of irony. They were two guys, dressed out, walking down the street and carrying a grocery bag worth more than most of the cars that drove by them. Dre started to laugh silently.

Pete drove up ten minutes later, he was eager to see them and the "re-up" as he was almost out. They headed back to Dre's place in Marion and when they walked in Tonya was lying comfortably on the leather sofa all snuggled up with Dusty. It was a sight. Dre laughed silently again.

"Hey baby, this my man Pete," acknowledged Dre as he made the introduction to Tonya.
"How are you Pete, it's a pleasure," replied Tonya with a courteous articulation that demonstrated not only her intellect, but her demeanor. It made her sexy.
"Hello, Ms. Tonya. The pleasure's all mines," replied Pete as he nodded in her direction.
"You sure can tell she from the CHI. She so jazzy," whispered Pete to Dre as they walked into the kitchen.
"That's my baby, she was down for Nigga when I was down and out," responded Dre with appreciation and pride.
"And Bobby Womack said it best, don't nobody wants ya

when you down and out'," added Pete with a smile.

Dre looked at Pete as if though he was looking through him. It was so intense it made Pete a little uncomfortable. Dre was taking it all in; a flash of a moment suspended in time for him to see. His Cuzo was in the next room with his girl and Dusty. He had a full brick with him to put in play and he had nine more in the batter's box. He had a house, cars and plenty of cash and he dressed well; life was good.

He had risen fast, but that was customary in a fast paced industry. He knew that for those who rose fast, the fall was even faster if they didn't stay ahead of the game. Dre was not to fall. He had a plan and he was adamant that it would work. He was determined to maintain a reign, to create a legacy, to beat the odds that were against him, as so was this world in which he now began to rule, the world of *Dog Food*, or so he thought.

Chapter 32
Land of Fire

The three-hour drive, no matter how many times they did it, was always a little taxing. Dre was eager to show Tonya the town, so he instructed Pete to hook up with Jason and Mariea and to take a quarter brick of the dope with him as well, so he and Tonya could freshen up.

Within the hour, Dre, Tonya and Munchie were feeling revitalized and ready to hit the road. Dusty would be left to fend for himself, but Dre caught a glimpse of Dusty as he was leaving. Dre was mesmerized by the look on Dusty's face, just like that day on the street; so sad and so lonely that it melted Dre's heart. He bent down and patted Dusty, rubbing behind his ears until the look transformed from one of sadness to one of contentment. Dre smiled.

Dre decided to take the *Excursion,* it was less conspicuous and provided ample room for all of them. Dre preferred sitting up high, as opposed to the low ride of a sedan, and it made Tonya feel safer.

She was caught up in her thoughts and the excitement. She was filled with anticipation of the enjoyable time that she and Dre were going to have, just the two of them. It was quality time that she needed with him.

"Hey baby, I want to show you something that I bought," commented Dre with a subdued excitement.
"What is it hunny-bunny, another new car?" inquired Tonya in a quick kidded response, bordering on sarcasm.
"Naw, it got somethin' to do with a Realtor like yourself and with some property," proudly replied Dre.

The words echoed in the air as they pulled in front of an old department store. A smile came across Tonya's face.

Dre escorted Tonya and Munchie inside the empty space. Its size alone was impressive, but Tonya was suspicious as to what his intentions were. She refrained from making any comments or judgments until she had given Dre a chance to explain.

"This is really nice," offered Tonya, fishing for additional insight, "how much is you buying it for without the repairs?"

Dre told her the numbers and how they tied in with his overall vision, one consisting of divided business.

"I want to divide it into multiple businesses; I wanna have a beauty shop, carwash, a restaurant and a record store all in one.

"Baby," started Tonya with sincerity, "I'm not trying to discourage you in any kinda way, but it is going to take a very large sum of money to operate four distinct businesses and there is no guarantee you will profit anything until the second or third year," she finished in a concerned business, yet personable manner.

"From where I come from, I am willing to take that chance!" exclaimed Dre with a sense of defiance and determination that made Dre, Dre.

"That's what I love about you Dre, the confidence and you're willingness to say, 'all or nothing', with what you believe in," shared Tonya with a genuine admiration.

"Whose name is it in?" quickly followed the inquisitive mind of Tonya.

"The ink isn't even dry yet, but just so you know, it will be in your name. After all, the name of the place is going to be *Tonya's,*" explained Dre with a smirk and a sense of warmth in him.

Dre took two steps and had her in his arms, looking down on her with such compassion and gratitude for all she had done for him. She reciprocated the look and their eyes expressed all that needed to be said at that moment. She buried her head into his chest and smiled.

They embraced, both knowing what the other was saying and the physical contact only added to the declaration how much they appreciated one another. Munchie looked on with understanding and envy.

Dre locked up and as they were returning to the truck discussing the various aspects of Dre's vision and Tonya's insight, Munchie's phone began to ring.

"Hello?" asked Munchie sheepishly not recognizing the number on his screen and listened intently. He nodded every so often, answering in the affirmative, "yes" or "I understand."
"Okay, in 30 minutes," were the last words out of Munchies' mouth as they entered the vehicle.

Not knowing what the voice on the other end was saying, coupled with the seriousness in Munchies' demeanor, made Dre and Tonya nervous.

"Cuzo that was my dad's attorney. Dad is going to trial tomorrow and it looks like he has a good chance of getting *off* due to a *non-knock search warrant* and several other technicalities," explained Munchie with a hope and concern caught in his voice.

"That's good than a motherfucker. We partyin' tonight for Unc, for yo' dad! We need Terry out here with us, straight up, straight up!" declared Dre triumphantly. "What else did the lawyer say," inquired Dre.
"I told him I could meet with him in thirty minutes, to give me more information on the case," replied Munchie.

"That's cool Cuzo, 'cuz we goin' to the crib to get him a lil' grease for his palms anyways!" emphatically declared Dre in support.

They expeditiously headed back to Marion, all of them in a quiet concentration. When they arrived Dre ran into the house and grabbed twenty-thousand out of the safe and put it in a brown envelope. He returned to the car, handing it to Munchie.

"There's twenty large in there for the attorney," announced Dre.

"Hunny-bunny, money like that should be in an interest bearing account, instead of in that safe, under your mattress or in your suit pockets," informed Tonya, the consummate business minded individual that she was.

"You sure know all of the hidin' spots, don't you baby?" teased Dre.
"Wait, I forgot the refrigerator!" exclaimed Tonya with an adolescent pride and chiding. "I learned all of that from my Dad and brother," continued Tonya.

They all laughed at her accurately depicted admission as Dre pulled into the *Dairy Queen* parking lot on *First Avenue*. It sat just a stone's throw from the Linn County jail.

Munchie jumped out with the brown envelope in hand as Tonya and Dre proceeded to the drive-through, they were craving something sweet.

By the time Dre and Tonya had their ice cream and were feeding it to one another, Munchie came rushing back with a sign of delight on his face.

"Hey Cuzo, the lawyer is talking good that my dad be home tomorrow," exploded Munchie as he entered the truck.
"He also tried to decline the money," continued Munchie, "until I opened the envelope and showed him those big faced Benjamin's!" jokingly admitted Munchie.
"Puffy told you it was all about the Benjamin's," echoed Dre.
"Call Jason up, we partyin' tonight, CHI town style! Tell him to get *R-Kelly, Dabrat, Twister, Speed Not Mobsters, Crucial Conflict and Nelly* to *Club Lab* and the after party will be at *Dancer Strip Club!*" announced Dre distinctively.

"How we going to let everybody know we're partyin'?" innocently inquired Munchie.
"We're gonna get the word out and kill'em with VIP pictures and drinks. It will be free to get in. That's how!" confidently instructed Dre.
"I'm on it now Cuzo and let's go get my dad a new suit to wear," replied Munchie obediently as he pulled out his cell phone.

It was not but a few months ago Dre was trying to get clean. Now, he was to host a party with big names; a circle not everyone was allowed to enter. The world was not as big as it seemed when you rose to a certain level. It was like a pyramid, everything got closer as you rose up it, but there was not enough room for all of the hungry souls at the top.

Dre knew he needed to be cognizant of his surroundings; and in a land of so much fire, you needed to respect the fact that one misstep could end a reign, it could burn a world down. This would be a fundamental understanding to the axioms of his world, a world with little room at the top and a whole bunch at the bottom, this critically unfair world, the world of *Dog Food.*

Chapter 33
Toast to Crime

Dre had the money and Jason had the contacts, a perfect match for the perfect party, CHI style. Simply seven hours later and Jason was on his way to the airport to pick up the entertainment.

His pearl white *Benz* was being followed by a fully loaded stretch *Hummer,* there would be enough room for everyone; *R-Kelly, Dabrat, Twista, Speed Not Mobsters, Crucial Conflict, Nelly* and *Trina.* The '*baddest*' bitch, *Trina,* was coming in from M.I.A. so Jason would instruct the limo driver to take his *Benz* and wait for her arrival.

Once all the parties were aboard the limo, Dre's voice came on the loud speaker. Jason handed each of them a glass of champagne.

"Welcome everyone. I trust your private flights were to your liking. It was the least I could do considering the short notice. I truly appreciate you finding it in your schedules to make this night a memorable one. I look forward to meeting you all and I wish you a safe remainder of your trip."

"With that, I would like to propose a toast; to the best talent on the planet and may this night be more than we ever thought it could be! Salute!" Then the voice was gone.

They pulled in front of the *Five Seasons* on First Avenue and the place was already buzzing. While heads began to turn, the paparazzi emerged from the shadows, like a plague hovering over Europe in the late Eighteenth century.

Dre did it up right, including the Presidential Suites and stocking it with their favorite foods and beverages. No expense was spared.

They would start taking the stage in only three hours, so Dre wanted to make sure that their accommodations afforded them the opportunity to rest and recover before they performed.

On the other side of town, Dre, Munchie and Tonya were getting ready for the big night. Dre and Tonya had just stepped out of the *Jacuzzi* tub and were rubbing one another down with lotion.

Dre's phone was a constant *buzz,* as everyone in town wanted a ticket to the show. Mariea called in the middle of it all and Dre played it off so smooth that Tonya was not even aware.

"Hey hunny-bunny, I knew when I was packing my bags to put me a sexy, erotic outfit in here" teased Tonya as she slid on a pair of sexy black lace panties over her phatt heart shaped ass.

"What did you decide to put in that LV luggage?" playfully asked Dre as he took all of her in. He began to get hard and swaggered over to Tonya and smacked her on the ass.

"Boy I'm not tryin' to go there right now!" snapped Tonya as she slowly finished snapping her bra into place.

"Tonya was without reservation when it came to Dre and his sexual advances or exploitations. Without missing a beat she reached out and gingerly stroked Dre's dick with her palm, gripping it tighter and tighter as her hand moved along his shaft; She looked up at Dre with 'fuck me eyes' and Dre wanted to take her right then and right there.

"I have a *Channel* crocodile outfit or an ostrich outfit with matching shoes and matching hand bags," solicited Tonya, bringing the mood back to getting ready as opposed to 'getting down'.

"Baby, you tryin' to make me a no show tonight?" asked Dre teasingly. "You going to be the flyest woman in the room," contended Dre with a look of desire and admiration.

"What are you wearing tonight hunny-bunny?" inquisitively asked Tonya in a continued effort to change the subject and extinguish the fire building in Dre.

"I'm going to wear this custom short sleeve raw silk suit I had made for me and Munchie's birthday, along with black square-toed crocodile *Gators* to match," declared Dre.

An hour and a half later and the group was ready for the red carpet. Dre was sporting the black suit, Munchie in the grey and Tonya in the red *Channel* with black crocodile to match Dre.

They were accessorized with *Rolex's* and hanging jewelry wherever visible; they were a sight to behold. They appealed to all senses as the colognes and perfume emanating from each of them combined, resulting in an aromatic bouquet associated with wealth and style.

Munchie, excited with all the events, hurriedly ran upstairs and came trampling down breathing fast and heavy, almost unable to catch his breath.

"This Cuzo, is for you," proudly stated Munchie as he extended his arms presenting a gift to Dre.

Dre opened the package and was taken back by the thoughtfulness of what Munchie had done.

"Now this is what the fuck I'm talkin' 'bout on these Niggas!"
"Boss up on them tonight!" exclaimed Munchie.
"Yeah, I'm bossin' up!" echoed Dre as he carefully placed the black *Dobb* gangster brim hat with a red feather upon his head.

He was beaming with delight.

"I don't know what I would do without you Cuzo," admitted Dre. "You too baby!" as Dre looked at both Munchie and Tonya with compassionate and endearing eyes that were saying, *I love you.*

"We love you too!" resonated the voices of Tonya and Munchie in unison as they all hugged.

As Dre pulled away, Munchie lifted his hands to the brim of Dre's new hat and tilted it ever so slightly to one side.

"Now, you straight-up!' complimented Munchie as he released his fingers in a gentle feminine like manner and flare.

There were champagne glasses that had been set out by Tonya. Dre picked one up, as did Munchie when Tonya headed back into the kitchen.

Dre lifted his glass towards his chest and extended his arms towards Munchie with glossy eyes.

"This is going to be a great night, our night and one for Terry," expressed Dre emotionally.

Dre looked at Munchie with a connectedness, a type of kinship that the streets created. Munchie reciprocated. They were a long way from the streets they grew up on. The streets made them, but they held onto the core of who they were. The streets had not taken them from their own natures yet; they had not completely lost themselves in their fast moving world.

For that moment, for that brief fleeting moment suspended in time, they remembered who they were. They remembered their roots and what made them the men they were. They both smiled simultaneously.

It is easy to lose yourself in their world and they knew it. So, they embraced the moment, trying to hold on to it for as long as they could, because you never knew if you would come back to yourself once you were stolen by the world, the world of *Dog Food*.

....Clink....went the glasses.

Dusty stared up at the two of them, his tender dark brown eyes seeking Dre's recognition and approval, the look always tugged at Dre's heart.

"Hey Dusty, you wanna party? I'm bossin' all the way up!" Dre explained to Dusty as Dusty turned his head from side to side as if to understand every word that was coming out of Dre's mouth.

"I'm hostin' this shit and I want all my family there! Let me go and get you an outfit," announced Dre as he fled upstairs and promptly returned with one of his *Platinum* changes.

Dre put it around Dusty's neck along with a jewel studded collar and matching leash.

"There, now the family is ready!" triumphantly declared Dre, like a parent on their child's first day of school.

Dre had his brim tilted and earphone in constantly like *Russell Simmons* or *Puffy;* attentive to the business at hand. They piled into the *Excursion,* all of them; Dre, Munchie Tonya and Dusty, they were ready. So hope the world was ready too.

"Dre, Dusty is shedding hair everywhere. How is he going to get into the party?" asked Tonya with a shade of complaint.

"Well, because his daddy is hostin' the party baby!" responded Dre as he reached in the third row seat and gave Dusty a pat.

"Ain't that right Dusty? Ain't that right?" finished Dre as Dusty barked once in reply. Dre smiled as he turned his attention to Munchie.

"Hey Cuzo, you bring all the money and the five-thousand worth of singles?"

"Cuzo, I am ten steps ahead of ya. It's under the seat you in. It's in the suitcase under you," proudly explained Munchie.

"You never cease to amaze me!" expressed Dre.

I know Cuzo, I know!" replied Munchie, causing all of them in the car to erupt in laughter. They were all a little nervous and the humor seemed to release some of the tension. They all held their smiles for just a moment longer than usual.

The road slowed ahead of them as they neared *Club Lab.*

They couldn't believe their eyes as they observed the line down Sixth towards *Dancers.*

It was amazing. All of the radio advertising and *word of mouth* had paid off. The big names did what big names do; draw a crowd, and this, was a crowd!

The troupe exited the vehicle as if in a choreographed scene of materialism. Dre lead the pack, all studded out to the brim, Munchie followed closely with a metal briefcase handcuffed to him and Tonya highlighted everything with her sway, style and ensemble. Dusty walked briskly next to Dre as the leash glittered in the lights.

This visual was accompanied by an audio; as a sound track by the *Lox,* "Money Power and Respect," blared from the truck. It was a red carpet moment. They could feel the energy; they could feel the place of honor upon them as all eyes watched in envy. It was their moment and they embraced it.

Dre needed this to be big, for many reasons and what those reasons were at that particular moment he could not recall. He threw handfuls of singles into the air as he walked towards the front door to enter the club. The floating bills flashed as they tumbled in the air and reflected the lights from all of the cameras; it was literally "raining money"!

Munchie had everything arranged and reminded Dre not to worry about the logistics and to just be himself, be the host he needed to be. Dre immensely appreciated Munchie and Jason and what they had done to put it all together. He nodded to Munchie and gave him the smile that was all the gratitude Munchie needed.

Ultimately it was Dre's deal and he walked like it was, right through the front door and into a scene that exploded before him. He had arrived.

"Ladies and gentlemen," announced the Emcee, "may I direct your attention to the front door! The man who put this altogether, who made this all possible... Dre..Dre..Dre!"

The entire place erupted in chant echoing the Emcee; "Dre, Dre, Dre, Dre, Dre," as they threw their hands in the air.

Dre responded in kind by slowly putting one hand up pushing the air and then slowly returning it to his side. The place exploded into a crescendo of applause as the music absorbed the moment and put people back on the dance floor.

Dre was feeling like *Goldie* off the "Mack" when he won the *Player's Ball Trophy*. He felt that he was untouchable, that he was unstoppable especially with a *Teflon* bullet-proof vest on under his silk shirt.

He made his way through the adoring crowd with Dusty in tow and grabbed the *Mic*.

"I wanted to offer up a big thank you for comin' out tonight! We 'bout to have a whole bunch of superstars take this very stage, but remember, this is my house tonight! So, when I say whose house? I want ya'll to say; *Dre's House!"*

The *Run DMC* playing in the background went silent and Dre shouted,

"Whose house?"
"Dre's house!" electrically exploded the crowd. Dre tingled from the energy.

"It's all free for the next hour, we've got it all; *Crystal, Belvedere, Don P*, whatever you want, we got it or we'll get it! So, to my guests...enjoy!" shouted Dre enthusiastically into the night.

Dre handed the *Mic* to the Emcee and headed back through the crowd towards the back door, he needed to make a call.

"Hello? Answered the man on the other end of the phone.
"What's the biz Pete, you good?" eagerly asked Dre.
"Yeah, everything cool here Captain," respectfully replied Pete.
"Pete, shut it down for tonight and bring the workers to *Club Lab*. Make sure they dressed the part and no bummy dress," instructed Dre.
"Will do Dre!" and the phone went silent.

Dre paused for a moment and wondered why he waited until then to tell Pete. Why hadn't he discussed the logistics with Pete prior? After all, it was business that made this party possible.

Was Dre getting too caught up in the fanfare to forget to discuss something so important, or was there something else deeper in his consciousness, in his sub-conscious even, that precluded him from engaging fully with Pete regarding the events.

Dre, eager to return to the party, shrugged his shoulders as he looked down at Dusty patiently sitting at his feet.

"I agree with you Dusty, too much thinkin' for tonight. Let's go and have us some fun!" commented Dre as Dusty replied with one short bark. Dre smiled.

When Dre walked back into the club, it was in full swing. The celebrities more prone to "party with the people" were mingling with the guests and the others were enjoying the seclusion of the V.I.P. section. All were having fun; the music was just the right volume, control and beat. It was a bash!

"Hey Dre, I'm feelin' this party Joe!" announced *Twista* with a blunt hanging out of the corner of his mouth.
"This some Westside shit for real, with all these hoes in here, like the chocolate one over there and that redbone one over there," quickly articulated *Twista* as if it was one of his songs as he handed Dre a blunt.

"I couldn't see it no other way. I'm 'bout to get these hoes jukin' and poppin' those phatt asses with some house music right now!" announced Dre as he took a hit from the blunt revealing his manicured nails, pinky ring and gold *Rolex* as the lights bounced off of it and into *Twista's* eyes.

"But, hey, Dre," replied Twista, leaning in close to Dre so only he could hear, "I feel kinda naked cause I don't have a strap on me, nor am I walkin' around with a shepherd through the crowd.'

Twista was laughing as he pulled away from Dre's ear and took the blunt back from him. Dre returned the gesture with a polite smile.

"Don't even trip, I feel ya," comforted Dre, "you see, I got this hot ass vest on under here," admitted Dre as he patted his chest with his free arm. "You can never tell what these crazy ass Nigga's thinkin'," finished Dre so as to give a purpose for his discomfort from the vest.

"I can have my Cuzo go grab you one or we can walk to the truck outside," further offered Dre if his attempt of empathy was unsuccessful.

"That's good, just don't forget about a Nigga, cause all this pink ice I'm wearin', a Nigga's mouth get watery and thirsty and just might want a sip! You dig?" announced *Twista* as he matched Dre's earlier unveiling by flashing his pink ice and *Rolex* as he walked away with a trail of smoke off the blunt following him.

Dre slowly swept through the crowd, everyone hugging him or greeting him in their own way. Tonya, Munchie and Jason were nowhere in sight as Dre concluded that they were most likely in the VIP section enjoying themselves as well.

Before he could take another step towards the VIP section, two, soft, gentle hands covered his eyes. They were warm and smelled like flowers in the spring.

"Guess who?" said the female voice trying to sound masculine.
"Sweetheart, from the touch of those hands over my eyes, keep me blind folded all night! The after party is with you and the smell of that sweet perfume is getting me and the dog's dick hard," replied Dre playfully as he turned around slowly.
"Hey Mona Lisa, damn you lookin' fine! Give me a spin, I can't turn you around, I got my dog on the leash!" explained Dre.
She had on a black cat suit, leaving very little for the imagination, but just enough to carve an image into the erotic portion of a man's mind. It was like she was naked, but she wasn't. The mind automatically filled in the parts that were covered. She was dynamite! The last time Dre saw her was in the middle of the shoot-out and he didn't have the time or inclination to notice her. Tonight however, at this moment, he noticed her thoroughly.

"What about that dog that don't bark?" Mona asked

flirtatiously as she pointed to the bulge in his silk pants. "Is that on a leash too?"

Dre just stared back at her and licked his lips as he bit the lower one.

"I heard you got shot the last time I saw you, are you okay?" continued Mona not wanting to lose the conversation or attention of Dre.
"Damn, Mona baby, as much as I'd love to flip that ass upside down, my lady here with me from the crib and my arm is cool. I don't even need to tell you the outcome, but I do have something for you for helping me out that night. Give me a call sometime," politely added Dre as he carefully tried to carve a distance between them.

It must have been a seventh sense, for as soon as Dre drew backwards, Tonya appeared between them, out of nowhere it seemed.

"Here you are baby? I was in the VIP section talking with *Trina, Ms. Harris, DaBrat,* and I come to find out that me and her are somewhat related," announced Tonya as she pressed against Dre letting Mona know whose man he was.

Dre, aware of her intent, kissed Tonya long and hard, affirming that which she was trying to prove.

"Mona, this my lady I was telling you about," introduced

Dre.

The girls made pleasant, greeting one another politely, only for Dre's sake however. Otherwise, it most likely would have been a catfight under different circumstances. Dre wished Mona a "good evening" as she walked away swaying her stuff, like a cat in heat, throwing her ass in the air.

"So, you just gonna watch her ass walk away with me right here?' exclaimed Tonya.
"Baby, don't start that. You trippin'," replied Dre with a confidence and laughter that seemed to appease Tonya's insecurity. Then, Dre kissed her again to provide her a reassurance that he was her man.

As their lips parted, Dre caught a glimpse of the owner making his way across the floor towards Dre. Dre was ready to accept an expressed gratitude for his patronage. Instead however, Dre was put back by the request the owner had regarding removing Dusty from the premises.

After all of the money Dre was dropping in the place, Dre had a mind to show him some manners. Contrary to his urge, Dre refrained and politely nodded and headed towards the door with Dusty. He needed some air anyways and dealing with the leash had become too cumbersome as well.

Just as Dre was stepping out onto the curb, Pete pulled up in the van with two of the workers. Dre noticed that while they were not dressed poorly, they were not exactly dressed to impress either.

Dre jumped in the van with Dusty before Pete could even get out.

"You ready to party Pete? You and your two partners here?" asked Dre once he realized how many were in the *van*. One of them Dre recognized, it was the man with the prosthetic arm that was always spending money.

"Yeah, we ready Captain. I got about fifty-thousand in the stash spot and still over a half of that quarter brick left," informed Pete proudly.

Dre wasn't sure when the whole "Captain" thing started or why, but he took it as a measure of respect and a recognized hierarchy so he allowed it and made no comment.

"That's cool, I'm letting Dusty chill in here and grab me one of those thumpers outta the stash spot," announced Dre.

Dre grabbed the heater while Pete and his partners went back to the club. Dre felt that there were eyes on him, but it could just as easily be the effects of the hits he was taking. It was his night, so he would set paranoia aside and enjoy himself.

Down the street sat a parked vehicle in the shadows; a car out of place if you were paying attention. Inside, the lieutenant took notice of the blue van immediately. While he was taking pictures and notes of all of the people and activity, the van was the biggest piece of evidence for the night as it tied people to various locations and activities.

"There's that fucking blue van again. Hand me the binoculars so I can get a good look at the driver this time," demanded the lieutenant of his partner.

"You won't believe who is driving that freakin' van?" riddled the lieutenant.

"Pete freakin' Smith! He used to be in the concrete construction business. He got hooked on heroin shortly after he lost his wife a few years back," informed the lieutenant.

"I remember him. He was a really gifted a worker who threw all his talents down the drain. Hell, he was part of building a lot of this town," added the lieutenant's partner.

"Yeah, but now he is helping to tear a lot of it down, including himself," echoed the lieutenant.

R-Kelly was calling *Crucial Conflict* on the stage as Dre caught up with Pete and the others inside the club.

When they hit the stage, "Ghetto Queen" filled the room, causing the ladies to pump up the volume and bring the room to another level.

Dre was heading back to check out *Twista* and give him a thumper when he noticed Mariea and Molly walk into the club.

Their eyes locked immediately, transporting them towards

one another; no sounds, no distractions, just Mariea and Dre surrounded by lights and movement, neither distinguishable from the other.

"Hey pimp, this the party you were telling me about? I see you pimped out with that hat on," playfully remarked Mariea as she moved closer to him wanting to feel his heat, wanting to feel him closer to her.
"Yeah, baby, thank you, what can I say," nervously replied Dre.

This took Mariea back as the reply was stoic and distant as if he was a player and she was being played. Something wasn't right; she could feel it and she didn't like it.

"Don't say nothing, just tell me when I can have you tonight and Molly was asking about Slick too."
"Not tonight, my 'wifey' here baby and Slick is locked up right now," openly admitted Dre as he looked at Molly and nodded to gesture a *hello*.

Dre's eyes left Mariea's and began to scan the room, the last thing he wanted was another scene like the one with Mona. This one however, might end differently, as Dre was concerned that he would not be able to hide his feelings for Mariea. Then, he saw her. Out of nowhere Tonya was there. Instinctively reacting, Dre followed his strategy from earlier and politely introduced them.

"Mariea, this is my lady Tonya."

As the words fell from his mouth he could sense the difference from when he introduced Mona; there was feeling in it this time. Dre suspected that Tonya sensed it, sensed something more.

Women had that way about them, Dre thought to himself. It was uncanny and something Dre couldn't protect against. Mariea's little wave goodbye with her departure did not help matters either.

"You must think I have *Stupid* written on my face?" challenged Tonya.

"What you talkin' about baby?" replied Dre as innocently as he could as he began the verbal dance.

"You fuckin' that white bitch right there!" accused Tonya more as a proclamation than an allegation, with her hands on her hips and fire in her eyes. "She wasn't lookin' goo-goo eyed at you for nothin' and you got that shit eatin' grin on your face! I hope you using rubbers on these hoes!" exclaimed Tonya.

"Baby," cautiously began Dre, as he knew he was on thin ice. "That should be one of your last worries; of me fucking with one of these women, when I got all the woman I need right here with me!"

Dre tried to draw her into him by looking deep into her eyes, hoping to cast a spell on her or at least break her vision of what she saw as the truth.

"Boy, I can't stand your black ass sometimes," replied Tonya with a subdued demeanor from a moment earlier.

She reciprocated Dre's movement to the music and pressed against him. Her mind knew one thing, but her emotions and her body were feeling and wanting another; she gave into the latter.

The night was a hit and the after party was 'off the chains' as *Nelly* was the star of the show at the strip club as he let ten and twenty dollar bills rain from the sky.

Everyone enjoyed themselves immensely. Munchie, Tonya and Dre reveled in the limelight, appreciating the scene, one of the greatest of their lives; the natural high was intoxicating.

Even though spirits were high, Tonya stirred and was filled with an unsettled feeling inside. Dre felt it too. The world of *Dog Food* was filled with misdirection, it was filled with lies and betrayal and it was taking its toll; but sometimes, concluded Tonya and Dre silently unto themselves, it was easier to believe a lie with a smile than to face a truth with a tear.

Chapter 34
The Court of Law

Pete was at the spot by 7:30 sharp. Tonya and Dre had just opened their eyes as to the new day. Dre looked intently at Tonya who had traces of sleep and the eventful evening still on her face. He felt different.

Munchie and Jason were already out the door and on their way to Terry's trial.

"Last night was crazy!" announced Munchie against the back drop of Toni Braxton's, "I Love Me Some Him."
"Bitch, I need me some Aspirin. I got a headache this motherfucking big!" expressed Jason with his hands at the sides of his head and expanding outward past his shoulders as if he was playing an accordion.
"All that drinking and partyin', I thought you'd have something that big in your mouth or in your ass!" joked Munchie crudely.
"Shit, don't think nothing didn't! We were just quick about it!" retorted Jason without missing a beat, making them both

laughed hysterically. A part of Jason was offended and hurt by the accusation, but he realized it was ultimately all in fun. He smiled as he laughed. The remainder of the ride to the courthouse was quiet; each man worrying his own worries. Munchie worried about the trial of his dad Terry, and Jason of his relationship with Munchie.

When Munchie and Jason entered the courtroom, Munchie had to catch his breath. He could not recall experiencing or ever hearing about anything good coming out of a courtroom and he could just feel it on this day too. Regardless, he clung to hope.

Terry was well dressed and had slowed down on the dope for a few days to clear his head for the trial. The jury had been selected already and the interesting observation that Munchie made was now that Terry's jury was selected, a jury of "his peers," Terry was the only black person in the courtroom.

Terry sat next to the greedy bastard that took the twenty grand from Munchie at their last encounter and he looked less than enthusiastic. Munchie began to feel ill.

"All rise!" instructed the bailiff at 8:00 sharp. That was one thing about the Courts, when they wanted to run on time, they could. "The Honorable Doris Ford presiding," finished the bailiff as a figure in long flowing black swayed out of a door behind the bench.

"Everyone, please be seated," said the figure with an

authority and a presence reserved for the elite.

The judge proceeded to review the charges alleged against Terry and went through a series of instructions for the sake of the jury so they could hear, "innocent until proven guilty."

Those words of such meaning, that is until you are faced with certain realities that would otherwise suggest differently. Hearing them is much different than understanding them, an element not presently required in a jury instruction.

It is one thing for a Senatorial hopeful to chime such notions of liberties and fairness, it is entirely another for a black man to feel them as he awaits his fate in a courtroom.

"We will have the first witness, Captain Jerry Rivera, approach please, be administered the oath and then to take the stand so we may proceed," instructed the Honorable Judge Ford.

"Please state your name, first and last, being sure to include the appropriate spelling," began the prosecution.

"My name is Captain Jerry Rivera, that is J-e-r-r-y R-i-v-e-r-a," obeyed the Captain.

"Captain Rivera, if you would, who is your present employer and in what capacity do you function as a Captain?" followed up the Government.

"My employer is the city of Vinton and as Captain of the Police Department I have many duties, including the heading of the Vinton Special Response Team. I lead a special squadron of some of the finest officers. Our aim is to thwart crime in our community," dramatically testified the Captain.

The first day of trial consisted of much of the same testimony as the Captain had provided. They covered all aspects associated with the high-risk search warrants, undercover operations, evidence from informants and compelling reasons to support the three counts alleged against Mr. Terry Dent involving the selling of narcotics to an undercover agent and having done so from a protected location within one-thousand feet from a school.

Terry's defense was equally compelling. His counsel laid out the facts as they would be seen from Terry's perspective. He was articulate and impressed Munchie and Jason alike.

Munchie was allowed to visit Terry in the Federal building. Terry was still all dressed up, looking much different to Munchie than he normally did. He couldn't deduce if it was the time that he had spent in the County or if it was just the suit. To Munchie, Terry looked lost.

"Well son, whatcha ya' think so far?" Asked Terry before Munchie could even finish sitting down. Munchie could sense an eagerness in Terry's voice driven by fear and uncertainty.
"I'm thinkin' even better yet, knowing my dad is coming home," replied Munchie with the sincere dedication of a son.
"You never can tell with these racist crackers. It's ninety-eight percent conviction rate. They all want our black asses in here or doped up or fuckin' dead!" exclaimed Terry with a degree of concession in his tone.

Munchie was taken back by his dad's remarks. Munchie was typically the sullen, yet positive one. This comment by Terry hit Munchie hard. It felt like a rationalization towards coping with a certain defeat before it ever occurred. It was unsettling to Munchie, but the merits of such a preconception were equally engrained in his mind, so he nodded in agreement, disgustingly.

"We gave that lawyer twenty grand!" trumpeted Munchie searching for any words to show he still had fight in him even if Terry's was waning.

"Ya'll gave that greedy cracker what?" yelled Terry as his fist found the table with equal force.

"Twenty-thousand," squeaked out Munchie, afraid of what Terry might do next.

"I have tried to tell you over these last few years, a greedy man never gets full. It's never enough, just look at me!" proclaimed Terry as a look of irritation succumbed to a compassion and plea for his son to see a man of despair and not of greed. Terry was reaching into himself trying to show his son his humanity, one that was mostly stolen from the drugs over the years, but today, his head was clear; he would let his son in.

"Son," continued Terry, "don't get greedy with whatever you do. When you get greedy, you get fucked. Look between your legs and see a dick that isn't yours, whether these fuckin' police, fake friends or enemies. You feel me son? But I ain't mad at ya son, you and Dre want me up outta here, I get it," finished Terry in a long gasp of breath to finish the soliloquy that he had started with the best of intentions.

When Terry was finished he excused himself, he was tired and the realization set in that he may not be able to hold his son for some time. Munchie was certain he saw a tear fall from the corner of his eye.

The next day, Terry stayed fast and opted to not take the stand as he stood by his motto: *these white racist bastards gotta find me guilty, so there ain't no need for me getting' on the stand. There not going to believe a fuckin' word that comes out of my mouth.*

The day consisted of much of the same as prior days as the prosecution and defense tried to clean up and wrap up their respective cases; each attempting to polish their stories or versions of the events that occurred; one to prosecute and one to defend.

As the last witness stepped down, a solemn voice took over. "Members of the jury," began the judge, "this concludes the presentation of the evidence in this case. Over the evening, the lawyers and I will be putting together instructions as a guide for when you deliberate that which you have seen and heard. This will follow the closing arguments by the parties. We will hear such arguments the first thing tomorrow morning. Is there anything else from either party at this time?"

Both parties nodded their heads so as to affirm in the

negative and stated it as well for the record; "nothing more your honor."

"All rise," announced the bailiff as the judge rose as if to levitate and leave the room.

Munchie was exhausted and needed a haven of rest, recovery and support, he needed a place he called home, he needed to go to Dre's.

Dre could see the wear on Munchie's face and in his posture, it saddened him.

"Unc's final arguments are tomorrow Cuzo, so I'm gonna be there!" announced Dre, trying to give Munchie what comfort he could as Munchie fell back onto the leather sofa.

* * *

The tone was melancholy as Dre, Tonya, Munchie and Pete entered the courtroom. Days like these never seemed to get better and they all had seen and heard too much about how these things typically turned out. It was the same as when Munchie had entered days prior. They were all nervous and it showed.

The room was so old you could smell it. There was history on the walls and the oak paneling that accented its perimeter reminded an occupant that it was to be a room of principles and respect.

On this day, it was filled with different officers from the task force and special team's unit from Vinton and from Cedar Rapids. It was a full house. There were mumblings of Mr. Dent and his associations, including his son Munchie and of course, Dre.

After three days of deliberation the parties were called back to the courtroom as the jury had reached a verdict.

The room was filled with tension; Munchie almost chocked on it. Dre on the other hand, was calm and Tonya held her head high. This comforted Munchie. Pete sat in utter silence.

"Mr. Dent, do you have anything that you wish to say before I read the verdict that has been handed to me?' inquired the judge as if reading from a script.

"Naw'll," replied Terry.

The judge proceeded to read all three of the counts and read their corresponding verdicts,

"As to count one....the defendant is found...guilty. As to count two...the defendant is found..guilty. As to count three...the defendant...is found..guilty," so read the judge with an indifference that only years of doing such could produce.

Munchie's heart went directly to his throat and he felt as if he couldn't breathe. Dre felt Munchie's anguish and he began to feel light headed, it was too close to home. Tonya wept.

Terry's strong frame became rigid and he exploded out of his chair as if attempting to leap across the table that separated him from the judge. The Marshall's were quick to react, as they physically subdued him before he could get his hands on anyone.

This startled everyone from the numbing effect of the verdicts, especially Munchie who was now in tears. Dre was equally sullen, but held back his own tears. Tonya wept as the courtroom went into an uproar. Pete sat motionless.

"You racist bastards!" yelled Terry, along with numerous inaudible sounds and gestures as he was wrestled to the ground by the Marshall's.

Terry managed to get to his feet in a rage. *Zap...Zap...Zap,* went the Taser gun, shaking Terry into convulsions. The room went silent as Terry hit the floor with a thud.

As the room quieted down, the judge regained composer and made a few brief comments regarding Terry and provided the date of the sentencing and then quickly adjourned.

*   *   *

The room smelled like three weeks old sweat and stale sandwiches. Captain Rivera reviewed the evidence that the team had put together, while Captain Boots and the lieutenants looked on.

"The van is a key, I just feel it!" exclaimed the Captain with a conviction that typically lead to a truth. "I saw his boy and nephew in the court room and I am betting they are not apples that have fallen too far from the family tree," followed up the Captain as he stroked his chin with his hand, slowly letting the information set in. "They were also there in Vinton, when Dent was arrested," he said more to himself in a quizzical manner as he thought out loud, hoping to spark additional flows of consciousness that might lead to more clues. He wanted a clearer trail towards apprehending additional members or conspirators.

"We saw those two at that big bash the other night too, the night when we spotted Pete Smith in the van. We also identified one as DeAndre Hall, that's the nephew. He entered the vehicle with Mr. Smith," added the lieutenant.

"You said we'd get those responsible. It's in their blood, they couldn't resist the temptation. It's like they are kids in a candy store, always wanting more and more," escaped Captain Boot's lips with a sense of accomplishment and satisfaction.

"Yes, I did and it looks like they are playing right into our hands, we just need to give them enough space and keep paying attention," replied Captain Rivera.

"I see this Pete guy. He's always around the areas of interest. He is where the action is and he seems to carry some type of rank out on the streets. With that being said however, I know that he is not the mastermind, he doesn't have the mentality. My bet is that Mr. Johnell Hall or this

DeAndre Hall have more of a mind to make this thing happen or they are close to the one who does," expressed Captain Boots as he was now thinking aloud as well.

He paused as if he had discovered something new, then he retreated as his new thought vanished as quickly as it had arrived.

"We need to get these bastards. Hell, I am sure their hands are all over the stuff that Dent is getting sent to him over at County that our snitch has been telling us about," added Captain Rivera.
"Dent needs to go behind bars for a long time and when he does, mark my words, we will bag the two little kitties," settled Captain Boots as he looked up intently into the eyes of Captain Rivera; determination was his message, conviction his promise.

The streets were about to get cold and nothing would warm them up, not even the rush of that food that so many fed on. It was their mission to see that they would starve the streets of that which poisoned their community, that took the life of the Captain's brother and that was stealing so much, from so many, every minute of every day.

They would champion a new world, one that respected the law, even if they had to hold their own hearings, their own court of laws.

The streets needed to be cleansed, they needed to be corrected, and they needed to be rid of the death and pain caused by the crippling addiction that was spreading. They would stop at nothing, even if that meant that the streets of gold were to be flooded with a sea of red. This would end, they would beat the rush of the food; the *Dog Food.*

Chapter 35
Slippin' in the Darkness

To say you could hear a pin drop would not be adequate. The sorrow felt so deeply by Munchie spoke volumes to the others as they drove away from the courthouse and towards Claire's.

Awestruck by the events, Munchie held on to what fortitude that remained in him, he didn't want to lose it right there in the back of the *Excursion* sitting next to Pete.

Jason was following in the white *Benz* and Dre and Tonya sat quietly in the front seat. The radio was on, but no one was listening. The silence was too deafening, so Dre broke it.

"That was some bullshit! Those racist crackers found Unc guilty!" exclaimed Dre with offense at the outcome.

Munchie sat silent as Dre spouted off at the injustice of it all, but a part of him knew his dad was a drug dealer and had been for as long as Munchie could remember. *Still, it wasn't fair,* thought Munchie to himself. The way that it occurred portrayed the injustice of the system. A system so big and powerful that no one, especially a black man, could break free from. Munchie sat motionless as tears fell down his face; he could not feel them.

"We gotta get Terry another paid attorney," parroted Pete from the far back nickel seats.

Tonya turned around to look at Munchie. The tears streaming down his face made Tonya swallow hard as she tried to stop from doing the same.

"Listen baby," she said with a comforting, pleading voice, "I remember when my dad was locked up, I know it isn't easy, but we can't take it too hard."

"I'm not, Tonya. I just may never see my dad again in the free world," replied Munchie in a monotone voice. He stared out the window into a nothingness as he began to feel the tears that had been falling down his cheeks.

"Oh, Munchie," she replied as she sat up and reached into the back to give him a hug.

The embrace was genuine, but the feeling resembled more of an imitation as Munchie was not really there, and the position she was in was awkward. The gesture carried a weight to lift Munchie from the slide he was in and he smiled as the warmth of her body comforted him, like mother would a child on a cold stormy night. They both wept.

"We going to get him out on the appeal, trust me Cuzo," trumpeted Dre trying to provide comfort in his way as he pulled up to Claire's.

While at Claire's it seemed unreal to Munchie. He sat silently as Dre and Pete were shaking up the food, his thoughts stolen; *my dad was just found guilty on multiple counts of drugs and here we sit mixing some up right after leaving the courthouse.*

Tonya was off to the spa with Jason so any feminine energy was absent, leaving Munchie to his own devices. He felt so alone.

They still had over a quarter brick of Dog Food left in addition to the nine bricks stashed in the Peugeot in the storage unit.

The system was routine and methodical; unwrapping the pure heroin, mixing it with *Dormin's,* tearing the aluminum foil and weighing everything on the scale. The sound of the blender helped to block the voice inside Munchies' head, the one that plead for his father, for him, for the relationship of a father and a son.

Pete shook out a full batch from the blender, took out a card and piled some on it with a distinct look of revenge.

"Here's to you and me Terry. We should have stopped tooting this stuff years ago," announced Pete as he sniffed until he had no more breath.

"I think I can take me a sniff of that good shit too, for Unc," followed Dre. "One sniff for ol' time sakes won't hurt a Nigga!" exclaimed Dre, hungry for an excuse and wanting the pain he felt inside to also go away.

Shou'll want," replied Pete as he handed Dre the card gingerly, as if it were part of a sacred ritual.

"Let me check out the product and see what's what," advertised Dre as he thrust the card deep into the pile as his pupils' dilated.

He sniffed it. His past met his present, changing his future. He instantly felt the old feeling, the rush of the poison filling his veins.

"Ooh, how I remember this now," admitted Dre with a type of admiration.

"I might as well, take me a sniff too," injected Munchie. "Noooo," replied Pete and Dre in unison.

"Naw'll, you can't have none of this," followed Pete.

"Hey Cuzo, this not for you," supported Dre.

"I'm a grown man the last time I checked and neither of ya'll just went to trial that took my daddy," replied Munchie with a sense of entitlement and sadness.

"Yeah, you right Cuzo that would be the person that kill us both; for me letting you try this shit. But hey, like you said, you grown," conceded Dre in that frog voice that only heroin can produce.

Dre put the card down on the table while not taking his eyes off of Munchie. He wanted Munchie to look at him, hoping that his stare would deter him from what he wanted to do. Munchie was too intent on his decision and stared at the card on the table and the mound of heroin beside it. Munchie was sweating, but he hurt so much inside it didn't matter.

"Remember Cuzo, that's some grown man shit right there, it is detrimental to your health and sometimes you never come back," cautioned Dre, trying one last time to get Munchie to change his mind.

Detrimental you shall, Munchie said to himself as he took the card and scooped some heroin on it, bringing it slowly to his nose. His breath blew it right back off onto the table. This was Munchies first time and he was nervous; he continued to sweat and he was breathing heavy. Determined, he tried it again.

When it hit him, it felt like he was in a rocket ship taking off of the launch pad. His head thrust back as a continuation of the sniff, but it stayed back for a moment, as if the body knew what was happening before Munchie was cognitively aware.

Then, the pain was gone. His worries, his concerns, his

heartache, his hesitation, his insecurities were gone, all of them, just gone.

He stood up to make sure it was real, that he wasn't dreaming. He began to spin a little and realized he had to sit down. Instead of just sitting back down, he walked, passing both Dre and Pete and finding a chair in the living room. He sat there waiting for something else to happen or for nothing at all. Either way, it didn't matter to him, because he finally, for once in his life, couldn't feel pain.

Munchie slowly scanned the room he was in, trying to focus his attention on anything he could not. Then, he began to puke.

Dre and Pete knew far too well that it was Munchies' body trying to resist the poison, but it startled Munchie. Despite him vomiting all over himself, he was still content. Even though he was startled, he was not afraid. Rather, he was calm, he was at a peace. As Munchies' head began to droop he began to scratch himself.

Next, Dre and Pete did something they never do, they invited one of the workers into the house to clean up the mess Munchie had just made. Heroin in a pile on the table, a blender, tin foil scattered about and Munchie sitting almost comatose in his own puke; a sight to behold.

"Man, he fucked up, I'll have me two of those if you please," sarcastically and whimsically announced the worker as he walked past Munchie.

Munchie wanted to reply but he could not. He tried to respond to the worker but nothing would come out, it was as if his mouth had been disconnected from his mind. His mind was full of vivid images and thoughts, but he could not verbally articulate them.

The images were much slower than normal, clearer for Munchie to digest and interpret. He saw himself sitting there in the chair, as if he was outside of his body looking down on himself. Munchie began to smile.

He looked like his dad! So many times Munchie would see his dad, Terry, slumped over in a chair looking as if nothing in the world was bothering him; calm, with a subtle demeanor.

We'll always be connected, Munchie repeated to himself, *me and my dad, we will always be connected!* Then it hit him; *love this feeling! I want to feel like this for the rest of my life!*

By the time Dre and Pete had finished shaking all the dope, Munchie was out. Getting Munchie into the car was an endeavor, but they got it done. The ride back to Dre's place was quiet; Dre was into his own mind and Munchie was out of his.

Munchie was slouched over as if he had been shot. He sat idle as his head bounced to every bump in the road.

On the way, Dre decided to stop by *Lindell Mall* to pick up a few things. When he drove by the front, Mariea was walking out, *what are the odds?* Dre thought to himself. He called her over.

"Hey baby, stay here in the car with Munchie while I run in and get something real quick?" asked Dre more in the form of an instruction.
"Okay baby, has Munchie been drinking? He's toasted!" exclaimed Mariea.
"He's had some shots, that's all, I'll be right back," informed Dre.

Dre ran into the optical center and purchased some new shades, two pairs of *Laura Bugatti* to be precise, and at a grand a piece, he was sure they would be just right.

"Thanks baby," offered Dre as he promptly returned as promised.
"Munchie doesn't look so good," informed Mariea with a genuine concern.
"Oh, Cuzo will be ok, his Dad lost at trial earlier so he has been tryin' to keep it off his mind," disclosed Dre.
"I can imagine that it is hard for your cousin, but don't let him try to drink his problems away."
"I won't, you're right. I'm 'bout to take him home anyway. I'll catch up with you later," offered Dre as she was getting out of the vehicle and he was climbing in.

Dre wasn't sure why he had lied about what Munchie had taken, but it was enough for him to consider; *is heroin that bad? So much so that I can't even tell her he had some?* Whatever the answer, Dre's mind didn't wait to hear it. He was off drowning his thoughts with some tunes as Munchie sat lifeless beside him.

Dre threw on a pair of the shades and placed a pair on Munchie as well, making no difference to his condition. Dre was anxious to get back to Tonya, the events of the day and seeing Mariea reminded him of his manhood and how it had been too long since Tonya had felt him, especially with that dope dick. He seemed to get more aroused the closer he got to the house.

When Jason and Tonya returned from the spa, they found both Munchie and Dre on the leather couch staring at the television, with their heads bobbing up and down, they were both goose- necking and feeling no pain at all.

C-Murder was playing in the background, a soft gentle hum to Dre and Munchie. To Tonya and Jason, it was practically breaking their eardrums; two groups of people, two different perceptions.

"Hey hunny-bunny!" greeted Tonya.

With no response from Dre, Tonya glanced up from all of the shopping bags on the floor at her feet that she had been so intently focused on. *This Nigga is high*, Tonya thought to herself.

Just as the words flashed through her mind, Dre's eyes opened, slowly.

"Hey baby," gently spoke Dre as if waking from a pleasant dream.

"Hey hunny-bunny," replied Tonya as her hands started to rise to her hips.

"I miss you. You got that sun dress on that I picked up for you?" observed Dre.

"Yes, I do," replied Tonya with a smirk and a little sass.

"You got some sexy panties on under there?" followed Dre as all of the blood started to flow to his midsection, making the 'froggy' in his voice even more pronounced.

"I have some sexy panties on, but let's take them off together," teased Tonya. She couldn't stand seeing Dre high like this, but she hated to miss out on his dope dick even more. She knew what it meant to her and she wanted it.

Tonya reached out a hand to help Dre off of the couch and led him down the hallway to the bedroom.

Jason had assumed Munchie's state was because he was so tired as the result of all that had happened, so he carefully sat down next to him. Jason felt comfort sitting close to Munchie, feeling the warmth of his body and hearing the steadiness of his breathing; he too closed his eyes.

Tonya was not worried about Munchie or Jason, rather, about that dope dick that was soon to be hers. She was aching, she had forgot how long it actually been. Her pussy was so wet she could feel it run down her thigh.

Dre had regained some composure and hit 'repeat' on the player as *Kutklose*; "I Like" played for them.

Dre didn't waste a second.

"Do you know how much I love you and everything about this pussy? The taste, the smell, the look, the feel, I love it all," softly and erotically declared Dre as the last few words began to become muffled as he started to suck on her pleasure cove.

Tonya was moaning before Dre even made his first contact, the anticipation of it all put her into another world. She moaned again and again as Dre sucked her pussy, trying to get every drop from her, but she was relentless, she kept oozing all over him.

Dre didn't know if he was hallucinating, as she flowed and flowed all over him, creating such an eroticism that he almost came.

"Take all of my clothes off!" demanded Tonya.

Dre complied most ardently and they both lay naked and aroused. Dre had to have her. He flipped her over onto her stomach and began to run his tongue along her thigh and into her pussy, it slid effortlessly as her wetness provided a trail for Dre to follow. She moaned in delight. As Dre slowly moved his tongue down towards the center of her ass and rimmed her, she lost it.

"Dre baby, you need to fuck me! Put that dick inside me....oooh....oooh...oh, baby, your tongue feels so good, but I need to ride my dick!" commanded Tonya with a senselessness that only erotica can provide.

Tonya mounted Dre facing away from him and grabbed his ankles as she arched her back and rode him hard. Her breasts were bouncing up and down as she thrust herself on him, driving him deeper and deeper into her.

Her phatt heart shaped ass was bouncing off of Dre's stomach and her wetness made his hard black dick shine like a silver sword from *Camelot*.

"Oh, your pussy feels so good wrapped around my big dick, turn around so I can kiss you," demanded Dre.

There was no time as Tonya was approaching her peak and she wasn't going to do anything to disturb her ride.

"Oh bay, oh...oh...oh...I'm about to cum baby, oh, grab my ass harder!" she screamed as she rode him even harder.

Dre grabbed her ass with both hands and thrust deep into her as he had never thrust before. His dope dick was so hard and big, he thought he might split her open.

"Give me more!" she begged. "Give me more!"

Dre gave her everything he had, he was jacking her back so hard that he was lifting both of them off the bed.

"Oh, I'm cuming.... I'm cuming," sang Tonya in a desperately pleasing voice.

She came so hard that Dre swore he could feel a part of her leave her body, a type of presence, an aura that warmed Dre to the core.

She had to get off as she was tender and Dre was so hard with his dope dick.

Now it was Dre's turn.

He turned her over, missionary style and proceeded to slide into her slowly, very slowly, as if to let her feel every single inch, every inch.

Tonya came three more times before Dre began to build up. It was euphoric. He felt like he was building up more and more, his dick seemed to be getting harder, *if that was even possible,* he thought to himself.

Dre took her around the world. He tried every position he remembered from the *Karma Sutra* book and scenes from the videos he had seen over his time.

Dre took her so passionately, so ravenously, as if trying to redefine what sex meant.

Tonya took all of him in, with passion, then love, and then compassion. She couldn't completely free herself to all of it, as a part of her trembled from the possibility that Dre was becoming a user. She wanted to say something, but she wouldn't ruin the moment for her or for him, the man that she loved and wanted to be loved by. They collapsed in each other's arms.

On the way to the airport, Tonya was filled with emotions. She had a first class ticket back to CHI, a million in cash for Mr. Bones and a head full of visions of the love that they had just made.

Her mind was swirling, she couldn't put things in order any more. She stared at the ownership papers that were in her name and tried to control her breathing.

Getting to the plane was a blur, as she was mentally inundated with images, memories and thoughts; each with meaning and purpose. It was not very long ago that she and Dre were thinking of what the future might hold for them, and now it was upon them, larger and bigger than they had imagined. Looking around in the first class cabin only reinforced this.

Dre always had secrets, this she knew and this she accepted, but she took pride in the fact that she did not have any that she kept from him; that was until now. It bothered her and she wanted the feeling in her to subside; it was a feeling of guilt and portrayal, that of her and that of him.

She was becoming someone that she didn't want to become, as if she was slipping into a darkness, but she would do it for him. She wouldn't lose her man to an addiction; she was to be his drug of choice. Beating the power of the *Dog Food* was all but impossible, but she stood at the corner of hope, where conviction and compassion meet, ready to face whatever lay ahead.

Chapter 36
The Soul of a Man

Three months had passed and Dre's game had elevated. He was not progressing at the rate he once did and was not due to the *laws of diminishing demands,* rather the laws of Dog Food. He was using frequently and he was getting sloppy and the worst part was, he didn't even realize it.

He and Munchie were treating their noses like aardvarks snorting under a rotted tree. They had two bricks left in the trunk of the Peugeot, which never left the storage unit. Pete always found that interesting, how the car never left the storage unit, like a ship that never leaves port, but always has cargo.

Terry was a level 39 offender and in a category *five,* of a maximum of *six,* for a career offense level. According to the sentencing guideline matrix, this resulted in an indicated sentencing range of 360 months to life.

Terry made sure to express his gratitude to the judge by calling her and her mother; "racist, worthless bitches and hoes," a consideration for her honor that most likely did not play into Terry's favor as she exercised her discretion in sentencing. He would be sent to Terre Haute, Indiana. He was sentenced to life.

The judge provided a brief rational to the sentence by referencing Terry's criminal history as well as the information obtained from the jailhouse informant relating to Terry's ongoing affairs with heroin. To most, however, it was obvious that she personally held a grudge against Terry for his outbursts and actions in her courtroom.

Dre retained a lawyer immediately to start the appellate process on Terry's behalf. He made sure it was a female that could also mule heroin into him on their visits.

It was the month of Dre's birthday and he was excited about finally opening the businesses. He and Munchie were riding high and in style; each donning exclusive *Pelle Pelle* leather jackets with *Gucci* bucket hats and dark shades. Dre was in his *Iceberg* and Munchie his *Polo* and their windows were slightly cracked to let the smoke out.

It had snowed a couple of days ago, but the early winter sun melted it away leaving behind a fresh wetness that made everything smell and feel clean again. The fresh air funneled into the vehicle reviving them as it also served as a ventilation. It was one of those beautiful days caught between summer, fall and winter, not deciding what it wanted to be specifically.

They were both sniffling from the nose candy as Munchie manned the wheel to the *Enchantment's*, "Gloria" playing in the cabin. Ever since Dre started hitting the dragon he only listened to the *Oldies*, the old soul music seemed to resonate with his altered state.

"Cuzo, who you gonna have run the four shops?" inquired Munchie.
"You already know I believe in keeping it in the family. I might have to call a family meeting and bring my two brothers and twin sister down here. But you also already know, we need to keep them completely separate; the family business and our business," indicated Dre as he pulled a drag from his cigarette. He held his hands shoulder width apart in the air to symbolize how the two activities were to be separate. "It is the best for everyone," continued Dre, "In case anyone decides to get cute, it protects one side from the other."

"Cuzo, they'll love that! Don't forget about cousin Totsie and Fe-Fe too. You know they the coldest on the hair-do's like your sister Tiesha, but your right, don't mix the two," offered Munchie.

"Matter of fact, we going to the crib later on, shit, we ain't been there in a while," mentioned Dre while singing the lyrics; *I don't want to see another day without your love.*

"Don't quit your day job," joked Munchie, "'cuz you won't get a dime singing!"

The laughter shattered the smoke clouds that had formed in the cabin as the winter air stole them both away out the window and down the highway behind them.

"Cuzo, we havin' way too much damn fun, blowing this good-ass dope and we can do any motherfuckin' thing that we want to do! The only thing we can't do is bring your dad home right now, but that lawyer guaranteed me that he is coming home!" forcefully verbalized Dre almost if he wanted to yell it, but didn't have enough air to do so.

Munchie drifted off again, thinking about his father and his plight. The warm sun in his face and the melancholy place that the dope placed you, made him just as warm on the inside. He breathed easy.

"Munchie watch out! Watch!" yelled Dre as he grabbed the steering wheel.

The bulkiness of the *Excursion* only made matters worse as Dre attempted to avoid hitting the vehicle. In his daydreaming, Munchie had run a red light. Dre's reaction, albeit slower than usual, was just enough to avoid a collision.

As the other vehicle passed them, Dre looked into the car from his elevated perch; the small sedan with the baby in the car seat would have been no match for the *Excursion.* Dre felt sick inside.

"Damn, Cuzo, I'm sorry, I almost hit that car," apologetically offered Munchie, unaware of the contents of the other vehicle.

'Fuck'em, they need to get outta our way! We some motherfuckin' *Mac* trucks! We can pullover if you need to blow some more of this good-ass dope, straight-up, straight-up!"

They pulled over and Dre grabbed some personally made dope that was in a tin foil stuffed in the bottom of his Newport pack. He poured it all out on a CD case and divided it up like a surgeon with his driver's license. He rolled up a hundred-dollar bill and snorted with the same vigor as *Scarface.* Munchie followed suit.

They went to the storage unit and pulled another quarter of a brick out to take to Pete and carved some out for their own use. They also took about a hundred thousand in cash, as Mr. Bones had been paid up, so the remainder was profit anyways.

They headed to CHI town and their first stop would be Mama Hall's.

Entering her home was always welcoming. Today, however, Dre felt a distance, he could not put his finger on it so he put his glasses on instead, Munchie followed suit.

"Hey Mama!" shot out Dre just as they entered.

Mama jumped up to greet the boys, hugging them intensely.

"How was ya'll drive? Ain't no sun inside of here, other than the rays of God. You all hidin' somethin' with those shades on?" played Mama Hall as she was too much a veteran to not notice the frog in their voices and the dope masks they were both wearing.

"Mama, we just cool, we good ain't we Munchie," quickly defended Dre.
"Yeah Auntie, we alright," as he put his hands up to his nose, "Excuse me while I use the bathroom," politely expressed Munchie.
"Dre, you must forget that I'm a recovering addict myself. Now, take those shades off, 'cuz you ain't foolin' nobody. DeAndre, the fight you're fighting, it's already been fixed. There is no way around it, you can't win no matter how you try to dress it and you got Munchie messin' with that too! His daddy, worse, his Mama, my sis, is turnin' over in her grave. His daddy will hurt you if he knew you were the one behind his son getting high," lectured Mama Hall.

Dre's glasses were already off, and behind the shades there now showed a look of a young boy. He knew she was right and the truth hurt.

"Mama, I ain't gonna lie to you, I'm just messin' around, I

ain't going to get a habit," comforted Dre.

"Dre, this is what I was telling you about; if the drugs don't get you, the lifestyle will. I ain't about to go on preachin', 'cause you gotta deal with DeAndre, you gotta deal with it and all that comes with it. I don't want no more pain," conceded Mama with a sigh.

"I'm sorry Mama, I'm not trying to disappoint you," offered Dre as a consolation.

"Don't be sorry, get right. You were doing so good too. Now you're just disappointing yourself," replied Mama Hall with sense of pity and unmasking disappointment.

"Mama, I need for you to call the rest of your children's up. I want to see if they interested in comin' down to Iowa. I am opening up a car wash, beauty shop, music room and a restaurant and I want you to come and help me too," instructed Dre.

"How you want me to come where you at and you getting high again? Dre, my sobriety is everything to me. You are going to need to let me think on it. I'll call your brothers and sister up and cook something good to eat for all my babies," informed Mama Hall.

"Call up cousin Felica and Lovia too," offered Dre as he winked at Munchie who had returned from the bathroom.

"We might as well have a family reunion," shouted Mama Hall with an excitement in her voice and a fresh hop in her step.

Within two hours everyone was packed into Mama Halls'

place. His two brothers, Myron and Myrail arrived first, followed by the rest of the group, twin sister Latiesha and his two cousins Felica and Lovia.

They all sat around the big ten-setting table that Dre bought for Mama Hall for occasions such as this one.

The soul food menu included; fried chicken, ham, smothered cube steaks in onion and gravy, macaroni and cheese, mixed greens, black-eyed peas, corn on the cob and potato salad. It would put any decent woman to shame.

The home was filled with delightful aromas and the sound of laughter as the family enjoyed the delectable cuisine and one another's company. It was a culinary delight mixed with a family experience; one that all of them had too few of.

As Mama Hall bowed her head to offer grace, she thought to herself, *I should have called 'Stormy', their father would have liked to have been here too.*

"Hey brothers, sis and cousins, I brought all of us together, cause I'm hoping that ya'll will agree to go down to Iowa with me and help me run my businesses," started Dre.

His sister was the first to speak up,

"I hope it don't have anything to do with drugs!"
"Tiesha, do I look like that type of guy, to involve my twin

and only sister in such indulgences?" curtly replied Dre.

"Naw'll, you wouldn't do that bro, but you'll have somebody riding with them without them knowing it though. That much I do know," quibbled Tiesha.

Consistent with Tiesha's decision, the remainder of the group was so inclined to acquiesce to Dre's request.

With full stomachs and the dishes done, everyone packed into the *Excursion,* heading for Iowa. One stop first, North Riverside.

Munchie was driving as usual and Dre manned the tunes, he selected *R-Kelly's* "Dedicating This to My Favorite Girl," smiling at Mama Hall. You could see the pride in her eyes, it made Dre feel like a man.

Within three hours they were pulling up to Dre's place in Marion.

The passengers were quiet as they stepped out of the vehicle and into the luxury. Mama Hall broke the silence.

"Baby, this is a nice beautiful home, oh, just look at those big cathedral windows," expressed Mama Hall with a reverence.

"Mama, I've been tryin' to get you to come down here and maybe stay with me," replied Dre as he motioned to Munchie to take the rest of the group upstairs.

"DeAndre, I'm not trying to move down here and get mixed

up in your illegal activities," decisively stated Mama Hall.

"Mama, we won't even be living in the same area. I'm going to get ya'll a house on the other side of town and as for the businesses, Tonya's name is on the tax ID. You will all just be employees in the public eye sight. You already know I am taking care of ya'll, straight-up!" declared Dre with a confidence and arrogance.

You could have heard a pin drop as Dre looked into Mama's face, the disappointment, the frustration, the sheer offense that she had taken.

"Dre, don't you ever give me none of that *straight-up,* like I'm one of your *homies* or something. I deserve a little more respect than that, I am certain that I have earned it!" retorted Mama Hall with a seriousness that Dre seldom heard.

He couldn't stand the look on her face and the pain inside him was almost more than he could stand, he needed to know it was all ok, that he was still her loved son, he needed to hug her, and he needed to be hugged by her.

"I'm sorry Mama," expressed Dre," give me a hug," he continued as he embraced her. "It would be like we ain't even related if you come down here."

Mama sensed Dre's need for recognition as he quickly went back to the topic of having her move down there, deflecting the "straight-up" comment. She appeased him.

"Let me think about it. You know I can't just jump up and leave my life in Chicago. When are you opening the business and when can we go and see it?" inquired Mama so as to move the conversation in a positive direction, she had said what needed to be said and that was the end of it in her eyes.

"We can go visit it later on, I gotta quick run to make and I'm going to be open for business this weekend. Hopefully, Tonya will be finished with her work and can fly down here by then," informed Dre.

As the rest of the family came back down the stairs from the tour by Munchie, they all commented on how awesome the home was and how nicely it was furnished. Dre thanked them and encouraged them to make themselves at home while he and Munchie took a ride.

Dre's brother Rail wanted to go with them as he could tell what time it was by the look on Dre's face. Dre did not want them seen together, he did not want his brother to be any part of it, Dre declined.

When Munchie and Dre jumped into the *Excursion*, Dre was already on the phone with Pete to see if he needed a re-up. Pete told him he was running low, so they stopped to get the rest of the opened three-quarters brick for Pete. They left the remaining full brick in the Peugeot for future business.

They met up with Pete, shook some dope, collected some cash and were quickly back on the road to Marion. The first order of business when they returned to his awaiting family was to hit the safe and for he and Munchie to blow some good dope.

"Cuzo, this spot right here in the safe is where I'll put the lil' treasure chest that will have the mixed up dope for us," directed Dre.

"Aight Cuzo, we'll put some more outta the pot of gold and stop being like a lil' leprechaun; *I want me a pot of blows,"* joked Munchie imitating the *Lucky Charms* Leprechaun.

Dre and Munchie carried on, laughing and blowing more and more dope. They laughed until their stomachs hurt and their eyes watered and snorted until their noses ran.

Wiping their faces, they rejoined the rest of the family and Dre announced that he was going to take them to the business. Mama Hall was the first with her coat on. The two brothers decided they would stay behind with Dusty.

As they pulled up to the businesses, Dre had butterflies. He wanted his family to be proud of him, he wanted them to appreciate what he had built and what he was offering them. He wanted their appreciation, love and respect in return.

He succeeded. They were thoroughly impressed with the attention to detail in all of the shops. The girls were particularly fond of what he had done in the salon, the nice chairs, sinks and blow dryers all matching in style and hue. The selection of product was extensive, making them feel like they were in a professional establishment.

Dre was consistent with his style, making certain that the motif was apropos to the environment he wanted to create in each establishment, giving each its own distinctive personality and traits that separated one from the other.

They were all excited and couldn't wait for the *Grand Opening of Tonya's!*

That day came faster than anticipated, so much so, that Tonya was not able to make the ribbon cutting. Mama Hall had the honors and she beamed with pride as she cut the ribbons. This in turn, increased Dre's self-pride as well.

Jason, even though he was not present, had the workers he hired there to be a part of the opening. Tiesha, Felica and Lovia were to oversee the salon with Mariea and Molly doing the white girls' hair.

The local press release and advertising brought more business than Dre had expected. Mama Hall put on her apron to work the restaurant with some special soul food dishes and Myron and Myrail were running the car wash and record store.

Dre and Munchie would make their rounds, checking in on each business and trying to interact with their customers. They knew from their other business, that the *experience* is what the customer remembered and would be back for, they wanted to add a personal touch in an economic time of so much commercialism; a means to differentiate them from other options the consumer had.

When they were walking through the carwash, Dre recognized a face. He couldn't place it at first, then it hit him.

"Hey Cuzo, you remember that clown ass mother fucker over there?" asked Dre as he pointed at the Nigga.
"Yeah Cuzo, that's that guy you connected with that three-piece at the gas station. Give him a free wash," suggested Munchie.
"Yeah, the Nigga don't even know he's up in my shit gettin' his car washed, sucka ass Nigga watch me as I go to the register, straight-up!" declared Dre with a sense of mischief.

As they walked towards the register, Munchie fell back a little so the guy would see only Dre. Just as the guy was walking to the register, Dre cut in on Myron who was already standing at the counter.

"I got this," whispered Dre to Myron as he took his place at the counter.
"Hey playboy, this wash is on me, don't even trip," declared Dre with a smugness that resentment and revenge create.
"I don't need you to give me shit chump! Wash this!" replied the man as he reached down and grabbed his dick.
"That's the shit that got you knocked out last time and now you come in my shop disrespecting me after I offer you a free wash?" replied Dre with a sense of humor at first that was quickly turning into a rage.

Dre slowly walked around the counter to face the man as he created a scene with his continued antics. Dre, not needing a scene in his place, simply gave the man a good old one-two and dropped him right there in front of the counter. At the very least he silenced the man for the time being.

Munchie, Myron and Myrail grabbed Dre to calm him down as the time bomb in him was ready to go off. This coupled with being jacked on the Dog food made for a recipe for possible disaster.

"Get this mother fucker outta here!" yelled Dre with an anger that made everyone uncomfortable.

The brothers slapped the man until he came to and helped him to his feet. They put him in his car as cautiously as they could and made remarks regarding how the man slipped. There were too many witnesses and no one wanted any charges or to have bad press with the businesses.

They made sure that coffee and donuts were being handed out to everyone, they were attempting to control the scene.

Pete arrived at the time that things had calmed down to get the van washed and even Mona Lisa showed up and had her hair done. She looked so fine.

In fact, she looked so good that Dre gave her a private tour of the offices and laid her on her back, like a patient on an operating table, filling her with his dope dick. Dre was so thorough that she had to get her hair done again. Tiesha, Dre's sister, didn't say a thing, she quietly giggled to herself when she saw the back of Mona's hair.

Through the conversations with Tiesha, Mona found herself a new job working in the salon as well. When Dre heard of this he made a joke to Mona.

"Well, if that's not fuckin' your boss making it to the top, I don't know what is!"

Mona appreciated the humor and took it as good fun. Mona really fit in and got along with everyone, everyone but Mariea that is.

Mariea could see how Dre and Mona interacted and how Mona was so easily accepted into the fold and how much more she and Dre had in common. In the end, Mariea knew that; *the black bitch ain't going to bring half the money that she brings and that she ain't gonna suck his dick like she does, nor will she give him any wetter of a pussy than hers.*

Molly sensed Mariea's frustration and comforted her by reminding Mariea how well her and Dre fit, even though they may be from different socio-economic backgrounds or cultural heritage.

They closed the businesses down at eight to drawers full of

cash. Everyone sat in the restaurant unwinding and enjoying some food. Dre handed each of them two grand. It was a successful day.

Dre had called Pete to come get him so Munchie could drive everyone back to Marion.

"Hey Cuzo, come by the tip after you drop them off," Dre instructed Munchie.
"Will do Cuzo!"

Dre went around the truck, hugging and thanking everyone for their efforts and for making the day such a great success.

"Thank ya'll, for everything," yelled Dre one more time to everyone as he turned away from Mama and headed towards the van to join Pete.

He was smiling from ear to ear as he could see the pride in Mama's eyes. He was on cloud nine. *Bang! Bang! Bang!* rang out across the horizon, steeling the smile from Dre's face. *Bang! Bang!* finished the echoes as Dre swore he felt the breeze from the last one brush his face.

By reactive instinct, Munchie floored it, taking off after the Monte Carlo carrying the gunmen. His family was still inside.

"Get that Nigga, get that Nigga!" Dre yelled, jumping into the van with Pete.

"Cuzo, I'm good and I'm right in back of you, I didn't catch one or anything. I need for you to fall back on this one. You got my Mama and my whole life in that truck, including you. I got this one baby, so spin off," Dre chirped to Munchie emphatically.

"Come on Cuzo, I'm right on his tail!" exclaimed Munchie in hot pursuit.

"I see you baby, but turn off! Love Fool! Drive everybody home, now!" demanded Dre.

"Okay, Cuzo," obeyed Munchie as he turned off, realizing the practicality of the decision.

As soon as he pulled off, it opened up a lane for Dre and Pete to close in; the Monte Carlo was no match for the van.

The impact from the van as it smashed into the rear of the Monte Carlo, sent the Monte Carlo flying off to the side, right into a parked car.

Dre jumped out of the van as Pete put the brakes to the floor, the vehicle was still moving as Dre hit the ground running. Dre made it to the Monte Carlo before it came to a final rest, ripping the Nigga from the Monte. The man was dazed and confused as he was being pulled from the side window by a force not of man, or so he thought.

Pete slid up on them and the side door of the van flew open as Dre hurled the man inside. Their execution was like a well-planned excursion exercise of a military operation.

As Pete pulled away, Dre knelt into the man.

"Nigga, you just don't quit huh? I knocked yo ass out twice and now you want to come shootin'? And you did so involving my family and right in front of my business. That is more than personal!"

The rage in Dre's voice made the hairs on Pete's arms stand up. The man lying there, despite his dazed condition, swallowed hard, feeling the anger in Dre as the words cut through him like a knife.

"Drive to the *Roller Dam!* I hope this Nigga can dance up under water and not get wet!" yelled Dre.

Pete followed Dre's instruction and drove to the *Roller Dam.* Dre had the *Glock* cocked back, forcing the man to stare down the barrel and contemplate his last few decisions, to reflect on his life, one that Dre was determined to end.

Dre tied the man's hands in front of him, hog-style, pulling the Nigga out with force when they arrived at the spot. It was winter, so they had the place to themselves and Dre would take advantage of that.

"Nigga, its two ways you can go; that way," pointed Dre with a steady hand towards the water, "or this way, with a bullet in your forehead," as Dre took his other arm and pointed the Glock at him.

"Fuck you, mother fucker!" spit the man back at Dre, "Fuck

you!"

"Wrong answer," calmly replied Dre shaking his head in disappointment.

Bang! Bang! Echoed across the tundra and the emptiness that surrounded them.

The man's body hit the ground and the fresh fallen blanket of white became a pool of crimson.

"You still going for a swim, Bitch!" argued Dre as he picked up the corpse and hurled it into the water. The *Glock* was still smoking and the man's blood was still warm. Dre could feel it as it ran down his arm.

Dre threw the *Glock* in the water and vigorously washed his arm off in the snow. It was done.

"He's the DEA's or coroner's problem now, a real smart mouth tuff ass Nigga. Tryin' to kill me in front of my Moms!" exclaimed Dre to Pete as he jumped back into the van.

"I need to blow me about a half-a-gram of dope and smoke me a whole pack of squares back to back!" continued Dre.

Pete nodded in agreement and looked on Dre with admiration and fear. His eyes were filled with tears, but Pete couldn't make out why.

"I can't have Ms. Hall grievin' all at a funeral, dropping tears on my sleeve!" finished Dre.

Pete headed straight for the crib where the family was waiting for Dre to return. They were on needles. It had been such a good day and to have it end like that was devastating.

Everyone embraced Dre, hugging him and telling him that they loved him, but no one asked him what had happened.

The next day they all headed back to Chicago. Pete retrieved the last brick from storage out of the Peugeot and the stores were left in good hands, Jason's.

Dre was making money hand over fist, legitimately. Nothing compared to the profit margins offered by the other business however, and Dre had crossed a line now where there was no turning back.

While there were little of rules on the street, there was one that was still to be followed; no gunning in front of family, especially in front of children or the Mama.

Tryin' to get a Nigga in front of his family violated the number one no-no, Dre told himself. It was this that allowed him to rationalize his actions. Shooting a man in the head was equal retribution for putting another man's family at risk Dre convinced himself.

In a world where there are no rules, rationalization comes cheap. Entitlements flow freely and character is measured in grams and dollar signs and not in decisions or actions. It was a world that appeared to provide such abundance, but cost so much.

The cost was not in dollars, but one of character and integrity, and at times, even a man's soul. Dre had plenty to give and no matter the cost, he would rule this world of his, the one that offered him what he wanted, what he needed; this world of *Dog Food.*

Chapter 37
Games People Play

Mama Hall stayed at Dre's place in Iowa. Mama was not an idle woman so she rolled up her sleeves and she gave the house something it was in desperate need of; a woman's touch. Her days were spent decorating and making the house a home while she and Dusty kept one another company.

While Dre was on the road he reached out to Mona and asked her to stop by his place to spend some time with Mama Hall. The time spent together gave Mama Hall the opportunity to get to know Mona, she liked her. While Mama's favorite was still Tonya, Mona grew on her and they developed a reciprocating appreciation for one another. It also became apparent to Mama that Mona genuinely cared for Dre and not so much about the money. That pleased Mama even more.

"Mona Lisa baby, can you take me to the grocery store, there is nothing in this kitchen, but junk food!" exclaimed Mama as she shut the last cupboard and rested her arms on the marble counter tops while flashing her hands open to show they were bare.

"No problem Mama Hall, anywhere you want to go, just let me know," replied Mona with a sincerity that is found only in the voice of a friend.

Dusty had just come into the kitchen to see what the fuss was all about. He sat calmly at Mama's feet and looked up at her with his *puppy-dog* eyes making Mama melt, just as Dre always did.

"Let's take Dusty with us!" excitedly decided Mama as she scooped him up in her arms, hugging him tightly.

They grabbed the keys to Munchie's *Tahoe* and were out the door. Dre had left Mama about ten grand in addition to the two grand he gave her on opening day, and this was in addition to the two grand he had given her the night before. Needless to say, the women were going to do some serious shopping.

"We are goin to do a *Hallmark* make-over on this house!" proudly spouted Mama as the three of them jumped into the truck.

* * *

Munchie, Dre and his brothers and sister had just arrived in the city and Munchie was reminding them to be at

Mama's the next day as they would be heading back to Iowa.

Once Dre and Munchie had dropped everyone off, they immediately pulled over for a fix. Dre pulled out the *Dog Food*, spread it on a *Newport Box* and blew it like a one, two and three!

"Cuzo, drop this truck off at the Auto Doctors. I'm ready to hook this big mother fucker up! Straight-up, straight-up!" trumpeted Dre with some white residue on his nose.
"I was wondering when you were going to stop ridin' it like a white man! Hey, don't forget, we have to pick Tonya up too," reminded Munchie.

"Naw'll, I'm going to call Ms. Mindy, that lady I was telling you about the last time I was up here and got the dope. Plus, we need a re-up anyways," instructed Dre, as he pulled out the phone he retrieved from the dashboard of the Peugeot so long ago and carried it on him at all times.

By the second ring Ms. Mindy was offering a customary, common pleasantry; she knew who it was.

"Hello Dre, how are you?"
"I'm good, what about you?" replied Dre just as swiftly.

"I am getting big as a house with your daughter is how I am?" she replied with a gentleness in her voice.
"How you know it's a girl?" fired Dre.

"Dre, they did an ultra sound and with how big I am, let's hope they're not twins," she replied with equal frankness and caring.

"What we lookin at, about another two months?" asked Dre.

"If that. I might have this girl early. She ready to see the world, I can feel it, or ready to see her daddy!" exclaimed Ms. Mindy.

It made Dre feel good inside, the way she said it, the way she referred to him as a *daddy,* a title typically earned, something he had not done yet.

Then it hit him like a hammer; he was going to be a father! *Getting high did him no good and it certainly wouldn't do any child of his any good either,* he thought to himself. Dre blocked all of the insecurities and cognitive struggles out.

"I'm ready! I'm ready to rock-n-roll!" he responded.

"I hope you are ready to be a father. I can take the phone to Edward in the next thirty. By the way, I saw that little chick of yours at the Amber Inn," mentioned Ms. Mindy as she jumped from one topic to another, revealing what was the heaviest on her mind; Dre's fatherhood, Mr. Bones and other women.

"You and Mr. Bones don't miss a fucking thing!" retorted Dre, also breaking the soberness of the parenthood topic.

"I'll be on Edward's tier in about thirty minutes. Call me back in about two hours when I get off so I can see you," instructed Ms. Mindy.

Ms. Mindy was already off the line before Dre finished, "Yeah baby, I'll holler in thirty minutes."

Thirty minutes later, on the dot, Dre was phoning Mr. Bones. Mr. Bones complimented Dre on how he was handling business and let him know that the new Dog Food was even more potent than the last bricks. He informed Dre with no uncertainty that he would be able to make five bricks out of one and still step on it; it was eighty-five percent pure.

Mr. Bones continued with various instructions and insights, including to make sure that he hooked up with Ms. Mindy in a few hours when she was off her shift.

Dre informed Mr. Bones that he would need fifteen bricks and that he would meet up with Ms. Mindy at his place, the *Amber Inn,* later.

Then Mr. Bones was gone.

Dre had two hours to kill so he and Munchie headed to Regina's house to see what was up with Slick; it had been too long.

It was like a ghost town. An area that was at one time vibrant with action and characters, now sat desolate and idle, Dre just shook his head.

Dre and Munchie took a moment to blow some good dope before Dre stepped out of the truck and ran upstairs to pay Regina a visit; he wanted an update on Slick.

Regina answered the door wearing a robe with her hair wrapped in a towel covering her micro braids. Dre was almost overwhelmed by the aromas emanating from her, from the place. The body lotion, perfume and scented candles mixed for a pleasant aroma, awaking many of Dre's senses.

The dim lit entrance was highlighted by a stream of light bouncing off the wall highlighting Regina's light skin, and freckles. The robe snug to her damp frame revealing her nice shape; big booty and full breasts. He walked over the threshold feeling like Don "Magic" Juan as the Dog Food created such a perception.

"Hey Regina, what's up with Slick?" started Dre as he eyed the room.
"He told me he's been calling some phone he left with you," answered Regina with an inquisitive tone herself.
"Damn, you talkin' 'bout the phone that was in the *Gucci* bag?" immediately asked Dre.
"I guess so?" answered Regina as more of a question than a definitive answer.

Regina closed the door behind her and sat down on the couch as Dre lazily looked around the room as his mind was racing; *where the hell is Slick?* He asked himself repeatedly.

Regina put one foot up on the glass coffee table and began to rub lotion on her feet. As she slightly shifted her foot to reach it, her robe came undone, revealing all of her. With her foot propped on the table edge, it showcased her non-manicured pussy.

"Oh, excuse me," Regina embarrassingly squeaked out, "I'm still half asleep."

"Damn girl, that burger is hairy!" exclaimed Dre as he began to get hard.

Regina stood up, stretched her arms to the sky and arching her back so her breasts and pussy came out showing Dre everything he could have. She slowly lowered her arms to her side, allowing the robe to fall off her shoulders and unto the floor. She turned around without taking her eyes off of Dre and bent forward slightly.

"C'mon, flip these cakes, Dre," teased Regina as she grabbed her ass cheeks and looked over her shoulder. The line from her chin to her ass was consumed by her tattoo.

Dre slowly walked over to her, dropped his jeans, took a deep breath and plunged into her. Her head immediately snapped back and Dre ran his hand down the curve of her spine as her damp skin glistened from the light that ricocheted off the walls.

Dre's dick was so hard he felt the urge to push harder and harder, around and around, up and down, a roller coaster of in-

and-out.

Dre flipped her around and lifted her up so she was straddling him as he stood. She did not know what she was getting herself into. She didn't care as the fear of the sudden change was shattered by the feeling of Dre's fullness in her. She needed him more and more and she demanded it of him.

"More, yes, more, oh yes!" she exclaimed in absolute passion.

She was outside of herself, she couldn't feel any part of her body other than her pussy as Dre filled it, deeper and deeper. She screamed in ecstasy as she scratched his back.

The smell of her made Dre want to eat her up if he could. He sucked on her neck like a vampire off a month long drought. He would alternate, between her neck and her full breasts, teasing her nipples every time they found their way into his mouth. He gripped her ass tightly and drove in her as an accompaniment to his sucking. It was a concert and Dre was the conductor. She had never felt a dope dick like this before and she was in a full crescendo!

"Oh, Dre, Dre, Dre," she screamed as she drew Dre into her as she now gripped the back of his neck and pulled with leverage. She looked straight into his eyes without a blink.

"Dre," she said calmly, as if time stood still for her to

whisper these words, "I am going to cum."

Then she exploded all over him. Dre could feel her pussy wrap tightly around him and she began to shake as she let out a scream Dre was certain everyone on the block heard.

Her passion filled Dre beyond no return and he came in her with all of his might. Thrusting one last time hoping the feeling wouldn't go away. He gently lowered her onto the couch, her body motionless and sweating, she moaned in a subtle delight as Dre reached down to put his jeans on. He could still smell all of her, but it felt like something was wrong.

"What's wrong, this pussy wasn't good to you?" Regina asked playfully, reminding Dre it was just sex.
"Regina baby, that pussy is too good, but this ain't right," admitted Dre as Slick was on his mind.
"This my pussy right here. It was itching and I got it scratched. I wish I can get it ate too," she replied as she spread her legs for Dre.

Dre dove into her without hesitation. He needed to taste what made him feel so good.

Regina moaned like Dre had never heard before, it made him even harder. He needed that wet moaning mouth wrapped around him, he needed to feel the warmth her on him.

He stood up and slowly slid his dick into her mouth, she

gladly took it all in and sucked on it as if paying him back for what he had just done to her. She sucked harder and harder. Dre could sense it was too much for her, so Dre went back down on her.

Back and forth they traded with one another, each time the other trying to outdo the other. They couldn't take it anymore, neither of them. He needed to be in her and she needed to be filled by him.

"Fuck me!" she demanded endlessly.

Dre got on top and did her doggie style, putting every inch of that dope dick in her until he was certain she was talking in tongues.

They came together this time and then it was over, both had worked their sexual desires out. They were satisfied.

Regina informed Dre of Slicks next court date. Dre gave her his cell phone number to give to Slick. Dre also played with her and told her it was for her too.

Dre stopped arguing with himself, right or wrong it mattered not, he loved that hot, wet, hairy pussy and he would have it as much as he could.

Munchie sat patiently waiting as Dre got back to the truck forty-five minutes later.

"Cuzo, I see you stung Regina's ass this time that dick ended up in her!" teased Munchie.

"Yeah, Cuzo, you have no idea. I am a dirty dog but it was so hard with dope in me," openly admitted Dre.

"You ain't a dirty dog, she gave it to you, you didn't take it from her. You just *hoeish!*" joked Munchie as they both laughed.

They headed to the *Auto Doctor* after they had shopped a little and gave Ms. Mindy a call as the two-hour mark was soon upon them.

Ms. Mindy picked them up where Dre told her they would be and they headed to the *Amber Inn* to get the dope.

Dre couldn't help himself when he saw Ms. Mindy bending over in the hotel room to pick up her bag. He stroked her ass that lead to her clothes on the ground and Dre inside her. Munchie was still in the room.

Ms. Mindy was comfortable with Munchie and it has been awhile for her and Dre always felt so good. Dre performed so well you thought she might give birth right there and have another baby tomorrow. Unlike with Regina, however, Dre was more compassionate.

Munchie had become accustomed to the unordinary, especially when it involved the sexual exploitations of Dre and his ladies. Even though he was in the same room, he might as well had been a million miles away, in his own head he sat on a beach watching a tide roll in, the sun warm on his face and no worries on his heart. He had never seen the ocean.

By the time they had finished, Munchie had just come out of his self-induced coma and they decided to hit the mall to burn some time until the truck was done at the *Auto Doctor*.

After a couple of hours at the mall they received the call from Mr. John that the vehicle was done, so they headed back to the hotel first, to grab the fifteen bricks.

They pulled into the *Auto Doctor* and Dre proceeded to unload the bricks into the truck as Ms. Mindy watched. Mr. John acted oblivious to the exchange and Munchie was busy looking at other vehicles in the shop.

Mr. John hit Dre up for another picture with the truck and then they were off; Dre and Munchie going one direction while Ms. Mindy, in her cherry *Benz* going the other.

As Dre was about to turn onto Lake and Central his phone began to ring, startling both he and Munchie.

"You have a collect call from....Slick....from the Cook County Jail," spoke the pre-recorded message into Dre's ear, "do you accept the charges?'
"Yes!" responded Dre.

"What's up Joe?" exclaimed Slick as soon as the tone broke indicating the call had gone through.

"You baby, what you locked up for?" immediately inquired Dre with a multi-faceted concern.

"Man, Joe, they trying to get me on a State conspiracy. I've been trying to call that phone I gave you right before you went to Iowa, Joe!" explained Slick on the border of frantic and desperate.

"Yeah, Regina told me about the phone, it's back in the *Chevy,*" replied Dre.

"What you doing right now? I'm glad Regina gave me your number. Come visit me, you got Iowa ID's, you already know you can visit whenever you want," rambled Slick.

Dre hung up the phone and headed for Cook County. It seemed like only yesterday he was in that same shit hole going through processing. He recalled a time he and Slick spent hours chopping it up back in the day. He recalled the time with a fondness despite the location. He and Slick had a history. Slick informed Dre that he was confident that Mr. Bones and Ms. Mindy were doing all they could to set him up just in order to get Mr. Bones off his Federal charges and cautioned Dre about the same.

Dre confided in Slick about all the business he was doing with them, as if to find a solace in sharing nefarious activities with another who has committed the same, as if to lessen that which one has done. Dre couldn't help but notice the lady guard that kept eying him; either that or she was spying on them. He deduced the former, so he asked her for her number and she gladly obliged.

As Dre exited the last gate out of Division six, he figured Ms. Mindy must have mentioned something to the guard because when she said goodbye, she used Dre's name, something that he never gave her.

Munchie was almost curbside just as Dre walked out. One thing Munchie was cognizant of; punctuality.

"Cuzo," stated Dre, "Let's drive out to Orland Park at that Lexus dealership before it gets too late," mentioned Dre as a question and a statement.
"Who we gettin' a *Lex* for?" immediately inquire Munchie.
"For the team," promptly answered Dre.
The transaction didn't take very long. Dre knew what he wanted, he had the cash and the Manager there knew him and Mr. Bones. Plus, the manager liked seeing all of those Benjamin's!

Dre had Munchie drive the new *Lexus* LS 430 while he drove the *Excursion;* Dre would not be far from the fifteen bricks at any time.

When they hit the west side, they parked the truck at Mama Hall's and Dre jumped in the *Lex* with Munchie, heading for Tonya's house to pick her up. They would stay the night at Mama Hall's.

The morning frost was dissipating in the eastern sun as it glared off the windows and the icicles that dangled erect from the eaves. Dre, Munchie and Tonya dressed accordingly; in stylish layers.

"This what I'm talkin' about, ya'll on time!" openly expressed Dre as his family entered Mama's house early and punctual.

Once the entire group was outside, Dre presented the set of keys to his sister. Awestruck by the gesture, she stood motionless as tears filled the corners of her eyes. Felica playfully snatched the keys out of her hand.

"I'll drive!" exclaimed Felica as the family laughed uproariously.

"I'm riding with them," announced Tonya to Dre as she nodded at the girls with a mischievous look.

"Naw'll, I want you to ride with me," responded Dre, taking the fun out of her youthful facial expression.

Felica, Latiesha, Lovia, Myron and Myrail drove in the *Lexus* as Munchie, Tonya and Dre drove the *Excursion*. Munchie thought about the extra passenger, the fifteen bricks. Dre had Tonya drive.

Just passed Whiteside County, a state trooper appeared in

Tonya's rearview mirror. This would typically not alarm her, but on this morning she was rattled; his lights were flashing.

Munchie observed as she calmly pulled over, entirely unaware of her extra cargo. Dre was not. His conversation with Slick flashed through his mind; *they're setting me up,* was one line that came to the forefront of his mind. Then it donned on him, the bricks were not even covered up that well. Dre began to get very anxious. Thoughts and expressions consuming him; *I'm glad I switched cars with the dope and that only Ms. Mindy knew about the truck and not the Lexus.* This was shortly followed by the recurring notion Slick placed in Dre's mind; *Mr. Bones is trying to get out from underneath his Federal sentence!*

Tonya handled the situation like a pro; she promptly provided all of the documentation the officer asked for, giving no cause for him to search the vehicle. Her being oblivious to the packages in the rear of the vehicle allowed her such honesty and calmness.

They were soon on their way to Marion and Tonya was left with a warning to watch her speed in such road conditions.

Once they arrived at Dre's, Dre and Munchie dropped Tonya off with the rest of the family and headed for the storage unit in the *Lexus*.

"We dodged another one Cuzo," Munchie commented with a sense of astonishment and gratitude.

"Whatcha ya mean?" asked Dre as he backed the *Lexus* up to the unit and promptly got out.

"Whatcha you mean; whatcha I mean?" asked Munchie curtly as Dre popped the trunk open.

"Oh, I see," sheepishly admitted Munchie as his eyes widened at the sight of the fifteen bricks in the back of the *Lexus*.

"You switched them?" Munchie commented in a whisper of admiration. "You are always one step ahead, Cuzo!"

"Yeah, they some slow mother fuckers. Let's make sure to take one of these to Pete and my man said we could make five outta one of these bricks. This is some powerful shit!" exclaimed Dre.

"Let me be the judge of that," retorted Munchie.

They drove to Pete's, shook some up and snorted the rest. They dropped the *Lexus* off at Mama Hall's and asked if anyone needed a ride to the shops. No one did as they had intended ongoing in an hour later.

Dre and Munchie then headed to see their lady mule for Terry and dropped off some more cash for the lawyer. He was the best in the state and one of the top five in the country in his discipline; getting people off.

James Brown, "Big Pay Back," was thumpin' from the *Excursion* by the time they rolled into the shops an hour and a half later.

"Hey Bro, what's up baby?" Dre asked Myron as he stepped from the truck.

"Everything is running smoothly Bro," Myron reported.

"Hey mister, is this your shop," sprouted a young voice from behind Dre.

Dre turned to see the face of a young boy, maybe eleven or so.

"Who wants to know, the IRS or your mamma, 'cuz you look like you could be mine," stoically replied Dre.

"Cause, I want me a job," replied the boy with a confidence that reminded Dre of his days on the playground, the day he beat that boy for making fun of his shoes.

"Hang on lil' man, let's try this again. I'll walk up to you and the only thing different, I want you to ask me how I am doing first," instructed Dre hoping to teach the young man proper etiquette.

So, Dre approached the young man as he said he would and the lad purposefully asked him how he was doing and then asked him for a job; just as Dre had instructed.

"What's your name lil' man?" Dre asked with an endearment that only seemed to surface when he interacted with Dusty.

"My name is Drew and I don't know my Moms', my grandma is raising me," replied a young version of Martin

Lawrence; smoothed skin with a slim frame and low cut hair.

Dre kneeled down so he could be eye level with the boy.

"Listen. I will give you a job sweeping and helping out around here. But you need to let your grandma know where you are at and what you are doing. We don't let the woman in our life worry," instructed Dre with a father type demeanor.

The boy clung to every word out of Dre's mouth. They connected at that very moment. He nodded in the affirmative, looked around the room and headed for the first broom he could see.

Dre watched the boy with curiosity at first. He was a very hard worker and appeared very conscientious, a trait no doubt taught to him by his grandmother.

Dre began to see himself in the boy the longer he observed; the mannerisms, the work ethic, the facial expressions, all so very familiar to Dre.

In Dre's world, the unexpected typically meant a raid, a shooting, a death, something disastrous. This unexpected event however, was one of a positive nature; it showed that humanity is stronger than the world Dre was in.

The reality of emotion, the strength of bonding, the purity of life could surpass the perception created by the fictitious world that they lived in.

Today was a day that a passion of humanity won over fear and greed. It was a good day. Dre smiled as a tear formed in the corner of his eyes. He felt no need to wipe it away, he instead, let it fall down his cheek for the whole world to see; he didn't care if they did. He felt good inside and nothing would take that moment from him, not even the *Dog Food.*

Chapter 38
Finding Religion

Pete called, waking Dre from a drug induced slumber. It had been a recurring theme for Dre, high to bed and high to rise. The addiction getting the better of him, he just didn't know it.

"Hey Captain, I'm 'bout outta that last brick and wanted to let ya know," informed Pete with a little rasp in his own voice.

"Come on by the crib, I'll call Munchie to go with you and to rock-n-roll later," offered Dre.

"I'm on my way Captain," responded Pete diligently.

By the time Pete pulled up, the only one home was Mama Hall and Dre. The rest of the family was already off to work. Mama Hall was in the kitchen firing up one of her famous morning meals and the aroma permeated the home, making Pete's stomach growl as he walked in.

"Hey Mrs. Hall how are you doing? It shou'll smells good in here!" Pete exclaimed with an honesty that begged to be offered some.

"I'm fine. DeAndre said he would be downstairs soon," stated Mama coldly, as she closed the door behind Pete.

Just as Mama had indicated, Dre came sashaying down the stairs; thick white robe flowing with house slippers like Hugh Heffner. They met in the atrium directly under the large chandelier.

Dre pulled a key off of his keychain that he had in his hand and purposefully handed it to Pete.

"Here, go to the storage unit and grab two bricks. I will meet up with you at the spot later. If I don't, Munchie will slide by later and grab the key from you," instructed Dre as he intently stared at Pete as if waiting for a profound response.

"Alright Captain!" was all that came from Pete.

Dre showed Pete to the door and slowly closed it behind him as he watched him walk down the front stoop. Dre had heavy thoughts on his mind as he turned to head back upstairs. Before his foot found the second step, his motion and thoughts were broken by Mrs. Hall calling for him from the kitchen.

Dre followed the aroma, finding Mama in her realm, the queen of the castle and she was enjoying herself immensely.

"Dre, do you really trust that guy? He bears watchin', so

you better keep your third eye on him. It's something I can't put my finger on the pulse right now, but Mama ain't going to steer you wrong," divulged Mama with concern and caution.

"Mama, you already know I don't never go against your judgment, but you wrong this time. That guy has made me, Naw'll us, so much money, it ain't funny Mama. You reading him on the local when he's in the *USA Today!*" comforted Dre as if trying to sell something as opposed to explain it.

"Alright DeAndre, but don't forget the devil was first an angel. Your friends come with a smile before they stab you in the back. One thing I have learned in my time on this earth, and even when I was in my madness, and that was to be a good judge of character. I've read his stuff, it ain't even a chapter in a book," pronounced Mama, with her hands on her hips and love in her eyes.

"Mama, I can't win. I can't beat you talkin', but I love you, love you, love," sang Dre like on the *Switch Song',* "Love Over and Over Again."

"Me and Tonya is 'bout to get up and get this day started and eat this good breakfast I'm smellin!" announced Dre as he kissed Mama on the cheek and dashed upstairs to find Tonya.

Pete drove to the storage unit and picked up two bricks as was instructed. When he left however, instead of going straight to the spot, he headed over to pay a visit to a friend in the Cambridge Apartments. It would only take a minute and he missed her touch.

Pete almost skipped up the steps as each stride was lighter

than the next as he neared his honey pot. He was getting erect already. He tapped lightly on the door.

"On the ground! On the ground! Face down and put your hands where I can see them!" where the words that he heard as he was being swarmed by bodies all around; they had on black suits and were carrying *Colt* forty-fives.

Like a whirlwind out of a story, Pete was on the ground before he even knew what had happened. He could hear his own breathing as his chest cavity was compressed by the knee that was driving sharply into his back.

Damn! I'm tryin' to trick off and Dre is going to kill me, where the only words that traveled through Pete's mind.

They cuffed him and searched the van finding the two bricks. This gave cause for a high-five amongst the officers. They had bagged an elephant!

All this time they had this place under surveillance and Pete walked right into it, like a worm on a hook. The officers were pleased that their patience paid off. What a great surprise it was for them as they were not exactly looking for or expecting Pete. They were watching for the one Pete came to see and she wasn't even home.

"This Nigga just hopped on the line, he wasn't even a part of the bust, but he is definitely the big fish of the day," trumpeted the office in charge.

Within the hour, Pete found himself at the station in a room with double smoked windows, two chairs and a metal table. It was dimly lit.

Lieutenant Haynes and Captain Boots of the Cedar Rapids Narcotics Task Force stepped up to the window eyeing the man in custody; each fighting back a grin.

"Has anyone questioned him yet?" asked the Captain.
"No," professionally replied the Sergeant in the room.
"I've got this one!" exclaimed Lieutenant Haynes, "and make sure that Bob is recording the audio and the video," he continued in instruction mode.

Lieutenant Haynes entered the room giddy and eager and his eyes showed the same as they met Pete's.

"Well, what surprise do we have here, Mr. Pete freakin' Smith," began the lieutenant with a seriously sarcastic overtone.

Pete just looked at the table in front him.

"You jumped right into the major leagues bud! Two kilos of heroin, that's been tested eighty-five percent. I don't think we ever had one test with such potency in this town; congratulations Mr. Smith, a new record!" exclaimed the lieutenant and giving pause for Pete to say something in response.

Pete just looked at the table in front of him.

"So look, it's very simple how it goes from here; you can play ball with us or strike out with life somewhere in a jail cell. Hey, you might even get lucky and house-up with that Terry Dent you used to cop from. Subsequently, in case you haven't heard, he is in a maximum Federal Penitentiary somewhere rotting," threatened the lieutenant.

Pete slowly looked up at the lieutenant without a blink and just stared.

"Well, what's it going to be?" the lieutenant asked with fire in his eyes.

"Hey, I don't know what you are even talkin' about. I use dope, but do I look like I own two keys of it?" replied Pete.

"Look here Pete," cautioned the Lieutenant with a losing of patience whispering in the air. "I don't have time for your fucking games! I know more about what you have been doing than you probably do, considering all of that heroin you are using. I even know about that lucrative business you are growing over there on 15th Street south east, or how about that big birthday bash?" continued the lieutenant.

With each reminder Pete felt smaller and smaller, he began to feel the walls closing in on him.

"You have been on our radar. That dope that killed the Captain's brother is on your hands. I've been working overtime to get you and the rest that are responsible!" threatened the lieutenant with a personal dedication.

The Captain's brother OD'd on our stuff? Pete shuddered to himself. Suddenly, Pete couldn't breathe.

"What I got to do?" Pete forced out with the only breath he had left. He thought he would pass out. Unfortunately, however, he did not.

"That's the best answer you have had all day!" replied the lieutenant as he pulled a cigarette out of its pack from his shirt pocket and handed it to Pete.

"Here is what we are going to do Mr. Smith; we are going to wire you and the van up and you are going to go around and get information on the whole pyramid of people. We will then go to the Grand Jury and put everyone up on federal charges. It all, however, depends on you. If you do your job, we will recommend to the prosecutor and judge, a sentence of probation and home monitoring for you while recommending the witness protection program.

"What have I got myself into," whispered Pete in a desperation as he buried his head in his hands.

"Look at it like this," interrupted the Lieutenant, sensing Pete was about to fall apart. "You can still enjoy your life. You can go on shooting your fucking dope, selling your fucking dope and trick off some dope for all I care. Hey, maybe even that girl will be home next time!" taunted the lieutenant with laughter.

Pete's mind went numb and his hands began to shake.

"When it's all said and done and the smoke clears," continued the lieutenant, "We need all the players involved in this!"

Another officer came into the room to wire Pete up with a wireless micro button so small it was almost undetectable to the human eye. The other officers had already outfitted the van; everything was set, but was Pete?

"Okay, here's the deal, whenever you're talking to one of the casted actors, get their voice and make sure you get them in the van so we can get a proper visual. Other than that, you are free to go," instructed the lieutenant.

"Oh, one more thing. This is your parting gift," Interjected the lieutenant, handing Pete a phone as he began to rise from his chair.

"We'll call you from time to time, so think of a good lie regarding who would be calling. Makes you wish you had stayed pouring concrete or just a two-bit pusher doesn't it?" asked the lieutenant.

"I'm free to go. I ain't about to just sit here and let you make me outta a complete ass," replied Pete as he still felt weak in the knees and the sweat still beading down his back.

"By all means," answered the lieutenant as he swept his arm across his body, waving him through like a tour guide on a river boat. "Oh, and the two keys of heroin? They are where you left them."

Pete pulled out of the underground garage acting as if he was just there on a visit. The pressure overwhelmed him and he began to talk to himself. The more he talked to himself the louder it became until he was yelling and pounding the steering wheel.

"Fuck! Fuck! Fuck!" he repeated to anyone that would listen. All I had to do was bring the shit to the spot first. Fuck chasing that pussy!" yelled Pete.

Soon surrounding cars were noticing his belligerent and odd behavior. Pete didn't notice them. He was torn up inside. He made a mistake and he didn't know how to pay for it.

He looked in the rearview mirror and he didn't even recognize the man that looked back at him. He had aged so much; he had to blink to make sure he was really seeing what he was seeing.

Pete headed for Claries' house so he could set up shop; he needed to keep it business as usual. His head was pounding and his palms were sweating. He needed a fix and he needed one bad. Pete had never been much of a praying man, but today he was. The religion he was seeking however, was not one of the spirit but one of the flesh, he hurt so much now and he wanted it all to go away, he wanted to be baptized in the rivers of peace. He asked God to help him as he turned onto her street, already tasting the sweet flavor of his communion; *Dog Food.*

Chapter 39
Have Mercy

Two weeks had passed since Pete's arrest and from the inside looking out, Dre and Munchie perceived that everything was back to normal.

They had the slightest notion that they were fish in a bowl, under heavy surveillance; after all, they were sleeping with the enemy.

The Thanksgiving festivities had wrapped up a few days earlier with Dre and Tonya playing host. The family decided to head back to give him some space and Tonya caught a flight back as well.

Today was Dre's birthday and the gifts just kept on coming, as Mariea fell back on the bed in exhaustion. Dre loved how wet her pussy would get. Sometimes, he would put on scuba diving gear, role playing on the notion of swimming the tidal wave of juices in her ecstasy.

It was a warm winter's day with fresh snow and brilliant white all around. The windows lit up like sun bursts as the rays flowed throughout the house, making it feel warm and safe. Dre moaned with a tranquility.

"Get up! Get up! Interrupted Munchie as he ran into Dre's bedroom, jumped on the bed and yanked the comforter back, revealing both Dre and Mariea still lying their naked and reeking of sex.

"Oh, I've seen you two like this before," exclaimed Munchie.

"Cuzo, chili out, Shit!" replied Dre as he attempted to snatch back the comforter from Munchie.

"D, it's your birthday, we're in our suits! Happy Birthday!" followed Mariea.

"Cuzo, what's up that you gotta wake me up, I knew last night it was my birthday," announced Dre as he jumped up and pulled on a pair of boxers that were lying next to the bed.

"Come outside, I have a surprise for you," teased Munchie with a youthful anxiousness.

By the time Dre had put on his *Air Max* and *Rocawear* sweats along with a leather sheep skin *Hoodie,* Dusty was wagging his tail waiting for him too.

As Dre walked outside he was covered up like an Eskimo; Munchie was leading the way with Dusty following along.

There was an anxiousness in the air and Dre was feeling excitement too.

"Go ahead Cuzo, take the cover off!" excitedly instructed Munchie as he pointed to the object under the cover in the driveway.

Dre felt his heart fall into his stomach and then into his throat. The gesture by Munchie was endearing and made him feel special in a way.

Dre slowly walked to the object, knowing it to obviously be a vehicle, *but what kind?* Dre thought to himself, *what has Munchie done now?*

Pulling back the cover revealed a brand new champagne on pearl white interior, *Land Rover Range Rover HSE;* supercharged. It had twenty-four inchers and glistened in the morning light. It was beautiful.

"So, this how you get me Cuzo? This slick than a motherfucker!" reacted Dre with a smile that reached from ear to ear.
"Happy birthday Cuzo, look inside!" replied Munchie with a continued excitement and anxious anticipation.

Dre slowly opened the door and climbed inside to see, spread across the back seat, two matching *Chinchilla* furs; one was three-quarter cut with a hood and the other was full-length with a complimenting hat.

Mariea had now joined them with camera in hand, as her and Munchie orchestrated it together.

Munchie walked over to the vehicle, opened the back door, grabbed the short fur and handed Dre the long fur. The two of them beaming in the photos as Mariea took picture after picture of them donning the furs in front of the new set of wheels. Dusty sat quietly enjoying the excitement and looked the cute puppy part as the camera flashed.

Mariea even joined in on the fun, trying on the furs and joining Munchie as Dre took the pictures; she was all *model* style as she posed for the camera.

Dre's big day was starting off in a big way, but he wanted to keep the rest of the day low-key. He called his sister and wished her a happy birthday and had Mariea fix him one of his favorite meals, her devious enchiladas.

Dre, Munchie and Mariea went to visit Pete and show off the new vehicle and stopped by the shops to revel in the success of the businesses, they were electric with people and activity and money being spent.

It was a grand site, one that Dre was certain he would never tire of. It was one thing to hustle nefariously, it was another to do it legitimately; the ladder felt better. It made him feel as if he had really accomplished something. The kid from so long ago who was made fun of because of his shoes, now stood tall as a man of enterprise. It was a good day.

"Hey Captain, how are you doing? Happy Birthday!" announced a young voice from behind Dre.
"Hey lil' Drew, now that's what I'm talkin' about!" replied Dre while giving him a pound of his fist, reinforcing the behaviorisms that Dre had so ardently worked on with him previously.
"I got someone I would like for you to meet," announced Drew as he motioned to the other young man to join them.
"Dre, this is my older brother Anthony, but we call him *AJ*," introduced Drew.

AJ was a tall, slim kid with an odd shaped head, the kind that most would grow into someday. He had a brilliant smile and a warmth in his eyes, he had a degree of a *Magic Johnson* persona that made him likable despite his oddities.

"What up Dre? I've heard a lot about you," offered AJ as he tipped his baseball cap to Dre.
"I hope it's a good thing you been hearin'. What ya'll trying to do, turn my shops into a *Boys Club?*" teased Dre. "What's up AJ, anything to keep you outta those streets, I'm for it. I see you have that 'C' on your hat, that better be for Chicago!" exclaimed Dre.
"Yeah, I love the Cubs. I play baseball really well, just ask Drew," replied AJ with pride and youthfulness.

"They lookin' at him in college and he's only in the ninth grade," added Drew.

"Oh, really. I need to see that. If you're anything like your lil' brother, stick around the shop. There is plenty of work for everyone. The more the merrier!" announced Dre as he went into his pocket pulled out a wad of cash and handed each of the boys a hundred-dollar bill. He gave them a cell phone number so they could reach him whenever they needed to, a trait that Dre had learned from Mr. Bones. *More eyes on the street was better for business and keeping a line of communication open was a way to use those eyes to ones maximized benefit,* deduced Dre.

When Dre was finished with the boys he drove Mariea home to drop her off, while Munchie stayed down at the shops with Jason.

Dre pulled away from her house wanting to be alone. He wanted to go home and spend time with his thoughts. He could not recall the last time he sat alone; just "a man and his thoughts." Considering it was his birthday, that is what he wanted, to go home and relax with Dusty and enjoy the emptiness of his big house. He stopped by the storage garage first to grab him a little "birthday cake" for his own use.

When he arrived at the crib, the silence was peaceful. Dusty felt it too as Dre looked down at him, seeing it in his eyes. He rolled over onto his side so Dre could pet him. The vulnerability of Dusty, the trusting was astonishing. It made Dre feel warm inside. He needed a fix.

Dre put a half gram on the scale and added nearly a full bottle of *Dormins* to the mix, remembering how potent the shit really was. He was looking for a high not brain damage.

While it was still kicking like Bruce Lee, Dre retrieved the treasure chest from the safe. He dumped the dope from the treasure chest on the dope he was shaking and put the rest of the 85% pure heroin from the brick in the garage into the chest.

Dre went back upstairs and returned the chest to the safe before he made his way back down stairs, landing on the welcoming leather couch that awaited him and his thoughts.

Dre sat on the couch staring at a full plate of *Dog Food* as *Earth Wind and Fire's,* "Imagination" melodically accompanied in the background. He pulled out a pack of squares and turned on the big screen.

Dre snorted the dope until he didn't even know his own name. He was oblivious to everything around him. The feeling of contentment that overwhelmed him in the kitchen when he was petting Dusty, was now a faded memory; stolen by the numbness of the drug, but it also killed the pain.

Within the half-hour, Munchie strolled in after Jason dropped him off. Dre had turned his cell phone off so he would not be disturbed, forgetting to go pick Munchie up.

"Look at my Cuzo over there, feeling no pain. A place where I'm 'bout to be," exclaimed Munchie to a comatose Dre.

Walking up the stairs Munchie looked forward to the bubble bath he was about to take. He was going to meet up with Jason later and conceded to allow Dre to have his alone time, *I'm going to let my Cuzo rest on his b-day,* he thought to himself.

Munchie allowed himself to get absorbed in the warm cocoon of the hot soft bubble bath. He took his time with things, he was in no hurry.

He decided to put on some Keith Sweat, "Don't Stop the Love," while getting dressed and pantomiming to the lyrics. When he looked at himself in the mirror, he liked what reflected, the new *Polo* gear he had bought with Mariea when he bought the two Chinchilla furs for Dre.

He thought he looked a little older than the last time he looked so intently into a mirror, but he also thought he looked healthier and more sophisticated. He too had come a long way from the streets as a boy. He found himself standing up a little straighter as a smile came across his face. How he chose to lead his lifestyle, in such a tumultuous environment, was harder on him than he let on.

"It's time for a bitch to get high now!" sang Munchie as he walked into Dre's room.

Munchie entered the code into the safe and slowly pulled the door open and removed the treasure chest. He licked his lips and sniffed.

Munchie methodically opened the chest and scooped out a heaping amount with a hundred-dollar bill that he had folded to use as a shovel. He poured it onto another hundred-dollar bill.

I might as well take some of these bills with me and roll and snort with this other bill, Munchie thought to himself as he eyed the food.

He left the safe open as he took everything with him to go blow it with Dre. *I'll come back and lock everything up later,* he whispered to himself.

Munchie went downstairs with dope in hand, finding Dre still torpid. In front of Dre was the plate with a nice pile of dope on it.

"This fool cool, he don't need no more. I can handle all this," commented Munchie as he poured what he had in his hand onto the table and grabbed the card off of Dre's plate.

Munchie rolled a hundred-dollar bill as he sang along to the *Earth Wind and Fire* that Dre had put on earlier. It was more of an unconscious effort for Munchie, as he was intently occupied by the dope and the words he heard so many times before.

Munchie took a slight breath in and exhaled slowly, leaned forward to the table and snorted the dope.

His life came to a screeching halt. His thoughts were torn out of him. He was blinded by a bright orange, yellow light in his mind's eye. He tried to breathe and he couldn't. He could not determine if he forgot how to or if he just couldn't, then it occurred to him, he was suffocating. Everything went black and the last thing Munchie heard was the sound of breaking glass.

Munchie falling forward into the glass table was enough to jar Dre from his drug induced slumber. Dre was idle at first and the sound replayed in his mind, as if a delay between reality and his awareness that was subdued by the dope. He jumped up in a panic as if the house was being raided by the police.

Dre looked around in great paranoia, searching for any signs of intruders when his eyes fell on what lay before him; Munchie's body.

"Get up Cuzo, what's wrong with you? You okay?" inquired Dre as he attempted to assess the scene before him but his cognitive abilities were impaired by his recent consumption of the dope.

Dre bent down and turned Munchie over to see white foam from the corner of his mouth and glass shards in his cheek. The top of his nose was red from where he hit the table but was ringed with white residue from the heroin.

Dre reacted instantly, as if he willed the dope out of his system. He grabbed Munchie, dragging him to the bathroom while demanding that Munchie acknowledge him.

"Talk to me Cuzo, talk to me!" Dre demanded over and over again.

Dre put him in the tub and turned on the water. He held Munchie in his arms as he waited for the water to revive him while he wiped the blood off his face.

Munchie was not responding so Dre listened to his chest and felt around his mouth. Munchie wasn't breathing either. One thing he did learn at the "Y" in the neighborhood was cardio pulmonary resuscitation, CPR. He administered it the best he could from memory, each breath, a symbol of Dre's will for Munchie to wake up.

Dre worked vigorously, pumping up and down, up and down on Munchie's chest. The sweat dripped from his forehead and mixed with the tears that streamed down his face.

"C'mon! Damn Cuzo! What have you done?" screamed Dre into the quietness of the large home, echoing off the walls and hitting Dre hard as he could hear his own desperation.

"Please Cuzo, please!" Dre pleaded with Munchie, shaking him while he continued to put breath into him.

Dre watched Munchie's chest rise as the air filled his lunges, convincing himself that Munchie would be doing it on his own with the next breath.

Dre pressed his face against Munchie to listen for his heartbeat and all Dre could hear was his own heartbeat, his own frantic breaths as he tried to catch his wind.

Munchie lay there placid, comfortably peaceful. Dre's heart felt like it was exploding, the pain was unbearable, the snot ran from his nose as Dre wept uncontrollably.

"No, No, No!" yelled Dre to the world, to all of the gods of all religions. He would defy this destiny; he would change the fate that the world had just handed him.

He began to hit Munchie in the chest, willing him to live.

"C'mon my Cuzo, you can do it, C'mon on Cuzo, I need you," silently and intently spoke Dre.

With no response, Dre reacted the best he knew how, his thoughts were racing but none of them made any sense, he was crying and frantic, he couldn't focus. He ran upstairs and grabbed the long fur coat, brought it back downstairs and wrapped Munchie in it.

He carried Munchie to the truck, put him in the back seat gently, as if to not break such a precious item.

Just as he was about to pull out, it occurred to him that he hadn't taken his phone, so, he ran back inside and grabbed the first one he could find; it was Munchie's.

Dre just started to drive. He called Jason first.

"Bitch, you must want me to come pick you up!" declared Jason as he noticed Munchie's phone number calling him.
"Jason," exasperatingly began Dre, "this is Dre, I need your help. Munchie is...Munchie is...is...dead," Dre forced the words out as if saying them made it more real, and Dre was not going to concede that his best friend was dead.
"Dead? I was just with him. He can't be...dead!" excitingly replied Jason with disbelief and denial.
"Where are you Jason?"
"I'm at the shop," replied Jason in a state of numbness. Then the phone went silent.

Dre made it to the shop in what seemed less than five minutes. Jason ran out to meet Dre as he pulled up.

"Dre, we gotta take him to the hospital!" yelled Jason as he approached the truck.

Jason opened the back door to see the bundled fur in the back seat. He slowly reached for the fur and began to pull it back. His hand began to shake and his eyes filled up with tears. He knew that he didn't have to look at what was under the cover, but he needed to.

Jason was silent as he peered down at his friend, at his partner.

"How did this happen?" calmly inquired Jason as the tears streamed steadily down his face.

"I forgot to move the pure shit outta the spot that we have and he went and snorted it," admitted Dre solemnly.

"Oh, my God," were the only words that Jason could whisper through all of his pain and anguish. He almost fainted but the door handle held him up just long enough for him to remember to breathe.

"It's okay Dre if you don't want to take him to a hospital. I gotta a guy who owns a bunch of funeral parlors and they can make sure that everything gets taken care of without any police or other authorities involved," offered Jason in a robotic manner trying to stay strong enough to just make it through this moment and the next.

Dre joined Munchie, looking over his shoulder at Munchie lying lifeless in the back seat.

"Oh, what have I done? I've lost my lil' man on my birthday, I'm so sorry Cuzo, I'm so sorry," whispered Dre through Jason hoping Munchie would hear him.

Dre began to shake and felt nauseated. He put his hand on Jason's shoulder to give him some balance and comfort.

"Okay, let's go see this guy that you know," conceded Dre.

The ride was quietly eerie. The presence of Munchie in the backseat was unnerving as Dre wanted to turn around and talk to his Cuzo. He wanted his Cuzo to sit up and start singing some ridiculous Keith Sweat song, anything just to look into his face one more time. Dre continued to weep.

When Dre pulled to the back of the funeral home, Jason jumped out and went inside to take care of things.

Dre climbed into the backseat and sat with Munchie, holding his head in his lap and looking down on him. Munchie's eyes were still open.

"Don't look at me like that Cuzo. I'm so sorry Cuzo, I'm going to be lost without you," softly spoke Dre as he caressed Munchies' face and gently ran his fingers over his eyelids closing his eyes.
"I don't know what to do without you Cuzo," Dre confided to the lifeless body in his arms. All of Dre's fears, all of his sadness, all of his worries met at the same spot, at that very moment. Dre couldn't breathe, he couldn't think, he couldn't even speak.

"I might as well join you Cuzo," admitted Dre in a seriousness that now overcame his anguish.

Dre bent foreword so his lips were on Munchie's forehead.

"Give me just one word. That's all I want, one word is all. I'm sorry, I'm sorry. I love you so much," declared Dre as he kissed him on the forehead, the cheeks and then on the lips.

Dre had stopped shaking by now and all he felt was a nothingness, an emptiness that he would never fill. A dark, deep hole of despair that the world had given him when it took what meant so much to him. He would never forgive it.

"Hey Dre," whispered a voice from the front seat. Jason had returned from talking with the owner.

"He wants ten thousand and he said that he will ship the body wherever we need it to go. I told him that chances were it would be Chicago. I am going to go back in and wait for you. Take your time," Instructed Jason as he got out and walked to the back door and opened it.

"I love you partner and I will truly miss you my friend, I will truly miss you," whispered Jason into Munchie's ear as he kissed him goodbye. "You were my brother, my sister, my friend all in one, you were part of me," finished Jason as he pulled his head away from Munchie's.

As Jason closed the door, Dre sat there in the silence as the words that he overheard Jason say hung in the air like a mist on a warm spring morning. Dre sat silently holding Munchie tightly, never wanting to let him go. He cried until he had no more tears.

Dre carefully wrapped Munchie up in the fur and brought him into the parlor. He informed the owner that the money was on its way and that he needed to ship the body to Chicago in three days. The owner was hesitant until Dre also offered him the long fur that Munchie was wrapped in.

Dre immediately called Mariea and instructed her to bring ten thousand down to the funeral home and returned to see his Cuzo one more time.

Dre bent down and whispered something into his ear as a large tear fell from his face onto Munchie's as if Munchie was crying too.

Jason drove Mariea's car while she drove Dre's as he was in no condition to do anything requiring coordination. He couldn't feel his limbs and his chest was caving in with each breath that he drew. Dre didn't care if his next breath was his last; he couldn't bear the pain.

When they arrived at Dre's the quietness of the expansive home embraced them. Without Munchie, it was emptier than merely less one more person, it was absent a soul, the life that gave the world more to enjoy and appreciate.

As Mariea and Jason cleaned up the mess trying to erase

more than broken glass, Dre called the family and informed them of what had occurred.

All were in disbelief and offered to immediately fly down, but Dre told them that the funeral would be in Chicago in a few days and there was no need to do so. Dre fought back what tears he had left as the pain had spread from his heart across his entire body.

When Dre phoned Tonya to let her know, she could feel his agony. Dre's normal chipper demeanor was drowned in a sorrow that only a silence can portray.

Dre packed up enough for a few days, including approximately one million in cash. He, Mariea and Dusty comfortably riding in the *Range Rover* as the hum of the road was the constant companion.

Dre had already shipped a six-foot marble cross inlayed with twenty-four karat gold. The cash was to insure that the funeral was done right and that Munchie would be laid next to his mom Annette and his grandma Sadie B. They would rest forever in God's hands buried in the Woodlawn Cemetery in Forest Park.

Mariea drove as Dre thumbed through Munchie's photo album and curbed his pain with the constant consumption of the brick that he had stopped and picked up from the storage unit before they left.

The *Smith and Thomas Funeral Home* on Madison Street was professionally somber as people eased in and out of the Review. The Reverend John Fluker provided the eulogy and was apropos, as the reverend had known Munchie his entire life.

The entire family was in attendance and many members of the community also paid their respects. Jason was stolid and polite to everyone and had Mariea on his arm. This boded well so Tonya would not suspect anything, even though it was the last thing on any mind. Everyone that had an influence or touched by Munchie was there, everyone but Terry or Dre.

During the processional, eyes were searching for Dre without success. As they sluggishly walked up the hillside following the burial, a long-stretch black limo slowly pulled up to the site and came to a complete stop in the direct path of everyone. The car sat idle for a minute and then a large white dove, for every year Munchie was alive, fluttered out of the top of the car and then the car drove away.

The family smiled as they knew it was Dre's way. They knew he didn't like funerals and they knew the pain had not subsided in him.

As people were getting in their cars, Dre approached the burial site alone in an all-white *Armani* suit and the short *Chinchilla* that Munchie gave him.

Dre bowed his head in silence and began to speak to

Munchie.

"Cuzo, I never had a chance to say goodbye. You were my best friend and I would die for you, but I wasn't there for you to do that, so now I will die with you," exasperatingly expressed Dre with tears streaming down his face as he pulled a nine millimeter from the pocket of his fur coat.

He poured some dope on the tombstone and snorted it. He drew the nine millimeter to his temple with a steady hand.

"That supposed to be me. Now it will be Cuzo," ended Dre as he began to squeeze the trigger.
"That's still not going to bring him back. That just going to have all of us grieving twice as much'' calmly stated a voice behind Dre, startling him.

Dre quickly turned around to face the one that had just ruined what he was trying to do; make his pain go away.

"Unless you don't care how I feel that is," finished Mama Hall appearing out of nowhere.

Dre began to slowly collapse, folding into the arms of Mama Hall as she hurriedly approached him. Dre's steady hand was now shaking as was the rest of his body, he was shivering from the cold and the loneliness.
As Dre fell into her, his heart stopped beating for what seemed an eternity and then he was warm. In her embrace, he

found a comfort, he found a solace that can only be found in a mother's cradle.

Dre fell to his knees with his head held in Mama's hands, he hugged her so tight she had to work to breathe. Then he released her and sat there, leaning into her, weeping harder than any person should. The depths of despair that Dre was in made him face his own mortality. They were a dynamic duo set to rule the world, and now one was gone like a gust of wind. The ignorance of adolescence and youth now abruptly taught a lesson in life; it is fragile.

Mama Hall looked over Dre at Munchie's tombstone as the wind blew the remaining residue that was left behind by Dre. She felt her son weeping at her feet and her heart sank. She was saddened by what had happened and by the path that her son was on. She shook her head and looked to the heavens pleading to God for the strength to endure and for the wisdom for her son to see a new path. She recited; *please have mercy,* as the tears fell down her face.

As she bowed her head onto Dre's, one of the doves found a resting place on Munchie's tombstone for a fleeting second and then was off, flapping out of Mama's sight. She was filled with a warmth and so was Dre.

"Mama?" asked Dre innocently, "did you feel that?"
"Yes baby. It was just Munchie saying goodbye."

The world, on that day, could have been colder or lonelier; it had lost a good soul to the evil of the demon known as, *Dog Food*.

Another of the victims left in the wake of its power, without prejudice and without mercy. In such emotional destitution, Mama found a renewed faith and Dre began to feel what real life was as he took comfort in the warm embrace of a consoling mother, something impervious to the power of the food, something that makes mortal men feel immortal; the power of love. Dre cried until he couldn't cry any more.

Chapter 40
Not Expecting the Unexpected

Terry was anxious as he waited for his *celly* to pull the towel down off the cell door. Terre Haute Penitentiary was his home now and he was trying to make the best of it. He had established his routine and was patiently waiting for his next fix.

While he waited, one of the guys from Cedar Rapids came by and handed Terry a paper to give to his *celly*. While waiting, Terry thought he would skim the pages. He was particularly interested in the *Metro* section, where they discussed the local crime activity. He was also interested in the *Obituaries,* as he wanted to see what poor souls didn't make it home for dinner.

When he found his way to the *Obituaries* he scanned the names that were in bold. One caught his attention, almost as a sub-conscious suggestion, so he went back and read the name again: *Johnell Hall.*

His heart leapt to his throat and his legs felt heavy as if they were pulling him into the concrete tier and his hands began to shake. He continued to read how *Johnell Hall,* of Chicago, had overdosed and he recited the information regarding the viewing and the funeral arrangements. *My boy. Oh, my lovely boy,* he whispered gently and deeply to himself. Suddenly, Terry was filled with rage.

Just as his *celly* opened the door and stepped out, Terry took one step into the cell and hit his *celly* so hard, that the one punch knocked him out; just like Tyson in his prime.

Terry put a sheet up around his bunk to provide a curtain, and then he laid back and blew some dog food. Terry tried to run from the pain, but it was upon him too fast, it hit him before the heroin did; he began to cry.

Of all the ways to find out, Terry just happens to read about it in the paper, only because his *celly* was taking a shit. As Terry began to feel the spin from the *food,* visions of his boy circled in his mind. He could see Munchie's face, his smile and his eyes and how he would stare at Terry with awe and admiration. Now, that boy, that man, was gone before Terry could tell him how proud he was of him.

Terry knew enough to know that when the dope wore off, the loss would hit him with a vengeance; something he didn't want to experience. Tears fell off his cheeks as he tightly closed his eyes, hoping it would be the last time he would have to close them, hoping that death would finally find him so he could join his son finally and forever.

* * *

Pete was in the Federal Courthouse Building waiting to go to the Grand Jury to make statements in an attempt to assist the prosecution in their efforts to indict the suggested co-conspirators; DeAndre Hall and Johnell "Munchie" Hall.

"Mr. Smith, this is a real important day for you," spoke one of the clean cut agents as they walked into the room.
"Are you ready?" asked the other agent.
"Yes sir!" promptly responded Pete nervously.
"Okay, Mr. Smith, to this point you have given us some small fish, but what we need is a whale. Are you telling us everything or are you so doped up you don't know anymore?" politely asked the first agent as he tried to temper his frustration as his patience was waning.

Before Pete could answer the other agent chided in.

"Listen Smith, we are just going to charge you with the two bricks, ship you off to V block in Linn County, let a snitch bogusly jump on your case and then see you go away for a long time," threatened the younger man with an attitude to match his body, short and stocky.

Pete sat and stared at the man. *He looks so young,* Pete thought to himself as he tried to find answers to get him out of the predicament he was in, but there were none, so he just nodded his head.

"Don't just nod your head Smith, we need some good valuable information on the eighty-five percent pure heroin, where it comes from, how much volume is flowing, its source, its distribution channels. We want some information!" excitedly demanded the agent as his face began to turn a shade of red.

The agents felt that his answers in the debriefing sessions were hindered by the dope in his system as his stories were not adding up. He was trying to protect Dre and he was stalling the best he could, but he was in deep, real deep and couldn't see any other way out.

Pete's shoulders collapsed forward as he let out a long sigh, a sigh of defeat, a breath of concession. He reached into his pocket and pulled out a key, throwing it on the table.

"This is to a storage unit with at least ten bricks of the same dope I was caught with, cause I needed to get high, ya'll don't want me high," confessed Pete.

"Where is this storage unit?" quickly inquired the agent just as fast as he scooped the key up off of the table and bounced it in his hand.

"In Marion, right off the highway, down the street from the *Hy-Vee,*" promptly answered Pete.

"I know where it is, very close to the Windsor Feder

Development Condos," offered the older agent.

"Pete you could have told us this weeks ago. We need to see if people are still coming and going from this site. What is the unit number and what else do you have for us now that your memory is back," sarcastically continued the same agent. "We will get a warrant and wait to execute it. There is no deadline on the Federal Warrant and especially with the weather so bad," started the younger agent, only to be cut off by Pete.

"The number is 1227. There is a car wash, beauty salon, music room and restaurant tied to the activities. There is also a house in Marion with my name on it that is sure to have millions stashed in it," continued Pete.

Pete was afraid for his life as the information began to spew out of his mouth, but as each detail came out, the easier it seemed to flow. Pete sang like a canary as the agents just watched in amusement and wonderment.

"Now this is the stuff I am talking about!" declared the younger agent as he pounded his fist on the table. "Let's go over this stuff again before we take you in to address the jury."

The Grand Jury heard everything Pete had to say along with other evidence presented by the government. The government would indict DeAndre and Johnell Hall and obtain search warrants for the businesses and the home in Marion. The agents both smiled at the days' success as Pete felt like he had just killed someone.

There was one thing however, that Pete would take to his grave, any of the murders he was aware of. It was his way of rationalizing that he was not completely giving Dre up.

The agents suggested Pete leave the state of Iowa and be placed under protective custody as he would most likely need to testify if the case went to trial.

One week to the day, following Munchie's death, the task force felt was the perfect time to raid the properties. With Johnell Hall out of the way, they knew they could focus on the one called DeAndre Hall or "Dre" as they had come to learn.

The first place they hit were the businesses, certain to find large amounts of drugs and Dre. The agents were determined and hungry and arranged for a massive onslaught, a barrage of agents all shielded and armed to hit the place.

They charged the businesses like they were to encounter a massive counter attack. In their pursuit however, they experienced no resistance and in the end, they found no drugs and no sign of DeAndre Hall.

* * *

Dre, Mariea and Dusty settled comfortably in a lavish Presidential Suite in Barrington, Illinois. Dre had been staring incessantly at the walls of his room for at least a week. He was focusing on the *Embassy Suites'* Logo on the drink coaster in his hand, turning it aimlessly clockwise as he tilted his head to follow the words inscribed.

Dog Food had been his constant companion, taking in all of Dre's pain and giving comfort in return. Each hit, giving him a new breath, but taking two more in payment. He talked to his family sporadically, trying to find enough energy between the highs. He had enough sense to talk with Jason on how the businesses were functioning, but he noticed little else. For example, that Pete never called him.

Dre took some delight in talking with Ms. Mindy, she was nearing the end of her pregnancy and the notion of a birth was attempting to off-set the recent anguish associated with the tremendous loss that Dre was feeling.

Dre spent time talking with Mr. Bones as well, however, the content was not around business but around matters of life.

"We go through things in life Dre, good and bad. These experiences build character and prepare us for our ultimate destiny, whatever that may be and only time will reveal it to us," explained Mr. Bones in a wise sage tone and demeanor.

Mr. Bones did not judge Dre nor did he caution Dre regarding his increased addiction. He understood the pain far too well to meddle.

Dre even talked to Regina, she had given Mama Hall her number at Munchie's funeral when she paid her respects. She missed Dre and the times they shared and she missed his touch.

Dre was not feeling the young sex drive that had accompanied him for so many years and when he did, albeit diluted, Mariea was there to accommodate him. Even with the dope dick, it wasn't the same. Dre felt empty and so alone. He felt guilty and responsible and he couldn't shake it, he wouldn't shake it. It was his Cuzo and he meant the world to him. Dre went from the top of the world to lost, utterly lost and without a compass.

The ringing of the phone knocked Dre out of his stupor and startled Dusty causing him to bark.

"Hello," forced Dre out of his lunges and into the receiver.
"Captain? This is Drew and the police came and put everybody outta the shops lookin' for you," excitedly rushed Drew into the phone.

Dre was hardly in any condition to think about strategy or execute any degree of cognitive exercises.

"Who you ridin' with right now?" asked Dre as he forced himself to focus on the matter at hand.
"It's me, Mona Lisa and AJ," answered Drew.

Dre's mind started to move, *where are they going next, the crib? Oh shit, the storage unit, there is more at stake there!* Dre said to himself so loud he thought he actually had stated it out loud.

"Drew, listen closely," started Dre with a seriousness Drew had not heard before. "Stop what you are doing, go to the hardware store and pick up some heavy duty lock cutters. Then, go to the storage unit, the one right off of the highway on the back road when you first make it into Marion, it is just down the street from the *Hy-Vee*. Go to gate number 1227 and get the bag that is in the trunk under the spare tire. Can you do that for me buddy?" asked Dre in a teaching manner.

"Okay Captain. Do you want us to drive the car home too? AJ can drive," replied Drew.

"Hand the phone to AJ," impatiently directed Dre.

"Listen AJ. I need you to go with Drew and find the key that is up under the hood, on top of the battery and drive my car out of storage. Do not go inside the trunk or anything, I just need you to drive it," instructed Dre with a clarity he had not felt in some time.

"Do you guys have a garage?" finished Dre. "Yeah," innocently replied AJ.

"Park it inside of there and wait for me to call ya'll with more instructions. It will be from a different line, but I will be calling."

Dre felt the task was better suited for the boys than to trust it in the hands of the ladies that were there. *No one would suspect a couple of young kids,* Dre thought to himself.

Drew and AJ did exactly as they were instructed. Drew was quick on his feet. This was his chance to prove to Dre that he had made the right decision when he hired him on.

Drew made up a story that his grandmother needed something out of her storage unit and asked Mona if she would give him and AJ a ride. He told her that his grandmother would be picking them up, so it was okay for her to go.

Mona knew the "grandmother" had a name and that name was "Dre." She was comforted that Dre had people looking out for him as she had only talked to him once since the passing of Munchie.

AJ and Drew wasted no time in getting in and getting out; AJ was behind the wheel and Drew was the lookout. As they casually pulled away from the garages, they were passed by a parade of marked and unmarked cars heading directly from hence they had just departed. It was poetic. *Dre would be proud of them,* Drew thought to himself and Drew could see Munchie looking down and smiling; Dre had outsmarted them once again. Drew took out the phone that Dre had given him and started to dial.

Dre hung up the phone with great comfort in what AJ and Drew had accomplished; he was satisfied with the outcome and took pride in his decision to bring the kids on staff. He would teach them as Mr. Bones had taught Dre.

Dre reflected back on something that Mr. Bones told him in Cook County, *they want us to self-destruct.* The words began to sink in as his high was upon him, it was a state of euphoria as the drugs were so concentrated in his system the new sensation was not expected.

The adrenaline rush from the events coupled with the dope, gave him a new sense of high. He felt a greater clarity or so he thought. His cognitive abilities had been altered and now visions of grandeur, paranoia, narcissism and reality all blended together, unable to be differentiated, so Dre brought them all in and made a collage of what would be his perceived reality.

"Mariea, they are after me. I don't know if it is for the drugs, Munchie, murders? I don't know what. But I do know that we're about to go on the run," explained Dre in a surprisingly calm manner as he walked into the bedroom.

Mariea just looked at him with adoration and uncertainty was on her face.

"Or, you could take the *Rover* and make ghost. I'm cool anyway," offered Dre as he interpreted the look on her face.

He wanted to protect her and letting her go was one way to express his feelings.

"D, I'm staying right by your side baby," cautiously and purposefully avowed Mariea.

Dre immediately found himself, in that instant of demonstrated love and dedication he found a glimpse of life, a sliver of hope. He had been drowning in so much sorrow from the passing of Munchie that life had lost all meaning, purpose or direction. The conviction of Mariea was the catalyst that he needed to move on, to believe again.

He slowly took his clothes off and slid under the covers, he would make love to this woman like he had never done before.

* * *

Drew and AJ were about to lock the garage behind them when the natural blanket of curiosity of teen age years wrapped itself around them.

"Hey Drew, let's take a look at what Dre has in the trunk," suggested AJ.
"Naw'll, man he told us not to do anything but wait for instructions. Don't drive it or go inside of it, or anything," countered Drew.
"Dre ain't here and I wanta to see what's inside. Let's just take a peek," urged AJ, trying to appeal to Drew's good nature.

* * *

Just as the agents hit the storage unit, across town another group raided the Marion house. They came up with little more than a blunt of weed; more concerning to the agents however, there was no sign of DeAndre Hall.

The garage unit was barren with only traces of activity, as the cut lock rested on the ground in front of the open door. The officers tried to locate tread marks or any tracks that would indicate a Pontiac had been there. Pete, in his stupor and ignorant state kept repeating "Pontiac," unknown to him was the proper pronunciation, "Peugeot." The trail had gone cold, stone cold.

The agents, not willing to accept such a defeat, traced every inch of the Marion house again, this time they caught a break, seven and half million of them to be precise.

In addition to the seven and a half million in hundred's, the dogs sniffed out some residue left behind from the shards of glass when Munchie went through the table. Dre and Mariea apparently did not get all of it. However, the minute amount of residue was not enough for the authorities to go on; they were beginning to doubt Pete's story.

They had seized everything, the cars, the furniture, the clothes and all the cash, but still no dope and no DeAndre. With the death of Johnell Hall their case ended, it was all but closed.

They did notice however, the name Tonya Anderson as the

registered owner of the properties and the businesses. They decided it was time to give her a call in a last desperate effort to find something.

"Hello?" answered the busy voice on the other end of the line, "this is Tonya."

"Tonya Anderson? Ms. Tonya Anderson?" replied the calm male voice on the other end.

"Yes, this is she."

"Ms. Anderson, this is agent Clark, with the DEA in Cedar Rapids, Iowa and I was calling to ask you a few questions regarding a DeAndre Hall," he continued.

The line went silent for what seemed to be a minute, but in actuality, only a brief, fleeting second, a moment in time where the world starts spinning in the opposite direction that it always had been.

"Hello, are you still there? Asked the agent.

"Yes," replied Tonya.

"It's okay Ms. Anderson, I just need to ask you a couple of questions in regards to him. What is your relationship with him?"

"He...he is my boyfriend," answered Tonya as her airway seemed to constrict.

She was feeling light headed all of a sudden and speaking was becoming increasingly more difficult.

"Okay, thank you, and do you know where we might find

him?"

"Not off hand. I would probably need to call him," answered Tonya, fighting to get enough air through her lungs to offer a reply.

"The businesses down here in Cedar Rapids called, *Tonya's,* is that yours by any chance?" fished the agent, knowing full well the answer to the question.

"Yes it is," promptly replied Tonya.

"Could you prove that in a court of law?" asked the agent.

Finding the question far too invasive, Tonya realized that his polite demeanor was no more than a veil to conceal his true intentions, to harm Dre.

"You would need to direct that question to my attorney," coldly and evasively answered Tonya.

"If you could just give us a location of where we could find Dre. We are not worried about the shop, we just want to talk to your boyfriend and we don't want to bring you in and charge you with federal money laundering and aiding and abetting. As a matter of fact, on second thought, we should send someone to bring you in for questioning," stated the agent, sensing that Tonya was playing too coy for her situation and he didn't have the time or inclination to play along any more.

The phone hit the desk before Tonya hit the floor. The receiver dangled from the desk, swinging in the air as the agent continued to speak into it.

"Oh, no!" screeched the co-worker that soon found Tonya lying lifeless on the floor in her office.

She maintained her vitals and the ambulance was there within ten minutes. When Tonya came to, she wasn't sure where she was or what had happened.

"It's okay, you're safe," calmly offered the man in the white coat as the sirens caught her attention.

She slowly looked around and realized she was in the back of an ambulance.

They conducted a variety of tests on Tonya and she was pleased to see the grinning face of the doctor when he entered her room.

"You have had quite the morning young lady," the doctor began.

Tonya nodded with courtesy, anxiously waiting for his diagnosis. She was filled with horror; *was it a disease, was it cancer?* Were the types of thoughts that raced through her mind.

The doctor could sense her impatience and worry. He placed a hand on her shoulder and looked her straight in the eyes. His eyes were a soft, light brown and crows' feet stemmed from the corners of his eyes; the years had conditioned him and made him gentler.

"My girl, do not look so worried, I bring good news. You are pregnant!" exclaimed the doctor as the lines of age on his face dissipated with the good news as it was delivered with a brilliant genuine smile.

Tonya laid there numb. She was filled with an excitement as she turned her head and gazed out the second story window, the wind slowly blew the snow off the ledge causing it to swirl in the sunlight that danced across her room.

She was then, suddenly, all alone. The doctor left with a skip in his step, leaving her to contemplate the reality of the situation. She was pregnant with Dre's baby and Dre was in trouble. The promises that they made to each other, said and unsaid, this was not all part of the plan. She began to feel anger.

Where is he, doesn't he care? She played to herself in a moment of self-pity. Quickly she realized he didn't even know, so how could she be so hard on him. A tear formed in the corner of her eye.

The world he lived in, that they lived in, did not follow a script despite every intention to make it do so. With the heat on Dre and the uncertainty of their future, Tonya was not only afraid for her but for a baby that may be brought into this world. A world that offered no excuses, that offered no parlay, one that was fast and furious, one driven not by dreams and commitment but by greed and hunger; a hunger for money and power, a hunger for the food, *Dog Food*.

Chapter 41
On the Run

Dre knew he had to move. It was only a matter of time before the authorities pieced more and more things together and they would be looking for a white *Range Rover.* It had only been two days since Dre received the phone call from Drew about the raids in Iowa, but they were closing in fast, Dre could just feel it.

Even though Jason and Munchie were the only two who knew about the *Range Rover,* Dre's paranoia was in full operation and it was quickly translating events into conspiratorial connections and indications of being caught.

Dre needed to call Ms. Mindy to get in touch with Mr. Bones. Dre needed new wheels and a new map, his present path was winding down and every way he surmised it ending, it ended in a *dead end.*

Dre took out the new phone Mariea had purchased and

dialed the number that always made him a little nervous.

"Dre, how are you?" answered the stoic voice on the other end. It took Dre by surprise that Mr. Bones would answer Ms. Mindy's phone.

"I ain't doin' so good. I'm on the run like *Uncle Tom*, bring your saddle on home. Where's Ms. Mindy?" replied Dre with a mixture of politeness and eagerness.

"She was rushed to the hospital. It's time to have your daughter Dre. Where are you? Is this line clean?" answered Mr. Bones with equal courtesy and eagerness.

"It's clean. I'm in Barrington. Man, I need to go see my daughter, but I need a new car. This one is marked by now," announced Dre.

"You are on the run from the Fed's, you're going to need an RV camper. Who do you have driving for you? Cause you can't be behind the wheel," instructed Mr. Bones.

"My white chick Mariea, she's with me," promptly answered Dre.

"That's cool, you have the other complexion with you, which is a plus. No disrespect to your sisters, but that white woman can get into doors that our black asses can't even make it to the fence. Only thing you gotta do is look at currency, there ain't no black face on no dollars, let alone a penny! So, your chances are greater with that woman. Also, make sure you call that lawyer you've been paying so much money to, the one like Bruce Cutler who represented Gotti," completed Mr. Bones with a sadness that had now crept into his voice, leaving Dre feeling alone and nervous.

"Yeah, he paid for, cause I'm the new Don on the run!" exclaimed Dre with a halfhearted sincerity, trying to keep the tone light, attempting to over compensate for his growing nervousness.

"I have a partner that's not that far from you. Have that woman of yours go to his RV center and trade in the *Range Rover* and pay the difference in cash. In exchange, he will set you up with a camper that will take you all over the world if you are trying to go there," explained Mr. Bones. "I will give him a call so he will be expecting you later. Oh, and Dre, your daughter is being born at Presbyterian St. Luke's Hospital, the one over by Cook County Hospital," informed Mr. Bones with a sense of compassion and pride.

"Alright Mr. Bones, thanks and I haven't forgot about cha," confessed Dre.

"I already know what was confiscated, it was all green, seven and a half million to be exact and without a trace of *Dog Food!* Call me when you get situated Dre," finished Mr. Bones with a finality that made Dre cold.

Mariea drove to the address that Mr. Bones had provided and traded the *Range Rover* in for a fully-loaded RV. She paid the man an additional one hundred and ten thousand, cash. It was luxury on wheels; full size refrigerator, large screen T.V., a full size shower and it slept eight. It was forty feet long so it intimidated Mariea, but she made due because she had to.

"Dre, it's me, I am on my way and should be there in about twenty-minutes. You are not going to believe this thing baby," announced Mariea with an adolescent excitement and apprehension all in one.

She was going to pick up the man she loved and go on the run. Where? She did not know and just then it didn't matter. She just needed to be with him wherever their future led.

When she pulled into the hotel parking lot, Dre and Dusty were ready to go. They jumped in the passenger side of the RV and Dre closed the door behind him, leaving the hotel that he may never see again.

"This is nice, you were telling it straight!" announced Dre, kissing Mariea as he passed her on his way to the back with Dusty. Dre noticed Mariea had already unpacked their clothes as he remembered she took them with her in the *Range Rover*. Dre smiled, *she is good to me,* he thought to himself.

"Mariea, let's drive out west, to this hospital. I'm 'bout to be a father," informed Dre as if it were just another event.

Mariea didn't ask any questions, but she felt a sadness inside, she held back the tears. That was their deal, but it didn't make it any easier on her. She loved Dre, but the way he announced it, with such indifference and lack of inclusion of her, it hurt. She swallowed her pride and just nodded her head in affirmation.

Within the hour she pulled into the hospital back lot as to give her enough room to maneuver. She had never driven anything like this, so, the more room the better. Plus, there was no reason to be out in front, exposing Dre to any additional attention.

Dre sent Mariea in to find out the floor and room number Ms. Mindy was occupying.

When Mariea returned to the RV she could not help herself, she busted into laughter. She tried so hard to not offend Dre, but the sight was so unbecoming, that humor was the only appropriate response. Dre laughed too.

Dre stood tall, wearing a wig, a pink jogging suit of Mariea's and he had on lipstick with jewelry to accessorize. It was his pose that said it all, especially the hand on the hips. *He may just pull it off,* Mariea thought to herself.

"So, you think this shit funny?" retorted Dre with a smile. It had been awhile since they had laughed together. This broke the tension that had been with them for too long and as they looked at each other with a reciprocating admiration, they laughed even harder.

"No baby, I know who wears the pants," playfully conceded Mariea as she rubbed his dick with her hand.

"Was everything good?" played Dre in return, flashing his million-dollar smile. It made her melt every time and this was no exception.

Mariea smiled on the outside, but the pain was still with her on the inside, she wanted this to be their baby. The fact that Dre was with her was enough, it was his way and she accepted it.

They left Dusty behind as he had already found his spot in the RV and headed upstairs to see Ms. Mindy, to see Dre's new baby girl.

When they entered the room, it was filled with an air that Dre had never felt. It was a light feeling, not so heavy as the world always seemed. The sun was coming in through the window and Ms. Mindy was flush and sparkled as something moved in her arms.

Dre knew babies were small, but he didn't know they were that small. She was seven pounds-five ounces, which is a healthy size for a baby, but to Dre, she was little.

Dre was so taken in that he forgot he was dressed the way he was, until he saw the expression on Ms. Mindy's face that is.

"Oh, yeah, that's right, I almost forgot 'bout this," admitted Dre as he approached them.
"She is beautiful," whispered Dre, as he could now see the face of his angel.

A tear fell down his face as he was flooded with emotions. He wanted Munchie to see this and be a part of it. He wanted Mama Sally to be there too. Dre soon realized that neither of those things would happen. Regardless, he was still happy to be there, to be there on the day of his daughter's birth, something no one could ever take away.

"Here's your daddy, Jasmine Delisha Hall," announced Ms. Mindy as she carefully handed the baby to Dre.

Ms. Mindy was warned that Dre would be in disguise, but she was still in awe of his transformation. To see this smooth operator, this man of men, in a wig and a tight fitting pink woman's jogging suit, it was hilarious. His demeanor and purpose however, quickly formed into an endearing gesture. Ms. Mindy felt a pride inside. She understood why he could not sign the birth certificate and she was okay with it, because the father was there on that day and she knew if he could have it another way, he would.

"Look at my lil' princess, Jasmine Delisha. Hey Boo-Boo," Dre teased in a little kids' voice. "You're so adorable. Welcome to this new world," announced Dre as he held her up and turned in the room for her to see. "This is your daddy," stated Dre as he looked her straight in the eyes and she looked back with just a peek, as she could barely open her eyes. Tears fell down Dre's face and he simply let them fall. They were tears that he had not had very often in his life. They were tears of joy and they tasted better than the tears he had shed so many times before.

Mariea was recording everything with the *Camcorder* so Dre could watch it while they were away. Mariea was jealous of the attention that Ms. Mindy was getting from Dre and how happy Dre was at that moment. He appeared happier than she had ever made him, so it seemed. But to see her man this happy, she felt happy too. She didn't care who it was that made him feel this way, she wanted him to be happy and if this is what it took, then she supported it. She smiled a genuine smile.

"Your daddy loves you Boo-Boo, he loves you," repeated Dre over and over again as he handed her back to Ms. Mindy. "Your daddy has to go, but he will explain everything to you later, Boo-Boo," expressed Dre in a weakening voice as the emotions were getting the better of him.

His heart hurt and eyes burned as he tried to fight back the onrush of so much emotion.

"She needs her daddy Dre," whispered Ms. Mindy, loud enough for Dre to hear as tears equally fell down her face.
"I'm on the run from the Feds," reminded Dre.
"Do you need some passports? Your daughter... can you please step out of the room for a second?" asks Ms. Mindy, interrupting herself, as she looked up at Mariea standing behind Dre.

Understanding and respecting them, Mariea put down the Camcorder and slowly turned away wiping her own tears away.

"Dre, I will have Edward make the two of you passports. I already have one, so all four of us will go on the run together. We need you Dre," admitted Ms. Mindy as tears filled her eyes again.

"Dre, I'm not trippin' on the white chick, I just want your daughter to grow up with a father. I grew up without one and that is one reason I do so much for Edward. He reminds me of the father I never had," confessed Ms. Mindy as the tears streamed down her face, looking helplessly at Dre.

"Baby, I'm going to call my lawyer and see what I can do," offered Dre while the mascara ran down his face. "This will be over soon, you'll see, I promise," comforted Dre as he bent over and kissed Ms. Mindy and his daughter. "I love you," he confessed as he slowly and quietly turned and walked out of the room leaving them both behind.

Dre could hardly breathe. In that moment, he would have given up everything of the past just to be able to stay with them, but his choices of the past prohibited him from making certain choices now. Dre began to feel anger.

The walk to the RV was silent. Dre undressed and jumped in the shower. He scrubbed his face to remove the make-up and scrubbed more, hoping to wash away the pain; to wash away the past that was now catching up with him.

Dre turned the water off and listened to it funnel down the drain, his thoughts shattering the otherwise silent RV. He dried off and splashed on some *Coolwater* cologne, the smell reminding him of days gone by.

Dre was hurting inside and he needed someone to talk to other than Mariea, so he called Mr. Bones to tell him that he had seen Ms. Mindy and his baby.

"Dre, go in the bottom kitchen cabinet," instructed Mr. Bones as soon as the conversation started.
"Mr. Bones, all there is in here is a little globe," replied Dre.
"That's what I want you to grab."
"What's the point of this?" instinctively asked Dre as he pulled it out and placed it on the counter.
"Ms. Mindy said that you and your lady friend need some passports. Dre, with a passport, you can go anywhere on that ball you're looking at. Do not stay in the United States. The whole U.S.A. will be looking for you, if they are not already. That is the mistake I made, I stayed in the United States. I went to Miami thinking I would be safe and I was wrong," admitted Mr. Bones, trying to impart some helpful advice on Dre.

"Alright Mr. Bones, I get it," replied Dre.
"There is a big difference between I get it and I done it!" barked Mr. Bones, now sensing Dre's lack of commitment. It was imperative that Dre didn't give up now, they had only just begun. He needed to stay strong and Mr. Bones would not just sit back and let Dre fall apart. He was determined to see him through this. "Did you hear me?" finished Mr. Bones.
"Yes, sir," conceded Dre in a more confident tone. Then the call was done.

Dre grabbed the globe and walked to one of the beds closest to Mariea, pushed play on the CD player, launching, *Master P.,* "I Miss My Homies." He then took out some *Dog Food* and snorted it.

He reached under the bed and took out the photo-album that Mariea had put there earlier.

Dre slowly went through the pages, reminiscing of moments so long ago that felt like just yesterday. He missed Munchie, Mamma Hall and his family. His missed the way things were, but welcomed how some things had changed; he was now a father. He laughed and cried at the same time. The tears of joy, mixing with the tears of pain, were an intoxicating emotional drink for Dre to swallow. He gulped it in, drinking as much of it as he could. He suddenly felt alive and he felt destined for something more. He had surpassed the pain, ascending to a new level, one of a nirvana. It was surreal.

Munchie's death would not be in vain and his new baby would grow up with a father; this, Dre avowed.

Dre turned to the last page, finding a thick package wrapped tightly. They were numismatic coins; old rare coins that had significant value.

Munchie, what have you done now? You always lookin' out for your Cuzo, Dre said to himself as he lifted his head as if to look to the heavens. He was overwhelmed with what felt like a presence, he was certain it was Munchie. *I love you Cuzo, I miss you, and you will forever live on through me, along with Will, Ball, grandma, and Auntie Annette,* continued Dre to himself.

Inside the back cover also laid an envelope addressed to Terry, Munchie's dad. Dre took out a piece of paper from the front of the album and a pen from Mariea's purse. He began to write Terry a letter. It was one of the toughest letters Dre had ever had to write, *how do I gently tell a father that his son has died?* Dre kept repeating to himself. The weight of the task was daunting no matter how Dre tried to articulate it. In the end, Dre concluded that there was no easy way, so he just told it straight. Dre decided he would also wire ten-thousand to Terry via *Western Union* when they were far out of town and include a message that he was okay and that he would be in touch when he could.

Dre wiped the tears from his eyes and off his cheeks. He took a deep breath and turned his head towards the front of the RV.

"Fire this plane up, the co-captain is ready to take off," directed Dre with a waning energy as the hit he took was starting to take effect.

Mariea promptly followed his instructions and turned the key. The motor hummed silently as she awaited his further instructions.

"Which way, baby?" asked Mariea.

What way is it going to be Cuzo? asked Dre to himself as he held the globe in his hand. *Let my finger stop on the place we need to go Cuzo, talk to me,* Dre continued inside.

They had over five-hundred thousand in cash and adding the value of the coins, they had a stash that would last them awhile. He also had the bricks with Drew and he had his never ending talents to get them through.

As the globe spun in his hand, a smile formed at the corner of his mouth. He had just had an epiphany; he saw the plan, just as clearly as he saw his destiny so many years ago on the playground.

No more tears, no more sadness, he saw his fate and he felt a metamorphosis, a new calling, and a new direction. His heart leapt for joy, a feeling as foreign as it had been so punished over the last few months. He almost forgot to breathe.

He looked at the white residue on his pants, the trail of the food that had led him to the very place he was; the trail of *Dog Food.*

He looked ahead, out the large front window and his finger stopped the globe from spinning. Dre looked at where his finger had landed and let out a sigh.

"I got that game," declared Dre, as the new found energy propelled his mind to new heights, he began to laugh; *Cuzo, you crazy,* he thought to himself, *Cuzo, you crazy.*

Dre rose from the bed, placed the album back underneath and joined Mariea in the front, plopping in the passenger seat with Dusty in tow and the globe still in his hand.

"Well, what direction?" softly and eagerly asked Mariea.

"That way," indicated Dre with a steady hand, "towards our fate to claim my destiny."

About The Author

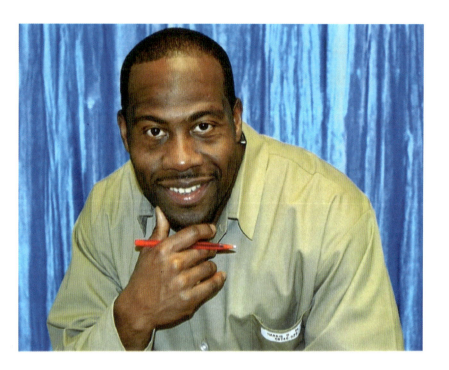

Deon Harris is an up and coming urban literature author who aspires to be a substance abuse counselor and motivational speaker following his incarceration. Despite enduring the privations of prison life for the past fourteen years, Harris is an extremely joyful, not to mention grateful, individual who has an incredibly positive outlook on life. He hopes that his first urban literature piece is beyond relatable and will inspire his readers to work towards the "blessed" life that he currently leads

You're The Publisher, We're Your Legs

Crystell Publications is not your publisher, but we will help you self-publish your own novel. **We Offer Editing For An Extra Fee, and Highly Suggest It, If Waived, We Print What You Submit!**

Don't have all your money? …. No Problem!
Ask About our Payment Plans
Crystal Perkins-Stell, MHR
Essence Magazine Bestseller
We Give You Books!
PO BOX 8044 / Edmond – OK 73083
www.crystalstell.com
(405) 414-3991

Don't have all your money up-front…. No Problem!
Ask About our Awesome Pay What You Can Plans

Plan 1-A 190 - 250 pgs $719.00 $674.00	Plan 1-B 150 -180 pgs
Plan 1-C 70 - 145pgs $625.00	

2 (Publisher/Printer) Proofs, Correspondence, 3 books, Manuscript Scan and Conversion, Typeset, Masters, Custom Cover, ISBN, Promo in Mink, 2 issues of Mink Magazine, Consultation, POD uploads. 1 Week of E-blast to a reading population of over 5000 readers, book clubs, and bookstores, The Authors Guide to Understanding The POD, and writing Tips, and a review snippet along with a professional query letter will be sent to our top 4 distributors in an attempt to have your book shelved in their bookstores or distributed to potential book vendors. After the query is sent, if interested in your book, distributors will contact you or your outside rep to discuss shipment of books, and fees.

Plan 2-A 190 - 250 pgs $645.00 $600.00	Plan 2-B 150 -180 pgs
Plan 2-C 70 - 145pgs $550.00	

1 Printer Proof, Correspondence, 3 books, Manuscript Scan and Conversion, Typeset, Masters, Custom Cover, ISBN, Promo in Mink, 1 issue of Mink Magazine, Consultation, POD upload.

VERY AFFORDABLE EXTRAS

Film/ Production & Websites **$175 and up**, Professional Book trailers on Youtube. They can also be used to shop your book to libraries, book clubs, and bookstores. Weddings, Music Videos, etc..